theZEDbook

Solutions for a shrinking world

Bill Dunster
Craig Simmons
Bobby Gilbert

Taylor & Francis
Taylor & Francis Group

The authors and publishers would like to thank the following individuals and institutions for giving permission to reproduce illustrations. We have made every effort to contact copyright holders, but if any errors have been made we would be happy to correct them at a later printing.

p.xiv, 2.15.2, p.233	Steve Speller Milner
2, p.4, p.216, p.248	Becki Bernstein
1.4.3, 1.4.4	Raf Makdha
p.8, 1.1.11, p.30, 1.4.5, 1.5.20	Adrian Arbib
1.5.2, 2.8.5	Ian Mawditt
1.5.14	Josh Knight/Sony Pictures Classics, all rights reserved
1.5.16	Blooming Futures
2.1.2, 2.1.10, 2.10.9	Linda Hancock
2.1.36	Steve Harris
2.6.2, 2.6.3, 2.6.5, 2.6.6	Jim Dunster
2.6.7	Jeff McMillan
p.219 (Hope House interior)	Dennis Gilbert
p.226 (BedZED village square), p.231	Phil Sayer

First published 2008 by Taylor & Francis
2 Park Square, Milton Park, Abingdon, Oxon, OX14 4RN

Simultaneously published in the USA and Canada by Taylor & Francis
270 Madison Avenue, New York, NY10016

Taylor & Francis is an imprint of the Taylor & Francis Group, an informa business

© 2008 ZEDfactory Ltd

Designed and typeset by Alex Lazarou, Surbiton, Surrey, England
Printed and bound in China by Everbest Printing Co. Ltd

British Library Cataloguing in Publication Data
A catalogue record for this book is available from the British Library

Library of Congress Cataloging- in-Publication Data
A catalog record for this book has been requested

ISBN10 0-415-391997
ISBN13 978-0-415-39199-3

Contents

Acknowledgements

The ZEDbook represents exactly ten years' hard work by everyone that has commissioned, collaborated, worked for and supported 'the ZEDfactory'. Particular thanks must go to Sue Dunster for keeping the idea alive over such a long period of time.

However, special credit must be given to those who have shaped the complex polemic covering the many diverse disciplines and seemingly conflicting technical parameters.

Harder still was finding the time to write and illustrate these thoughts while surviving commercially in an industry dominated by the lowest price and the minimum specification.

Firstly: Steve Harris, senior architect – for his long-term commitment to the ZEDfactory, his contribution to the technical sections and financial payback models, and his help with the ZEDfabric supply chain. Jon Double for all the computer visualisations over the years. John Shakespeare for his graphic and photographic contributions.

Secondly: Nicole Lazarus – 'Bioregional guru' and one of the few core team left that still understands why and what we were trying to do all those years ago when BedZED was just a twinkle in the Peabody Trusts' eye.

Thirdly: Matt Bulba – alternative transport engineer and founder of 'Blooming Futures', and biofuels specialist, for sharing his research and practical solutions for running diesel engines on localy produced vegetable oil. The ZEDfactory company VW Lupo has proven the reliabilty of Matt's conversion system over the past two years.

Fourthly: Ian Mawditt – of Living Space Sciences for carrying out sophisticated tracer gas ventilation analysis and monitoring the thermal performance of parts of the completed BedZED project.

Fifthly: All the other architects and engineering practices that have collaborated with the ZEDfactory on joint venture projects and masterplans – particularly:

- Alan Philips of Alan Philips Architects – APA ZEDfactory – PortZED in Shoreham
- Andy von Bradsky and Chris Wilford of PRP architects – PRP ZEDfactor – Gallions Reach
- Mathew Branton and David Franklin of Franklin Ellis Architects – Upton urban village, and Milton Keynes Central ZEDquarter
- Mike Rainbow and Chris Twinn of Ove Arup and Partners.

And finally – to all those clients who have helped shape the ZED philosophy, particularly Dave Hill, Andrew Marsden, Dickon Robinson, Malcolm Kirk, Johnathon Smales, Dan Epstein, Alan Yates, Jaqueline Leach, Colin Brace, Andrew Mercer, Paul Bright and Jody Scheckter.

Bill Dunster

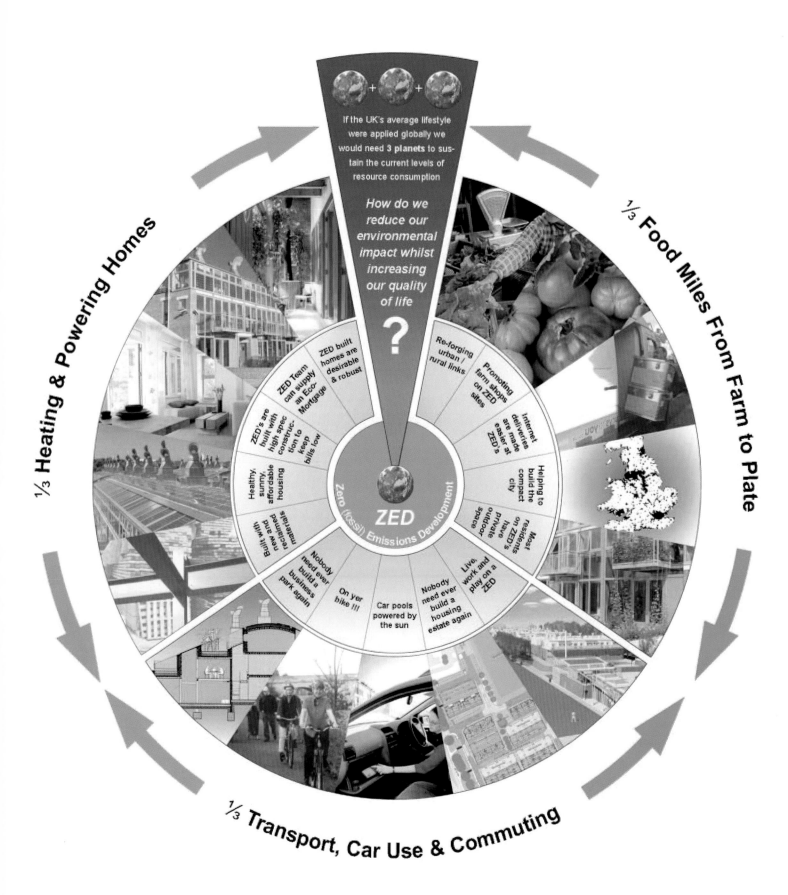

If the UK's average lifestyle were applied globally we would need **3 planets** to sustain the current levels of resource consumption

How do we reduce our environmental impact whilst increasing our quality of life

?

⅓ **Heating & Powering Homes**

⅓ **Food Miles From Farm to Plate**

⅓ **Transport, Car Use & Commuting**

ZED
Zero (fossil) Emissions Development

ZED built homes are desirable & robust

ZED Team can supply an Eco-Mortgage

ZED's are built with high construction to keep bills low

Healthy, sunny, affordable housing

Built with new and reclaimed materials

Nobody need ever build a business park again

On yer bike !!!

Car pools powered by the sun

Nobody need ever build a housing estate again

Live, work and play on a ZED

Most residents on ZED's have private outdoor space

Helping to build the compact city

Internet deliveries are made easier at ZED's

Promoting farm shops on ZED sites

Re-forging urban / rural links

1

The ZEDwheel – showing the annual carbon footprint of a typical UK citizen

Preface

We are the Microgeneration

- the first generation to do something about climate change
- the first generation to take personal responsibility for our future
- the first generation to break free of passive consumer culture
- the first generation to generate its future from renewable energy.

Carbon is the new currency

Over four generations the average UK household will produce enough climate changing greenhouse CO_2 gas to be directly responsible for seriously impacting on the lives of the number of people in a climate change hotspot. This figure will rise annually as climate change accelerates.If atmospheric carbon emissions continue at current levels, a 3–5°C increase in average global temperatures could potentially lead to the loss of two-thirds of the world's productive farmland, mainly due to crop failure from water shortages (see Figure 3). The possibility of losing billions of lives from famine is close to becoming unavoidable. We can now predict the days of someone else's life taken by each UK citizen's increasing carbon footprint.

Acknowledging this process changes all the rules. Every car advertisement, cheap flight to the Mediterranean and fashion gimmick suddenly becomes a guilt trip. Aspiring to own a Ferrari or four-wheel drive turns the innocent consumer into a climate criminal. A long haul flight to Disneyland in Florida has the potential to wipe out an entire village in a climate sensitive tipping point already suffering from drought.

2
Zero carbon café at Jubilee Wharf

3
Two-thirds of the world's productive farm land could be lost
if a 5°C temperature rise is experienced by the end of the century

Apathy or self denial of the relationship between climate change and fossil fuel use becomes a dangerous, antisocial stance. Already wars are being fought over scarce food and water resources. Climate change is likely to overload the aid packages proposed by the 'Make Poverty History' campaign every year in perpetuity, unless industrial nations come to terms with reducing carbon emissions.

Suddenly it becomes important to be seen to care. Conspicuous carbon production changes from being a sign of virility, affluence or social status to indicating insensitivity, stupidity and selfishness. Fashions will change. Products will change. The most exclusive, desirable products will have the lowest carbon footprint not the highest. Carbon 'lite' or zero fossil energy becomes a desirable commodity, not something to mock from the suburban 'good life'. The carbon footprint of almost every activity can be measured – and a carefully composed carbon diet proposed for each of us – with it becoming our personal responsibility not to exceed our fair share of the right to pollute everbody else's planet.

Powerdown

Every aspect of our contemporary society runs on cheap fossil fuel, from agriculture and food production to transport and buildings. The human population of the planet has expanded from one to six billion over the past century – largely because of the availability of low cost fossil fuel (see Figure 4). Converting millennia-old stored carbon into energy for the human economy and atmospheric CO_2 is responsible for the greenhouse effect and escalating climate change.

Equally worrying is the decline in discoveries of new fossil fuel reserves. Global demand for fossil fuel will soon exceed supply, resulting in escalating annual price rises for both oil and gas, and increased international conflict over dwindling supplies.

UK stocks of North sea oil will last around ten years, with gas reduced to five, and output declining annually, making the United Kingdom increasingly dependant on sourcing new reserves from some of the most politically unstable countries on the planet. The national cost of military intervention in the oil-rich Middle East and the increasing body count must now inform any debate on our current carbon-intensive

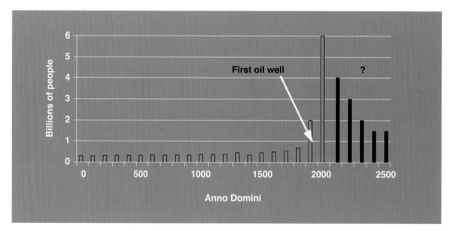

4
Is the human population of the planet directly proportional to the availability of cheap energy?

lifestyle in the United Kingdom. Reducing personal carbon emissions and moving away from our almost complete dependance on fossil fuel can start to increase the quality of our everyday lives and save lives outside our national boundaries.

It is tempting to believe that we will somehow develop new zero carbon technologies that will enable life as we currently know it to proceed without changing very much. With a technology such as nuclear electricity, in theory all that has to happen is that we build more power stations, and our cars and transport will gradually change over to hydrogen fuel cell motors, with unlimited hydrogen produced by nuclear electricity too cheap to meter. The reality is that there is only enough nuclear raw ingredient to sustain the industrialised nations for between 12 and 15 years, without taking into account the nightmare of leakfree radioactive secure storage of the waste product for millennia. There will be other similar technologies, such as carbon capture from coal, promoted by the large industrial corporations as peak oil begins to inform the collective consciousness. Any process that takes a finite mineral reserve from the ground to solve a short term problem risks causing an ecological and meteorological imbalance, leading to reserve depletion within relatively short geological timescales.

The ZEDteam watches emerging technologies critically, but does not invest blind faith in any particular one. Our experience has been that the higher the technology – the larger the unwelcome side effects and the faster the eventual depletion of the fuel feedstock. High technology seems to need large research and development budgets that can only be met by large multinational companies, and have a tendency for large scale high investment infrastructure – often with massive embodied cash and carbon. When they go wrong, whole nations are affected for many years – witness Chernobyl.

The only meaningful blueprint for a stable society is one that recognises that it must run on the limited amounts of renewable energy available within its national boundaries.

It is very unlikely in a low carbon future that there will be many countries with surplus energy to trade on the international markets. Most industry experts agree that even if all known renewable energy strategies were adopted in the United Kingdom we could only ever meet around 30 per cent of current demand across all sectors.

A new political landscape

It is no accident that large companies prefer large engineering solutions. Any large organisation with an authoritarian pyramid structure will seek energy and infrastructure solutions offered by similar scale organisations. Any property developer with large landholdings today will resist spending any extra profit on the increased construction costs that accompany the microgeneration or energy efficiency agenda, as this will affect their landbank value. The same logic is then used to justify investment in off site zero carbon generation – with the claim that it is more cost effective. The largest company of all – the UK government – uses this logic to justify investment in nuclear energy. The big idea here is that you should always try to export your personal or local problem somewhere else – as there will always be a cheaper way of achieving the same CO_2 reduction targets off site. This is the classic offsetting agenda – and the same logic that encourages tree planting in the third world used to offset air travel. All of this would be perfectly reasonable, and work well, if we didn't live in such an overcrowded country on such an overcrowded planet. There is simply no more offsetting opportunity, or insufficient

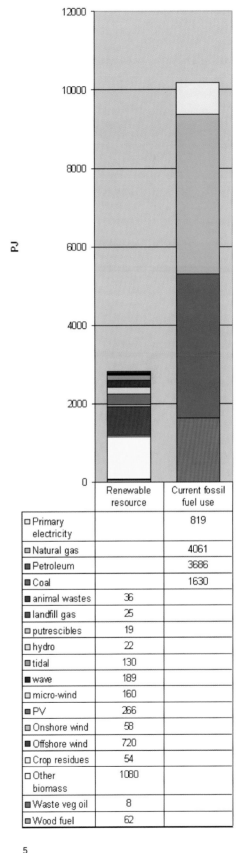

PJ

	Renewable resource	Current fossil fuel use
▢ Primary electricity		819
▣ Natural gas		4061
▪ Petroleum		3686
▪ Coal		1630
▪ animal wastes	36	
▪ landfill gas	25	
▢ putrescibles	19	
▢ hydro	22	
▣ tidal	130	
▪ wave	189	
▢ micro-wind	160	
▪ PV	266	
▢ Onshore wind	58	
▪ Offshore wind	720	
▢ Crop residues	54	
▢ Other biomass	1080	
▪ Waste veg oil	8	
▣ Wood fuel	62	

5

The scale of the challenge. The UK's potential renewable resources compared with current fossil fuel use (in Petajoules). We must reduce our demand for energy as well as transfer to renewable sources

6
A 225 KW vestas turbine erected on London's South Bank to power Christmas decorations had little noticeable acoustic or flicker problems and was popular with the majority of the public, perhaps suggesting onshore community scale wind could work well if carefully integrated into our new and existing urban fabric

off site generating opportunity available within our national boundaries, to meet more than a tiny fraction of current or future demand. There is a good reason why many successive government energy targets suggest a maximum contribution from offshore wind of around 15 per cent of national electrical demand – because this is the maximum practically achievable with a 2 MW turbine at 500 metre grid spacing on the limited areas of continental shelf below 50 metre depth. It is for this reason that the ZEDstandards have been devised – setting workable CO_2 targets for new build and then carefully upgrading our existing building stock to match the available stocks of national renewable green grid power.

With this strategy it is perfectly possible to achieve sufficient economies of scale to reduce the cost of decentralised renewable energy and meeting the ZEDstandards – and suddenly the little people can make a big difference. The same energy efficiency supply chain and microgeneration kit is used for renovating existing buildings as is required for the new build and regeneration programme. So do we adopt a top down, big business strategy, adopting the nuclear revival, or encourage a bottom up, grass roots emphasis on decentralised microgeneration and energy efficiency?

Offsetting carbon footprints, by buying someone else's spare carbon ration, is cheating and ducking the issue. While sending money to developing countries to fund technologies that reduce carbon emissions is very worthwhile, it does not give you a personal mandate to continue with your own excessive carbon footprint at home or at work.

Even if every sensible large scale wind farm, tidal barrage, wave energy farm and biomass or waste power power station were built, there would only be enough energy to power public transport, food production and distribution, and possibly public services. This doesn't leave much for you and me at home and at work. There is certainly little or no surplus to run our existing stock of energy hungry historic buildings, many of which we will wish to retain for the purposes of maintaining historic cultural continuity. There is simply not enough offsetting opportunity to arrest climate change in time to create a stable, equitable society before the fossil fuel runs out. It is no longer possible to pay someone else to put a turbine offshore or on a Welsh hillside, without stealing someone else's future renewable energy generating opportunity. It is critical that everybody recognises that in a United Kingdom running off renewable energy they cannot export their problems somewhere else. Every single renewable energy generating opportunity will be required, both maximising building integrated microgeneration within plot boundaries, *and* adopting community and city scale renewable energy schemes. This realisation should stop the damaging and unnecessary debate today about favouring large scale wind farms over higher renewable energy targets for new build in cities. More importantly, any new build project claiming ownership of a large scale renewable energy installation off site to create zero carbon status on an urban site should be challenged unless all the opportunities for on site microgeneration have been adopted. Even if new or refurbished projects are only future proofed to allow for future installation of microgeneration technologies, this is better than ignoring the future zero carbon generating potential.

It becomes very important to match renewable energy profile to the urban typology. It is critical that scarce transport grade biofuel is not used for urban combined heat and power plants when woodchip from urban tree waste will suffice. A good example is the contribution that surburbia can make to national energy strategy in the United Kingdom.

ZEDfact

Seventy per cent of the United Kingdom's urban fabric is under 50 homes per hectare. At this density it is feasible to achieve the following renewable energy targets:

- 60 per cent annual domestic hot water from solar thermal collectors

- 40 per cent annual domestic hot water from automated wood pellet boiler staying within the national biomass quota

- 80 per cent space heating reduction from improved airtightness, superinsulation and passive heat recovery ventilation

- 20 per cent space heating reduction from passive solar gain

- 100 per cent summer passive cooling from building fabric

- 80 per cent annual electric demand from building mounted photovoltaics

- 20 per cent annual electric demand from micro- or community-scale wind generation

- peak demand on the electric grid substantially reduced by incorporating half a day's electric storage initially through recyclable batteries; upgraded to fuel cells within a decade – effectively peak lopping to avoid the need for investment in centralised generation solutions.

This reduces the demand on the limited stocks of national biomass available, without losing premium agricultural land, to less than 250 kg dry biomass / person / year – basically only providing domestic hot water in winter when there is not enough sun. Note that no electric-hungry technologies such as heat pumps have been used, as these double domestic electrical energy consumption, requiring more photovoltaic area than it is possible to provide – even with optimised solar urban layouts. With low maintenance and low technical risk, photovoltaics now have a payback of under 12 years, making it irresponsible not to plan new urban fabric around these emerging microgeneration technologies. The same supply chain can also be used to upgrade existing homes and workplaces – although it is harder to achieve high levels of thermal efficiency, so slightly higher personal biomass quotas will be required.

If we could replace or renovate the majority of our urban fabric to this performance specification at an average rate of 5 per cent per annum, we could probably achieve reductions in the cost of both energy efficiency and microgeneration fast enough to achieve wholesale adoption just before peak oil and inflation caused by climate change make any investment in building fabric impossible. An energy mortgage system introduced now would remove the obstacle of high capital costs, funding the energy efficiency and microgeneration installation from savings made from not having to purchase fossil fuel. This strategy then frees up the remainder of the national biomass reserve for allocation to higher density urban plots – which will need to adopt ZEDstandards or continental *passivhaus* levels of energy efficient fabric with a minimum of 20 per cent contribution from on site renewable electricity. This is realistically achievable, even on an eight-storey development, as the top two to three storeys enjoy the same solar and wind access as a suburban plot. ZEDfactory have designed schemes achieving 175 homes per hectare and requiring less than 500 dry kg of biomass per year – staying within the limits of a future national biomass ration without requiring the conversion from food to energy cropland. This higher biomass quota can only be sustained on the remaining 30 per cent of our national built fabric by correctly matching energy demand of both workspace and housing on mixed use urban regeneration projects using woodchip fuelled combined heat and power plants. Using more than your fair share of the national biomass quota to achieve carbon neutrality is reckless, a ruse practised by developers seeking to reduce capital cost at the expense of escalating future running costs – effectively stealing future communal national renewable energy reserves.

Recent government incentives have significantly enhanced the chances of achieving these long term strategic targets. The Code for Sustainable Homes will make very similar standards to those used to design 'Hopetown' in 1996 and BedZED in 1998 mandatory for all new housing by 2016. Meanwhile the new Home Information Packs will provide all homes for sale with an energy efficiency grading. For the first time the public will be provided with the tools to take decisions about the most significant financial investment most people ever make. With the energy grading for each home now required with every sale and an effective public information campaign about the future hazards of climate change and peak oil, coinciding with the introduction of low cost microgeneration initiatives on a national scale, we could see significant empowerment of the population where each homeowner has decided to become part of the solution rather than contribute to the accelerating environmental crisis.

7

Community-scale biomass CHP at BedZED – the latest clean combustion technologies make this a useful solution for high-density urban communities, providing the natural biomass quota is used to limit overconsumption of a scarce resource

ZEDfact

The ZEDquarters urban concept

All the old European cities were divided into political / religious / ethnic identities, however most of the time a harmonious co-existence was achieved. We would like to propose a new cultural quarter for major regeneration sites based on environmental awareness.

This is the 'ZEDquarter' – a new urban district of both new and existing buildings where people of all sects, creeds and backgrounds can unite under a common aspiration – to create a zero waste / zero carbon society – achieving a step change reduction in environmental impact at the same time as increasing most ordinary peoples' quality of life.

These communities have decided to live within their 'earthshare' – working towards a one planet lifestyle and workstyle – and looking forward to a future without guilt or despair.

They will generate new cultural values that will significantly enrich a larger cities' vitality, and will provide a living demonstration of a clean green future that the wider city outside will choose without coercion and legislation.

The ZEDquarter will spread by consensus – radiating outwards, repairing the damaged urban fabric all around.

Three p's summarise this book. In parts it is justly provocative, it is also prophetic but most importantly it shows what is possible. This is an excellent book which should be read by designers (both students and practitioners), policy makers and politicians. After all, buildings contribute over 30% of global greenhouse gas emissions … this pioneering book helps lead the way forward.

Geoff Levermore
Professor of the Built Environment, the University of Manchester

Mature skygardens at BedZED, reaching the residential density of Soho. How can we reconcile a step change reduction in our carbon footprint at the same time as increasing our collective quality of life?

Foreword by Jonathon Porritt

As we are regularly told, prophets are reputedly never honoured in their own land. Often for good reason, it has to be said, as prophets can make stroppy, uncomfortable bedfellows, especially in an age of deep-seated denial about the kind of things that prophets keep prophesying about.

The "not honoured" generalization certainly doesn't apply to the authors of this work. They are much and genuinely honoured by other architects, environmentalists, land use professionals and those who've been inspired by their unique combination of prophecy and practicality.

But the problem is that they're not honoured enough by enough of the so-called "decision-makers" in this ecologically-illiterate land. Despite years of spuriously stoked-up scientific controversy about climate change and its potential impact on our lives, the low-carbon writing has been on the wall for at least a decade. However, government ministers, house builders, chairs of planning committees and the majority of architectural practices have kept on strolling past that wall, studiously averting their gaze from what remains a deeply uncomfortable truth: that we have to totally transform our approach to house building and to the built environment in general if we're going to get anywhere close to achieving the reduction in emissions of CO_2 and other greenhouse gases that are now so urgently required.

Many of those people love making eloquent speeches about climate change, often referring to BedZED – Bill Dunster's iconic zero carbon housing development in Merton that first demonstrated the feasibility of delivering high-quality housing for the lowest possible carbon footprint. Brilliant stuff. People loved it. And they kept on loving it. When I made a television programme recently on sustainable consumption, I was astonished (and even a little depressed) to discover that BedZED was *still* the best (and certainly the best-known) exemplar of this approach to housing here in the UK.

At long last, however, that is now beginning to change. The Government has set a real "stretch target" for house builders by determining that all new houses built after 2016 must be zero carbon. On top of that, the proposal for a number of Eco-Towns from the Department for Communities and Local Government represents a real breakthrough, and the new Green Paper on Housing is much more sustainability-friendly than any previous document. As a result, a number of house builders have already started to think much more ambitiously about zero carbon and sustainable building techniques, materials and supply chains.

As the bar is raised, inch by inch, you can absolutely guarantee that the ZED team will be straining upwards much further and much faster, reminding us all (sometimes quite uncomfortably!) how much more there is still to be done in this critical area and exactly how we should set about doing it.

Jonathon Porritt
Founder Director of Forum for the Future and
Chairman of the UK Sustainable Development Commission

Introduction

Every aspect of our contemporary society runs on cheap fossil fuel; from agriculture and food production to transport and buildings. This stockpile of energy, this 'stored sunlight of paleozoic summers' left intact by past civilisations, is being squandered. Current generations – certainly those yet to reach mid-life – will have to learn to survive without abundant energy.

Fossil fuels are not the only resources being consumed at unsustainable levels. Forests are shrinking, fresh water is scarce, fishing grounds are being depleted and topsoil is eroding – just a few of the global ecosystems under pressure.

The ecological footprint of humanity is still growing – both as numbers increase and as lifestyles become more profligate. Six and a half billion people are competing for a shrinking world.

Those growing old in today's market-based, global economy will need a new generosity of spirit – a commitment to construct a world order based on equity and co-operation. Without this, global society will collapse as conflicts over resources dominate every aspect of our lives from the freedom to express ourselves to Government spending priorities.

In the authors' experience of delivering this somewhat gloomy prognostication to audiences the world over, four deeply visceral reactions surface: denial, depression, wild optimism or constructive engagement.

The deniers are the proverbial ostriches who stick their heads in the sand and either ignore or contest the mounting scientific evidence that compels urgent action.

The depressed take the issues very much to heart. They might succeed in compartmentalising their concerns – even burying them in the tribulations of day-to-day living – but the concerns just keep re-surfacing. They see little benefit in acting alone but are fatalistic about the chance of engaging others.

The wild optimists are seduced by the belief that human ingenuity will provide the necessary solutions. They comfort themselves in the warm blanket of history – the belief that hurdles have been vaulted in the past and will be again.

We, the authors, prefer to see ourselves as members of the growing band of constructive engagers. The aim in writing this book is to take the reader beyond denial and depression. There are many good books which nourish these emotions, set out the evidence, and scope out the various alternate paths that society might tread – from the gentle 'powerdown' to the terminal collapse. We hope to convince the optimists that there is no quick techno-fix lurking around the corner, but that there are solutions nonetheless which are practical, proven and cost effective.

We call our blueprint for a sustainable society ZEDliving – a term which attempts to accommodate both our logical arguments for change and the package of design

Opposite

BedZED – urban infill in Tomlins Grove, East London

and engineering measures which can together deliver a high quality of life in a shrinking world.

The ZED is short for 'zero (fossil) energy development' – a term popularised by the award-winning Beddington ZED (or BedZED), a development of 'zero carbon' live/work units in the London Borough of Sutton. Though modest in size, BedZED's holistic approach to sustainability has attracted admirers from around the world. Many thousands of planners, architects, engineers, environmentalists and policy-makers have visited BedZED since it was completed in 2002.

The authors have, to varying degrees, all been involved in BedZED and similar ZEDs before and since. Most notably, Bill was BedZED's architect.

Given this background, it will come as no surprise that this book is a synthesis of practical knowledge, hard-earned experience and collective vision. We realise that this is a lot of ground to cover in one book but feel that the coherence of our message would be lost were the content to be sliced up between multiple sets of covers.

To lend some structure to the ZEDliving blueprint we have divided the content into three distinct parts.

In Part 1 we introduce the basic philosophy behind ZEDliving. In the first four chapters we set out a series of quantified ZED design principles, one per chapter, followed by an introduction to the ZEDstandards – a simple checklist for assessing compliance with the ZEDliving approach.

In Part 2 we dig deep into the detailed design issues which are essential elements of the ZEDliving approach.

In Part 3 we present case studies to illustrate the application of ZEDliving principles.

Each part will undoubtedly appeal to different audiences and can be tackled individually. However, for the full ZEDliving experience we would urge people to read outside their 'comfort zone'. ZEDliving is not going to happen unless we all think a little more 'outside of the box'.

1
BedZED – southernmost terrace

2
BedZED demonstrates how a low carbon lifestyle and workstyle produces new urban design and a new building aesthetic

Part one

Principles for ZEDliving

Streetscape of Jubilee Wharf from Commercial Road, Penryn

There is a great deal of interest in low carbon developments. That is, the design, construction and refurbishment of buildings, and their associated infrastructure, to minimise overall carbon dioxide emissions. Usually, other environmental factors are also considered in such 'eco' developments: water conservation, the protection or enhancement of site biodiversity, the use of low impact construction materials, facilities for recycling, provision for public transport, cycling and walking, and so on.

There is no universal agreement on what constitutes a 'low' emission development. However, planning guidance issued by the Greater London Authority provides a useful working definition:

> A *low carbon development* is one that achieves a reduction in carbon emissions of 50% or more from energy use on site [as compared with the building regulations prevalent at the time], on an annual basis.[1]

The ZEDstandards approach goes further. In this part we argue the case for *designing, constructing and refurbishing developments to use only renewable energy sources with no net, direct carbon emissions.* For this approach to be truly sustainable, overall energy consumption must not exceed the national renewable supply.

Broader lifestyle impacts cannot be ignored. Although about half of global carbon dioxide emissions are buildings related, the remainder (from transport, industry, agriculture and so on) also need to be tackled if climate change is to be addressed and the effects of fuel scarcity minimised.

The design challenges faced with ZEDs are very different from those that occur with low carbon developments. Carbon savings become progressively more difficult to achieve as the emissions target is reduced. Whereas a number of strategies exist for achieving 50 per cent carbon reductions – 'bolt-on' renewable solar or wind generators, large wood burning heating systems and better thermal insulation – achieving zero carbon requires a more holistic design approach. The 'nuts and bolts' of this are described in Part 2.

In Part 1 we introduce and explain the four core ZEDstandards principles:

- Make Carbon History
- Design Out Fossil Fuels
- Reduce Demand – Run on Native Renewables
- Enable a High Quality Life on a LOW Footprint.

Part 1 closes with an overview – a handy reference to all those elements which contribute to the ZEDstandards.

Our aim is not to duplicate the work of others (we have provided extensive footnotes for those wishing to dig deeper into any particular topic), but to weave a path through those bodies of literature that together make a compelling case for ZEDs. Where there is a paucity of research, we have used our own writings and pulled data from our own spreadsheets to provide the necessary supporting evidence.

Though many of the arguments made are a direct response to global concerns (climate change, the scarcity of resources and so on), the examples given are necessarily local. To make best use of natural resources ZEDs must be responsive to their local environment. As we shall see, a ZED in China functions very differently from a ZED in the United Kingdom. The justification for both, and the design philosophy which underpins them is, however, the same.

These are the foundations upon which the ZEDstandards concept is built.

Community-scale masterplan integrated turbines at Jubilee Wharf, Penryn, Cornwall

Family house for three generations

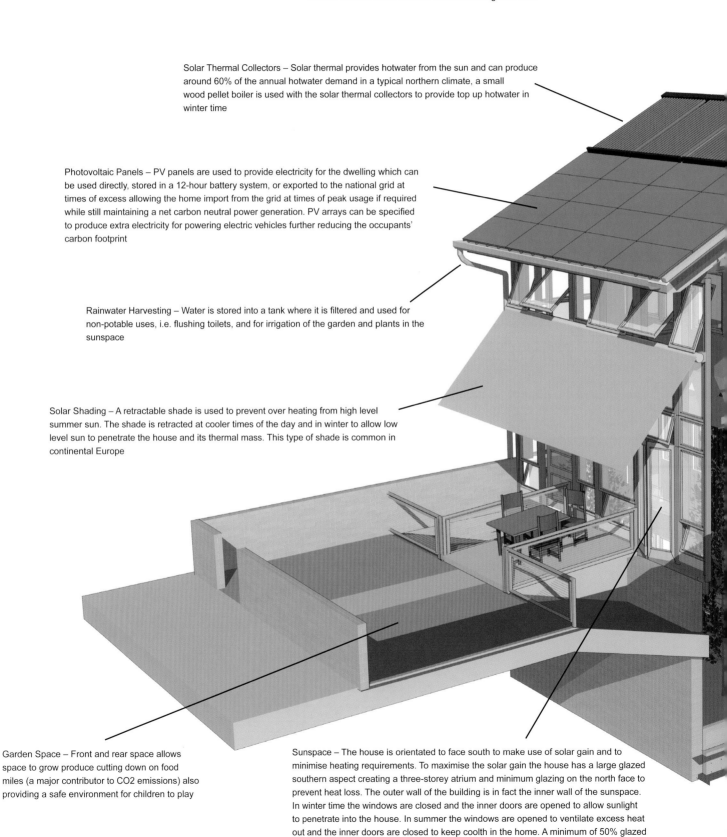

Vertical Axis Wind Turbine – A near silent VAWT provides electricity for the dwelling. A VAWT and PV panels are complementary technologies where the PV produces peak output in summer when the sunlight hours are longest whilst theVAWT produces peak output in winter when wind speeds are generally higher. Modern mountings are vibration isolated and so do not transmit into the buildings structure

Solar Thermal Collectors – Solar thermal provides hotwater from the sun and can produce around 60% of the annual hotwater demand in a typical northern climate, a small wood pellet boiler is used with the solar thermal collectors to provide top up hotwater in winter time

Photovoltaic Panels – PV panels are used to provide electricity for the dwelling which can be used directly, stored in a 12-hour battery system, or exported to the national grid at times of excess allowing the home import from the grid at times of peak usage if required while still maintaining a net carbon neutral power generation. PV arrays can be specified to produce extra electricity for powering electric vehicles further reducing the occupants' carbon footprint

Rainwater Harvesting – Water is stored into a tank where it is filtered and used for non-potable uses, i.e. flushing toilets, and for irrigation of the garden and plants in the sunspace

Solar Shading – A retractable shade is used to prevent over heating from high level summer sun. The shade is retracted at cooler times of the day and in winter to allow low level sun to penetrate the house and its thermal mass. This type of shade is common in continental Europe

Garden Space – Front and rear space allows space to grow produce cutting down on food miles (a major contributor to CO2 emissions) also providing a safe environment for children to play

Sunspace – The house is orientated to face south to make use of solar gain and to minimise heating requirements. To maximise the solar gain the house has a large glazed southern aspect creating a three-storey atrium and minimum glazing on the north face to prevent heat loss. The outer wall of the building is in fact the inner wall of the sunspace. In winter time the windows are closed and the inner doors are opened to allow sunlight to penetrate into the house. In summer the windows are opened to ventilate excess heat out and the inner doors are closed to keep coolth in the home. A minimum of 50% glazed opening window area in the outer glazed screen turns a winter sunspace into a summer veranda, with internal balcony floors shading the internal glass wall

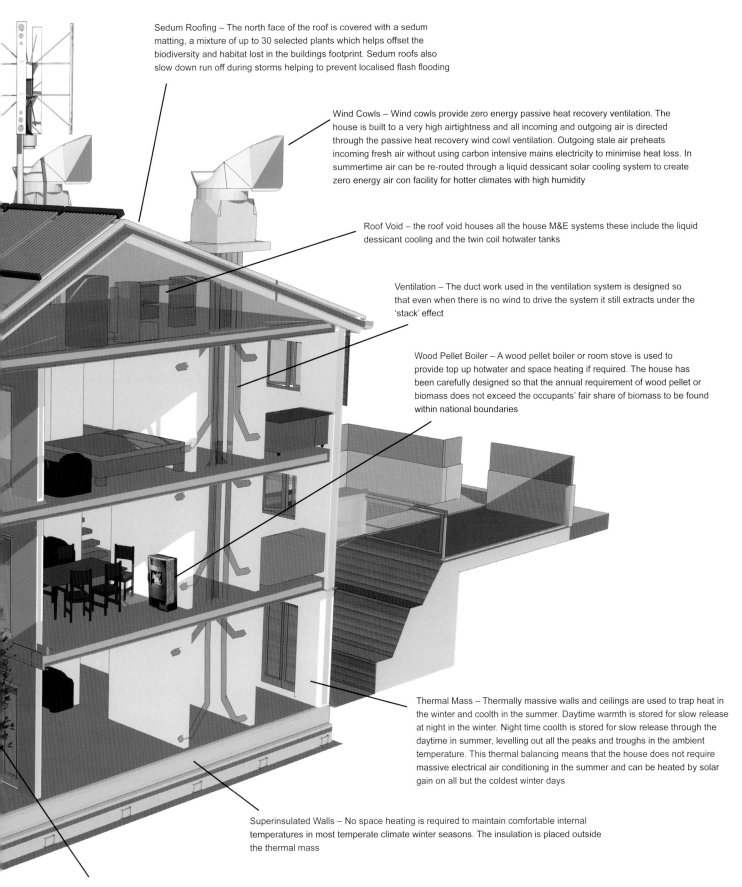

Sedum Roofing – The north face of the roof is covered with a sedum matting, a mixture of up to 30 selected plants which helps offset the biodiversity and habitat lost in the buildings footprint. Sedum roofs also slow down run off during storms helping to prevent localised flash flooding

Wind Cowls – Wind cowls provide zero energy passive heat recovery ventilation. The house is built to a very high airtightness and all incoming and outgoing air is directed through the passive heat recovery wind cowl ventilation. Outgoing stale air preheats incoming fresh air without using carbon intensive mains electricity to minimise heat loss. In summertime air can be re-routed through a liquid dessicant solar cooling system to create zero energy air con facility for hotter climates with high humidity

Roof Void – the roof void houses all the house M&E systems these include the liquid dessicant cooling and the twin coil hotwater tanks

Ventilation – The duct work used in the ventilation system is designed so that even when there is no wind to drive the system it still extracts under the 'stack' effect

Wood Pellet Boiler – A wood pellet boiler or room stove is used to provide top up hotwater and space heating if required. The house has been carefully designed so that the annual requirement of wood pellet or biomass does not exceed the occupants' fair share of biomass to be found within national boundaries

Thermal Mass – Thermally massive walls and ceilings are used to trap heat in the winter and coolth in the summer. Daytime warmth is stored for slow release at night in the winter. Night time coolth is stored for slow release through the daytime in summer, levelling out all the peaks and troughs in the ambient temperature. This thermal balancing means that the house does not require massive electrical air conditioning in the summer and can be heated by solar gain on all but the coldest winter days

Superinsulated Walls – No space heating is required to maintain comfortable internal temperatures in most temperate climate winter seasons. The insulation is placed outside the thermal mass

Indoor Growing – The sunspace can be used as a glasshouse to provide produce such as salad out of season or citrus that would otherwise not ripen in a northern climate, also plants can be started early before planting out as in a potting shed

ZED Principle 1

A ZED should permit a high quality of life on less than 2.1 tonnes of CO_2 per annum

1.1 Make carbon history

We have 45 years, and if we start now, not in 10 or 15 years' time, we have a chance of hitting those targets. But we've got to start now. We have no time to lose.

Lord Oxburgh, non-executive chairman
of Shell on the challenge of tackling
climate change, speech at the 2005 Hay-on-Wye Festival

The evidence of the first signs of climate change is all around us. In Europe, the glaciers of the Alps are disappearing and droughts in the Mediterranean are worsening. Southern Spain is turning to desert. In the tropics, high sea temperatures whip up unprecedented storms and hurricanes that bring floods and lethal landslides. In Siberia, roads buckle as permafrost melts. And, as ice melts and oceans warm, sea levels worldwide are rising.

UK Environment Agency[1]

The debate on whether or not human-induced climate change is actually happening has all but ended. At what point the global consensus shifted is difficult to identify, though the official admission in 2002 by the United States Government that 'Greenhouse gases are accumulating in the Earth's atmosphere as a result of human activities' was undoubtedly a tipping point.[2]

The evidence that has won over the sternest sceptics is the firm correspondence between global carbon emissions from the combustion of oil, gas, coal and other fossil fuels (see Figure 1.1.1), rising atmospheric concentrations of carbon dioxide (CO_2) (see Figure 1.1.2) and global average temperature increases (so called global warming) (see Figure 1.1.3).

1.1.1
Global carbon emissions from fossil fuel combustion 1800–2000
1.1.2
Atmospheric CO_2 concentrations 1750–2000

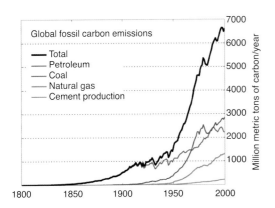

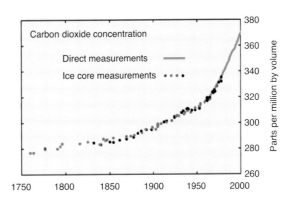

Opposite
Drax coal-fired power station – the biggest single source of CO_2 emissions in the UK. It alone emits more than 22 million tonnes of CO_2 per year

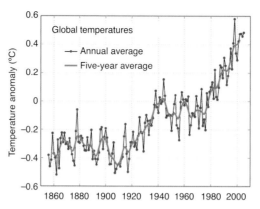

1.1.3
Global temperature increases 1860–2000

Box 1.1.1: Climate change by degrees

In 2005, an international scientific symposium at the Hadley Centre for Climate Prediction and Research in the United Kingdom gathered evidence from 200 experts from 30 countries on the threats of climate change.

The conference, *Avoiding Dangerous Climate Change*, took as its starting point the Third Assessment Report of the International Panel on Climate Change (IPCC), which estimated that global temperatures would rise anywhere from 1.4 to 5.8°C this century.

The scientists concluded that increases of as little as 1°C could seriously impact on sensitive ecosystems, such as the coral reefs, and a rise of 2.7°C could trigger melting of the Greenland ice cap, which would eventually raise global sea levels by around 7 m. A range of other ecosystem impacts were linked to specific temperature increases.[7] To be certain of averting the more serious impacts of climate change would require stabilisation of atmospheric carbon concentrations at below 400 parts per million (ppm). Stabilising at 450 ppm *may* limit the more serious impacts. At current rates of increase, 400 ppm could be reached before 2015.

For more information, see www.stabilisation2005.com

CO_2 is not the most potent greenhouse gas, but it is the most abundant. The Kyoto Protocol, which seeks to regulate global greenhouse gas emissions, lists five others.[3]

CO_2 concentrations in the atmosphere have increased from pre-industrial levels of 280 parts per million (1750), to 288 ppm (1850), 369 ppm (2000), 375 ppm (2003) and are accelerating.[4]

This exponential rise in emissions is not entirely proportional to the increase in the burning of fossil fuels – there are signs that a worrying positive feedback loop is spiralling emissions higher than might be expected. This has been referred to as 'runaway' climate change. The exact cause of this is currently speculation – but there is no shortage of viable theories, including the release of carbon from the melting of permafrost[5] and changes in the ocean's ability to sequester CO_2.[6]

Though there is general agreement on the science of climate change, the severity of its consequences is the subject of on-going research (see Box 1.1.1).

Inevitably, there remains uncertainty over the exact nature and likely future rate of climate change. Few would deny, though, that the scale of change implied by even the more modest predictions demands a precautionary approach and urgent action. The European Union believes that the global temperature rise should be limited to no more than 2°C above the pre-industrial level in order to prevent the worst impacts of climate change.

Climate change cannot be stopped – it has already begun – but the more serious consequences can be avoided by taking action to limit CO_2 emissions now. There is a time lag between the release of the CO_2 and its climate-changing effect so, even if emissions were stabilised or reduced now, the damage would continue for decades to come.

Box 1.1.2: Signs of climate change

Two of the best documented signs of climate change are sea level change and the thinning of the Arctic ice.

Sea ice has thinned by 40 per cent in places reflecting diminishing snow cover and mountain glaciers. The sea level has also risen by about 15 cm during the last century, partly due to the thermal expansion of the oceans and partly attributable to melting ice.

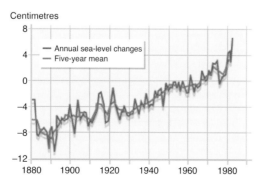

1.1.4
Sea level change over the last century

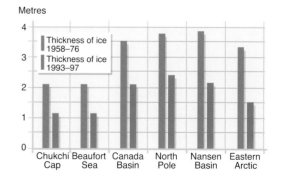

1.1.5
Thinning of Arctic sea ice

Carbon targets

Setting carbon reduction targets is part science and part politics. Assuming that consensus can be reached on the overall acceptable level of global emissions, then the way in which this is allocated as national and individual quotas is bound to be controversial. If the complex process of reducing global carbon emissions is to have a fighting chance of succeeding then it must start with a broad framework agreement – one that nations both big and small can live with.

The most likely candidate is 'Contraction and Convergence' (C&C), devised by the Global Commons Institute (GCI). This starts from the simple premise that every individual has an equal right to pollute. It proposes that, first, we need to reach international agreement on safe and acceptable levels of overall global emissions (contraction) and then, second, reduce or increase emissions from individual countries, until all countries are emitting CO_2 in proportion to the size of the populations and within the global limits (convergence).

C&C does not suggest definite target dates, or stabilisation rates for carbon, but the GCI's modelling work makes it abundantly clear that industrialised countries will need to reduce their emissions dramatically in the next 50 years (see Box 1.1.3).

So, having discussed our preferred mechanism for globally managing and allocating emissions, what is the scale of reductions needed to arrest climate change?

Emissions from fossil fuels are responsible for around 26.8 billion tonnes of CO_2 per annum.[10] With a global population estimated at 6.4 billion, this amounts to an average of approximately 4.2 tonnes of CO_2 per person.

Of course, the actual average emissions vary considerably by country and by lifestyle. Figure 1.1.6 shows average per capita emissions and population by world region. The most populous region in the world, Asia, also has one of the lowest average per capita emissions. Hence the concern that if Asia follows the same development path as Europe and North America, global emissions will grow stratospherically.

If all the world's population led lifestyles similar to the Europeans, then global CO_2 emissions would double. If they followed North American patterns of consumption then emissions would increase five-fold.

Using the Contraction and Convergence framework to guide them, scientists Mayer Hillman and Tina Fawcett[11] argue that 450 ppm is the maximum concentration of atmospheric CO_2 that should be considered safe (see Box 1.1.1). This is equivalent to converging on global average emissions of around 2.1 tonnes CO_2 per person per

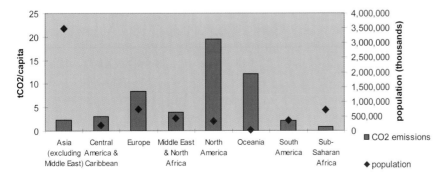

1.1.6
Average per capita emissions and population by world region (2002)

Box 1.1.3: More about 'Contraction & Convergence' [C&C]
Kindly contributed by Aubrey Meyer, GCI

C&C is the science-based, global climate-policy framework, proposed to the United Nations since 1990 by the GCI.

The objective of safe and stable greenhouse gas concentrations in the atmosphere and the principles of precaution and equity, as already agreed in the United Nations Framework Convention of Climate Change (UNFCCC), provide the formal calculating basis of the C&C framework that proposes:

- A full-term contraction budget for global emissions consistent with stabilising atmospheric concentrations of greenhouse gases (GHGs) at a pre-agreed concentration maximum deemed to be safe, following IPCC WG1[8] carbon cycle modelling.

- The international sharing of this budget as 'entitlements' results from a negotiable rate of linear convergence to equal shares per person globally by an agreed date within the timeline of the full-term contraction/concentration agreement.

- Negotiations for this at the UNFCCC[9] should occur between regions of the world, leaving negotiations between countries within their respective regions, such as the European Union, the Africa Union, the United States and so on. The inter-regional, inter-national and intra-national tradability of these entitlements in a currency such as International Energy Backed Currency Units (EBCUs) is appropriate.

- Scientific understanding of the relationship between an emissions-free economy and concentrations develops, so rates of C&C can evolve under periodic revision.

C&C is science guided, rights based, simple and easy to understand. It turns a problem into a solution. It answers, (1) the US demand for all-country inclusion, (2) the developing country demand for equity over emissions historically accumulated in the atmosphere and (3) the emissions-trading prerequisite of capping. It turns argument into agreement and the certainty of principle into practice.

C&C now has much international support. Protection lies in formally establishing C&C compliance as the basis of the UN Climate Treaty. Collective corporate advocacy of this is needed now. Find out more:

http://www.gci.org.uk/briefings/ICE.pdf
http://www.gci.org.uk/images/CC_Demo(pc).exe
A detailed PDF image can be zoom-viewed on-line at:
http://www.gci.org.uk/images/C&C_Bubbles.pdf

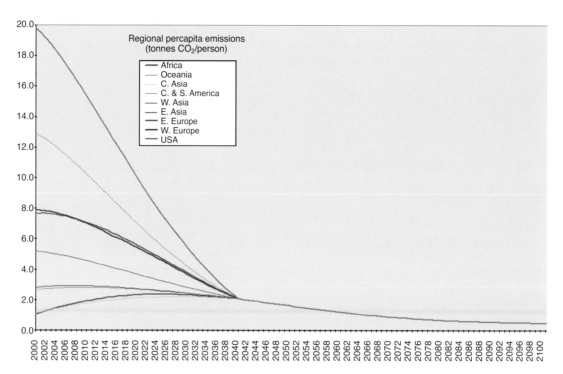

1.1.7

Contraction and Convergence. Illustration shows
convergence to average per capita emissions of 2.1 tonnes
by 2040

year before 2050 (see Figure 1.1.7). Though such figures can never be precise, this
requires reductions of the order of 75 per cent in Europe and 90 per cent in North
America. The figure for the United Kingdom is 80 per cent. Beyond 2050 the figure
will have to fall still further.

2.1 Tonnes CO$_2$

Throughout this book we will use 2.1 tonnes CO$_2$ per capita by 2050 as our ZED
design goal, our benchmark for an equitable, sustainable future. Taking into account
all emissions – direct and indirect – associated with modern living, a ZED should
permit a high quality of life without breaching this 2.1 tonne limit.

This need not be achieved immediately but, given that most new buildings,
and a substantial proportion of existing buildings and infrastructure, will still be
around in 2050, any development must be future-proofed to facilitate this carbon
goal.

It is a challenging, but necessary, target if we are to avoid catastrophic climate
change. It is also just the start. Emissions will have to fall still further if the accumu-
lation of CO$_2$ in our atmosphere is to be reversed rather than merely stabilised.

Later on we will suggest ways in which this 2.1 tonnes could reasonably be
distributed among the various activities, goods and services that are an accepted
part of modern living. Suffice to say that 2.1 tonnes is comparatively little (see Box
1.1.4) and, where there are opportunities to make savings, these should be made.
It is particularly important to ensure that long lived capital items, buildings and
infrastructure are built to work both now and under future operating constraints.

Contrast this with a typical specification lightweight, high-energy building that is the norm today. How will these survive in a post-carbon world? What will these cost to run when carbon is taxed to the hilt? Society is currently investing in buildings which will be redundant within 20 years, creating the environmental equivalent of shanty towns.

In the next chapter we will learn why carbon reductions may be forced upon society by another inescapable ecological phenomenon – the decline in fossil energy supplies.

Carbon rationing – a further incentive for ZEDliving

One method of managing carbon emissions, which is attracting several high profile supporters, including one former UK Environment Minister,[12] is that of personal carbon allowances or PCAs (also known as domestic tradable quotas).

The idea behind PCAs is remarkably simple, though different views exist on the best method of implementation. The basic principle is that each individual within a country is allocated an equal number of carbon 'credits'. This would most likely be, in the first instance, around 5 tonnes of CO_2 per year or 5,000 credits – each unit being equal to a kilogramme of CO_2.

Current thinking is that PCAs would be managed electronically, with each person being issued with a carbon debit card. Credits would be deducted from your personal carbon account each time any energy was purchased – for example, petrol, gas or electricity.

The amount debited would be in proportion to the carbon emissions released from combustion of the fuel. In this example, each litre of petrol would 'cost' 2.3 credits, each kilowatt-hour of UK grid electricity 0.4 credits, and each kilowatt-hour of gas 0.2 units. Credits could even be associated with the use of public transport or aircraft flights. A return trip from London to the USA East Coast would 'cost' around 1,400 credits (or more if greenhouse gases other than CO_2 were included).

Those who found themselves with insufficient credits could purchase them at the market rate from others who had a surplus.

The amount of credits in circulation would be slowly reduced over time (at about 2–5 per cent per annum) to shrink national carbon emissions. Either fewer credits could be issued each year or the Government could 'buy up' credits at the market value.

Based on the current trading price of carbon, credits would initially be inexpensive – about £10 or €15 per thousand – but would rapidly gain value as trading started and credits were 'retired'.

PCAs, once introduced, would quite quickly motivate people to adopt low carbon, ZED lifestyles. Say, for example, in the first years of a PCA scheme credits quadrupled in price. This would yield several hundred pounds for the ZED resident without any reductions in their quality of life. Alternatively, rather than trading their spare carbon credits, they could be saved up for a long-haul holiday.

Of course, only about half of carbon emissions can be easily attributed to individual purchasing. PCAs would have to be combined with a system of resource taxation, possibly based on an extension of the existing European carbon emissions trading scheme, to effectively reduce overall emissions.

Box 1.1.4: Five things you can do with 2.1 tonnes of CO_2

The sustainable level of CO_2 emissions assumed throughout this book is 2.1 tonnes per person *each year*, to be achieved by 2050.

To give an idea of the scale of reductions needed to reach this 'carbon footprint', the following examples are provided. Based on current technologies, *each* of these activities result in emissions of about 2.1 tonnes CO_2:

1. Driving 11,500 km in an average UK petrol car OR 26,000 km in a small, ultra efficient car OR 5,500 km in a sports utility vehicle (SUV).
2. Flying 8,000 km (equivalent to a one-way trip from London to San Francisco).
3. Travelling 44,000 km by coach OR 35,000 km by train.
4. Transporting 10 tonnes of freight 7,000 km by rail OR 135 km by air (short haul) OR 21,000 km by ship (bulk carrier).
5. Using 4,300 kWh of UK grid electricity (2.5 times the current average UK consumption of electricity). This is approximately equivalent to the energy used by a TV if watched continuously for 3 years OR running a fridge for 12 years OR 3,500 cycles of a washing machine.

1.1.8
2.1 tonnes of carbon dioxide is enough to fill one large hot air balloon.

emissary

1.1.9
Carbon credit card

Such a scheme would, nonetheless, be a big step towards reducing our carbon emissions.

London-based product innovation consultancy Design Stream and Identity specialist Sven Vogel have responded to interest in PCAs by creating the Emissary card concept – a carbon debit card which uses advanced thin screen technology to display messages about our consumption of goods and services as purchases are made, see: www.designstream.co.uk.

Carbon casualties

Though this chapter has focused on the less controversial environmental impacts of climate change, the direct and indirect human suffering that global warming will cause is nothing short of devastating.

Whereas the rich countries are responsible for the bulk of carbon emissions, it is inevitably those in the poorer countries that will experience most of the suffering. For example, the tidal barriers and sea defences under construction in the West are simply unaffordable or unworkable for countries such as Bangladesh. Being low lying and densely populated, Bangladesh is particularly vulnerable to both sea level rises[13] and the tidal surges which tend to accompany monsoons (a more regular feature in a warmer world). Thirty to seventy per cent of Bangladesh is already flooded each year. The potential scale of the problem is almost unimaginable. In 2004 alone, 30 million Bangladeshis were displaced or made homeless, more than 100,000 were affected by waterborne diseases and at least 700 were killed. It has been estimated that US $7 billion worth of damage was caused.[14]

One can't help feeling that were the effects of climate change to be felt so severely in a wealthier part of the world there would be riots in the street, Governments would fall and all steps would be taken to tackle the root cause of the problem. Surely, regardless of the geography, it is those countries historically responsible for causing the problem that should be proactive in championing the solutions?

To try and make the plight of the world's carbon casualties more tangible, we have here attempted to estimate the numbers annually killed or otherwise affected by climate change.

Climate change-related extreme weather events are responsible for the majority of carbon casualties, and they are on the increase. The insurance industry, hit by rising claims, is in no doubt of this. In 2002 Bruno Porro, the Chief Risk Officer at insurance giant Swiss Re, wrote that 'The climate has changed: visibly, tangibly, measurably. An additional increase in average global temperatures is not only possible, but very probable.'[15]

The number of recorded disasters has quadrupled in the last 40 years (see Figure 1.1.10). The human cost of this is significant. It is estimated that somewhere between 150,000 and 500,000 die annually from climate related disasters. This is probably an under-estimate – climate change may be responsible indirectly for many more deaths. Each year more than 250 million are sufficiently affected to warrant urgent assistance (for example, they are made homeless, require emergency medical assistance or food rations).[16]

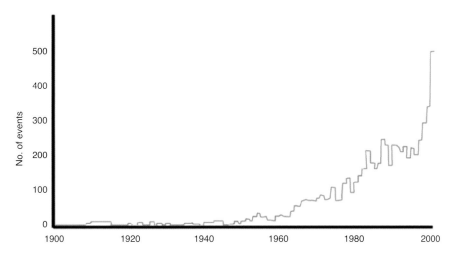

Annual global frequency of recorded climate-related disasters for all disaster types

How many people are affected per tonne of CO_2 emitted?

This was a question which challenged the authors at a meeting of climate change experts in Oxford, held at Christchurch College in 2005. Although any attempt to link human suffering with carbon emissions is bound to be both controversial and methodologically problematic, we felt that it was nonetheless a calculation worth attempting.

In 2002, around 25,757 million tonnes of CO_2 were emitted from fossil fuel burning.[17] The number of people killed and affected varies from year to year, due to many factors, but here we will use the figure of 250 million – a conservative estimate based on recent data – though the way data is recorded could mean that the same people are affected by multiple events.

The number of disasters associated with climate change is predicted to increase for some years, even if early action is taken, due to the time lag built into atmospheric cycles. Some estimates suggest a possible doubling of the number affected by climate change within the next 20 years.[18]

For the purpose of this exercise, we will ignore historical and future emissions (no account will be taken of the cumulative nature of unsustainable emissions). Though population and climate related events are increasing, we shall also assume that no more people are killed or affected by the average extreme climate event than now. These assumptions are both conservative and simplistic.

Let us take as our starting point a person living an average, modern urban lifestyle, emitting around 11.5 tonnes of CO_2 per year, with a life expectancy of 87 years. Within their lifetime they will emit close to 1,000 tonnes of CO_2. Most of this will be unsustainable – that is, it will accumulate in the atmosphere rather than be sequestered by the oceans, soil or vegetation.

Snapshot data for 2002 shows that approximately 10 people were killed or affected for every 1,000 tonnes of CO_2 emitted that year (250 million people divided by 25,757 million tonnes of CO_2).

This back-of-the-envelope calculation conveys a strong message. For each person living a 'high carbon' lifestyle, somewhere in the world 10 other people will be killed or affected, over their lifetime, by an extreme climate related weather event. Something to think about when you next leave your television on standby.

1.1.11
The World Food Programme recognises that climate change will cause a dramatic increase in the demand for food aid. According to their 2006 annual report, natural disasters have more than doubled between 1994 and 2006

ZEDfact

Have the rules now changed?

In 2002 around 25,757 million tonnes of CO_2 were emitted from burning fossil fuel.

In an average year 250 million people are killed, face starvation, require urgent medical attention or are made homeless because of climate-related disaster – this is five times the number recorded in 1980.

In 2002 10 people were killed or affected for every thousand tonnes of CO_2 emitted that year.

It is now possible to quantify days of human life saved / tonnes of CO_2 avoided.

Continuing with CO_2 emissions as usual is likely to result in a 5 degree change in average global temperature – leading to the loss of two-thirds of the world's productive farmland – leading to starvation for billions.

A typical four-person UK household responsible for 12 tonnes CO_2 per year over three generations will be directly responsible for the suffering of the same number of people in a climate change hot spot. This figure could increase exponentially as climate change accelerates.

Is it still socially acceptable to join the jet set?

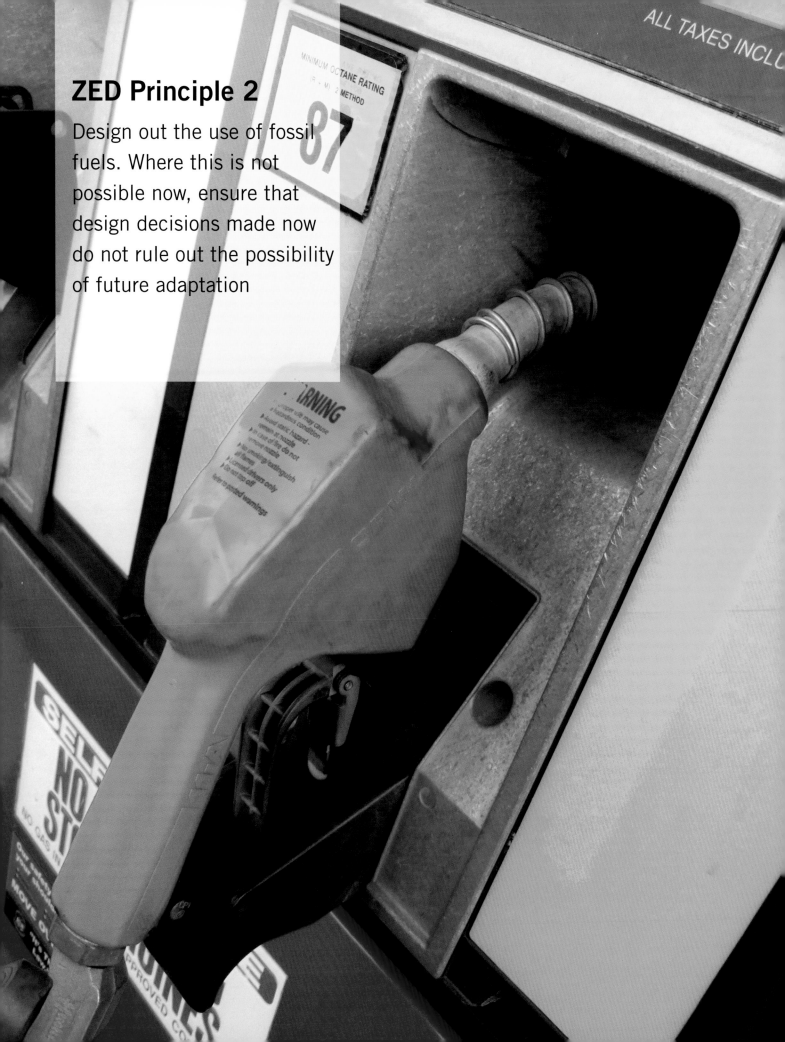

ZED Principle 2

Design out the use of fossil fuels. Where this is not possible now, ensure that design decisions made now do not rule out the possibility of future adaptation

1.2 Design Out Fossil Fuels

A series of crises in oil supply is likely over the coming decades ... These
crises will have global economic and geopolitical significance: The
oil price will be high and volatile, and demand growth will have to be
curtailed.

'Oil Supply Challenges – 2:
What Can OPEC Deliver?'
Oil and Gas Journal, 7 March 2005

Almost all expert opinion agrees that [peak oil] is fast approaching,
possibly within five years, almost certainly within 15. What is so
disturbing is that long-term global policymaking on this, perhaps the
biggest decision this century, is virtually non-existent and driven instead
by self-destructive short-termism.

Michael Meacher,
Former UK Environment Minister,
Daily Telegraph, 26 June 2006

A short history of oil

There are three major forms of fossil fuel: coal, oil and natural gas. All three were
formed many hundreds of millions of years ago, before the time of the dinosaurs. They
were formed from compacted organic materials (dead plants and animals), mainly in
the geological era known as the Carboniferous Period, about 300 million years ago.

The formation of these fuels took millennia and took place under very specific
conditions and over an incredibly long timescale. For all intents and purposes fossil
fuels are therefore considered non-renewable, finite resources.

The fact that fossil fuels are finite means that supplies will, at some point, be
exhausted. As we shall see, there is evidence that the decline in oil and gas supplies
may well start to occur within the next decade.

Far from seeing open political debate and front page headlines on the subject,
we find that, as with climate change, the prevailing mood is one of denial. Despite
an array of excellent books on the subject,[1] our decision-makers and opinion-formers
are strangely silent on the issue.

To be sure, the subject matter is not totally ignored in the media. The problem
has been described as like having a gorilla in the room: too huge and terrifying
to tackle, but equally difficult to ignore.[2] Perhaps the scale and extent of the
changes required to reduce our reliance on fossil fuels has engendered a sense

Opposite
More than 1,100,000,000,000 litres of petrol are consumed each year worldwide.
The figure is increasing by more than 1.5% per annum

of helplessness. Like the rabbit caught in the headlights, society risks being condemned by its own inaction.

How long have we got?

When fossil fuels are going to 'run out' is a hotly debated subject. But most experts now agree that the critical issue is not one of total depletion but more to do with when production peaks. After 'peak oil' the gap between rising demands (assuming current trends continue) and diminishing supplies widens, leading to restrictions in supply and increased costs, requiring substantive changes in the structure of the economy and the lifestyles of those in the higher consuming countries.

About half the world's conventional oil reserves have already been extracted (excluding shale oil and tar sands), which suggests that we are theoretically close to maximum output.

The idea of peak oil stems from the work of Shell geologist M. K. Hubbert who successfully predicted peak production in the USA. Many argue that his Hubbert Curve, which shows the rise and fall of national output, can equally well be applied globally.

Detractors from Hubbert's theory argue that it is too simplistic. The International Energy Agency (IEA), who remain skeptical on peak oil, have tried to engage with the issue.[3] They raise two main concerns:

- whether the Hubbert model should be applied globally
- whether it accurately reflects the impact of new and emerging extraction technologies.

The Association for the Study of Peak Oil (ASPO), founded by retired petroleum geologists Jean Laherrère and Colin Campbell, is a network of scientists, affiliated with a wide array of global institutions and universities, who have an interest in determining the date and impact of the peak and decline of the world's production of oil and gas. They are in no doubt of the efficacy of Hubbert's work and issue regular estimates of the timing of peak oil. They are currently predicting peak production in 2010 (see Figure 1.2.1).[4] Note that this graph includes both oil and gas. A summary of the data used to construct this prediction can be found in Table 1.2.2.

Though initially a voice in the wilderness, ASPO are growing in strength as interest in the subject has rocketed alongside oil prices. Other individuals, within

1.2.1
Fossil fuel is a global human addiction requiring a careful rehabilitation plan if we are to avoid violence

---

Note to Table 1.2.1 (opposite)

This table lists when, as a historical matter, oil production peaked. Peaking can occur for many reasons, related or unrelated to technical extraction difficulties, such as discovery of more accessible oil elsewhere, or changes in regulations. Inclusion on this list does not necessarily mean oil extraction cannot exceed the previous peak in that country.

Data from the Association for the Study of Peak Oil & Gas, Ireland (www.peakoil.ie/) and the annual British Petroleum Energy Report (www.bp.com/liveassets/bp_internet/globalbp/globalbp_uk_english/publications/energy_reviews_2006/STAGING/local_assets/downloads/spreadsheets/statistical_review_full_report_workbook_2006.xls).

1 OPEC member

2 former OPEC member

Source of table: Wikipedia http://en.wikipedia.org/wiki/Oil_reserves#Oil_reserves_by_country

Table 1.2.1: Countries where production has already peaked

State	Regular oil (light, heavy, deepwater, polar)			Natural gas peak
	Oil discovery peak	Oil production peak	Oil depletion midpoint	
North America				
Canada	1958	1973	1988	2002
USA	1930	1971	2003	1974
Mexico	1977	2002	1999	
South America				
Argentina	1960	1998	1994	
Colombia	1992	1999	1999	
Venezuela (1)	1941	1970	2003	
Chile	1960	1982	1979	1980
Ecuador (2)	1969	2004	2007	
Peru	1861	1983	1988	
Trinidad and Tobago	1969	1978	1983	
Europe				
Albania	1928	1983	1986	
Austria	1947	1955	1970	
Croatia	1950	1988	1987	
Denmark	1971	2002	2004	
France	1958	1988	1987	1978
Germany	1952	1966	1977	1979
Hungary	1964	1987	1987	
Italy	1981	1997	2005	1994
Netherlands	1980	1987	1991	1976
Norway	1979	2003	2003	
Romania	1857	1976	1970	1982
Ukraine	1962	1970	1984	
United Kingdom	1974	1999	1998	2000
Africa				
Cameroon	1977	1986	1994	
Congo	1984	2001	2000	
Egypt	1965	1995	2007	
Gabon (2)	1985	1996	1997	
Libya (1)	1961	1970	2011	
Sudan	1980	2005	2009	
Tunisia	1971	1981	1998	
Middle East				
Bahrain	1932	1970	1977	
Oman	1962	2001	2003	
Qatar (1)	1940	2004	1998	
Syria	1966	1995	1998	
Saudi Arabia	1946	2006	2010	
Yemen	1978	1999	2003	
Eurasia and Central Asia				
Turkey	1969	1991	1992	
Uzbekistan	1992	1998	2008	
Rest of Asia				
Brunei	1929	1978	1989	2003
China	1953	2003	2003	
India	1974	2004	2003	
Indonesia (1)	1955	1977	1992	
Malaysia	1973	2004	2002	
Pakistan	1983	1992	2001	
Thailand	1981	2005	2008	
Oceania				
Papua New Guinea	1987	1993	2007	
Australia	1967	2000	2001	

1.2.2
Estimated global peak in oil and gas production

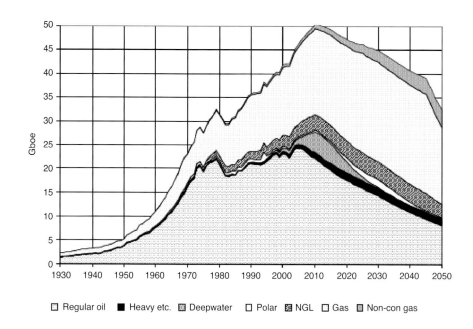

☐ Regular oil   ■ Heavy etc.   ▦ Deepwater   ☐ Polar   ▨ NGL   ☐ Gas   ▨ Non-con gas

Table 1.2.2: Estimated production by world region

Estimated Production to 2075									End 2005	
Amount (in Gb)				2005	2010	2015	2020	2050	TOTAL (in Gb)	Peak Date
Regular Oil				Annual Rate – Regular Oil (in Mb/d)						
Past	Future		Total	US-48	3.6	2.8	2.2	1.7	0.4	200	1971
Known fields		New		Europe	5.0	3.4	2.3	1.6	0.2	75	2000
968	794	138	1900	Russia	9.2	8.5	6.9	5.7	1.5	220	1987
932				ME Gulf	20	19	19	19	11	680	1974
All liquids				Other	29	27	23	20	9	725	2004
1073	1377		2450	World	67	61	54	48	22	1900	2005
2005 Base Scenario				Annual Rate – Other (in Mb/d)						
Middle East producing at capacity				Heavy etc.	2.3	3	4	4	4	151	2021
(anomalous reporting corrected)				Deepwater	3.6	12	11	6	4	69	2011
'Regular oil' excludes oil from				Polar	0.9	1	1	2	0	52	2030
Coal, shale, bitumen, heavy,				Gas Liquid	6.9	9	9	10	8	276	2035
Deepwater, polar & gasfield NGL				Rounding				-1	-2	2	
Revised	03/03/2006			**ALL**	80	86	80	70	37	2450	2010

Gb = 1,000,000,000 barrels

industry and Government, are beginning to express a view on the subject. The French Government is apparently anticipating a peak around 2013[5] and Energyfiles estimate around 2016.[6] The IEA originally published a peak oil date of 2014 but later, without much explanation, changed their official view to 'between 2020 and 2035', and now merely state that peak oil is 'beyond 2020'.[7] One comprehensive study published in 2004 took account of many of the numerous variables involved in predicting peak oil and concluded that 'global production of conventional oil will almost certainly begin an irreversible decline somewhere between 2004 and 2037'.[8]

More recent work by Paul Mobbs acknowledges the wide range of economic and sociopolitical factors that can affect the timing of peak oil. Having considered a broad evidence base, he concludes that 'There's a good chance that Peak Oil will occur within ten years [by 2015], perhaps leading to a plateau in production, and the total volume of oil might begin to reduce in fifteen to twenty years'.[9]

Though there is a gathering consensus that peak production of both oil and gas will occur – if Hubbert's theory proves sound – within the next two decades, there are many variables to consider. The main difficulty in making such predictions is the range of estimates that exist for remaining conventional reserves. Until there is independent validation of the size and quality of the reserves claimed by OPEC and other producers (often state-owned enterprises), then predicting peak production is always going to be a fuzzy science.

Given that it is in the interests of these parties to overstate their assets, a skeptic could conclude that the situation is likely to be worse than the official figures suggest. For example, in July 2006 the Kuwait Oil Company made the surprise announcement that its Burgan oil field, the second largest in the world responsible for half of Kuwait's output, was beginning to run dry.[10] The company, who had been predicting that production would rise to 2 million barrels per day and remain at that level for the foreseeable future, publicly admitted that 1.7 million barrels was all that could be achieved, casting doubt on the field's depletion rate.

Though we are inexorably climbing up Hubbert's Peak, and may already be negotiating the final rocky outcrops, the timing of peak oil is arguably less important than understanding and responding to the long term consequences of a restricted supply. The most certain outcome is rapidly escalating oil prices.[11] At the time of writing, prices are at record highs (US $75 a barrel),[12] with the cost having doubled in the last four years. Higher, more volatile oil prices are undoubtedly bad for the economy.

Some oil insiders are predicting that prices may hit US $200 by the end of the decade.[13] Even the usually cautious International Monetary Fund (IMF) has estimated that a sustained US $5 increase in the price of oil reduces Gross Domestic Product (GDP) by 0.3 per cent – equivalent to setting back economic growth by 2 or 3 months.[14] If the IMF are even in the right ballpark, then a rapid US $50 rise would plunge the global economy into deep recession.

Oil companies are largely hoping (and perhaps praying) that increases in the price people are willing to pay for oil will make currently uneconomic sources of oil – such as tar sands – more attractive. However such unconventional reserves are not without their own considerable environmental and technical problems which may prevent large scale extraction at any cost.

What is certain is that in a world which demands more and more energy – yet can supply less and less – prices will spiral. This will create a market situation in which energy is unaffordable for many. Not only will oil become more environmentally and financially costly but other remaining fossil fuel reserves will be stretched. There are substantial reserves of brown coal in China, for example; a handy but particularly polluting source of heat and power.[15]

PortZED, Shoreham

The dangers of business as usual

Setting aside the problems that will be created by escalating climate change, many have speculated as to the where continuing demand for the dwindling supplies of fossil fuels might lead if left unchecked.

Science writer Jared Diamond argues that our modern industrial society is facing many of the same environmental problems that caused ancient communities to fail.[16] To these historically significant factors he adds four new threats: 'human-caused climate change, buildup of toxic chemicals in the environment, energy shortages and full human utilization of the earth's photosynthetic capacity.' Diamond notes that many of these problems are likely to 'become globally critical within the next few decades'.

Another theory on how resource scarcity can lead to a dramatic disintegration of a society is posited by John Michael Greer. Borrowing descriptive terms from physiology, Greer describes how overuse of resources leads to catabolic, rather than anabolic, failure. The former leads to terminal collapse whereas the latter leads to a more temporary decline and eventual recovery. In effect, whereas most factors that can cause societal collapse are to some extent self-limiting and lead to cycles of activity, a decline in resources has the potential to be more permanently damaging.

Greer uses the fall of the Roman Empire as one example of a catabolic collapse:

> the Empire itself was ... fueled by easily depleted resources and driven by Roman military superiority ... Roman expansion transformed the capital of other societies into resources for Rome as country after country was conquered and stripped of movable wealth. Each new conquest increased the Roman resource base and helped pay for further conquests. After the first century CE, though, further expansion failed to pay its own costs. All remaining peoples within the reach of Rome were either barbarian tribes with little wealth ... or rival empires capable of defending themselves, such as the Parthians. Without income from new conquests, the maintenance costs of empire proved unsustainable, and a catabolic cycle followed rapidly. [17]

Parallels between the bellicose behaviour of the Empire, as it struggled to acquire control of sufficient resources to maintain profligate Roman lifestyles, and the actions of modern military-industrial economies, are all too apparent.

The Worldwatch Institute puts it bluntly: 'today's conflicts are less about ideologies and seizing the reins of state than about the struggle to control or plunder resources'.[18]

Whether the eventual decline in fossil fuels is managed in an orderly manner, a gentle 'powerdown' as Richard Heinberg describes it,[19] or results in chaotic disintegration of society, is for us to decide. Unlike the threats posed by global climate change, which are impossible to avoid, the dependence on fossil fuels can be tackled nationally and even personally. Iceland and Sweden are the first countries to acknowledge peak oil officially. Both are already taking steps to reduce their dependence on fossil fuels.[20]

It is certain that countries that make no concerted effort to design out fossil fuels will be increasing the risk of national economic collapse. What this will mean for citizens and business is a matter of conjecture. It is likely that countries, regions and even local communities will react differently to the crisis depending in part on their preparedness and inherent sustainability.

Heinberg paints this gloomy picture of what could happen:

> Energy shortages commence in the second decade of the century, leading
> to economic turmoil, frequent and lengthy power blackouts and general
> chaos. Over the course of several years, food production plummets,
> resulting in widespread famine, even in formerly wealthy countries. Wars
> – including civil wars – rage intermittently. Meanwhile ecological crisis
> also tears at the social fabric, with water shortages, rising sea levels,
> and severe storms wreaking further havoc. While previous episodic
> disasters could have been dealt with by disaster management and rescue
> efforts, by now societies are too disorganised to mount such efforts. One
> after another, central governments collapse. Societies attempt to shed
> complexity in stages, thus buying time. Empires devolve into nations;
> nations into smaller regional or tribal states ... Between 2020 and 2100
> the global population declines steeply, perhaps to fewer than one billion.[21]

Other fossil fuels

Though the focus in this chapter has been on oil and gas, both of which are
predicted to peak in the near term, there are other hydrocarbons that could
theoretically meet future energy needs. These may be more abundant but are not
without their own problems, which make them unlikely as a total energy solution.

The two most discussed alternatives to oil and gas are coal and tar sands. In our
view, it is not sensible to rely on these as future energy sources due to their environmental shortcomings. To summarise the problems with these:

Coal appears, on the face of it, to be relatively abundant but has three main
problems:

1. The poor quality of current coal reserves and the consequent problems
    of extraction means that we may well be facing 'peak coal' within a few
    decades.[22] Globally, at current consumption, there is enough coal to last
    around 200 years, but if the world tried to get most of its energy from coal it
    would last less than a century.[23] The exhaustion of coal reserves has been of
    concern for more than a century and was one of the reasons countries such
    at the United Kingdom diversified its energy portfolio.[24]

2. Coal is a polluting fuel producing not just high levels of climate changing car-
    bon dioxide (CO_2), but also sulphur dioxide (SO_2) and nitrogen oxides (NO_x).
    Both are responsible for acid rain and NO_x is a main cause of smog. Electric-
    ity produced using coal has higher levels of these pollutants than any other
    fossil fuel. There is widespread talk about 'clean coal' technologies which
    capture the carbon from coal-burning, but the risks and scale of storage that
    would be required rule out more than a few decades' storage at most.[25]

3. Coal is not suitable for many uses. It has traditionally been used for central-
    ised electricity production (though it is much less efficient at this than gas),
    various industrial uses (notably steel-making) and some home heating, but
    little else. Coal can be processed to produce gas, as was common before the

Box 1.2.1 Energy Return on Investment (EROI)

As energy sources such as oil become more difficult to mine, more energy is needed to extract them. Early wells literally gushed crude oil out of the ground (the stuff of many early US pioneer movies) and had an Energy Return On Investment (EROI) ratio of more than 100:1 – that is, for every 100 barrels of oil extracted the equivalent of only 1 barrel of oil was needed to extract and refine the crude oil for general use. US oil wells today have an EROI of about 30:1 – only a third as much oil is liberated for the same amount of energy.

It is generally the case that as oil reserves are depleted, the remaining crude becomes more energy intensive to extract. The 'quick wins' are exploited first and the more difficult to access reserves are left until later when perhaps higher market prices make the extraction more attractive.

The environmental consequences of these EROI ratios is significant. In effect, three times as much CO_2 is emitted to mine and refine oil in the United States than at the turn of the last century – a pattern repeated elsewhere.

So called non-conventional oil sources (tar sands and shale oil) have much lower EROIs. To extract tar sands, for example, produces around ten times more CO_2 than conventional oil extraction.[28]

widespread availability of natural gas, but the efficiencies were low and the toxic by-products caused considerable contamination problems.

Tar sands (also called oil sands) are a sticky mixture of sand, clay and bitumen. Three-quarters of the world's reserves are located in the Athabasca and Orinoco Tar Sands in Canada and Venezuela respectively.

Unlike conventional oil, tar sands are strip-mined, leading to extensive damage to the local environment. Around 2 tonnes of tar sands ore and 2 tonnes of top soil must be mined to produce each barrel of oil. Each barrel of oil extracted results in two to four barrels of polluted waste water. Containing the waste water alone is a mammoth undertaking. Fifty square kilometres of forest and bogs in Canada have been flooded to date.

Producing usable oil from tar sands is an energy intensive process involving substantial amounts of natural gas which, as we have seen, is becoming both more expensive and more scarce.

According to the extraction technique used between 40 and 80 kg CO_2 is currently emitted from natural gas use alone per barrel of oil extracted. On top of this must be added the substantial amount of transportation and other process fuels used.[26]

In 2000, the tar sands industry was estimated to be responsible for 3 per cent of Canada's total greenhouse gas emissions. Under some scenarios this could increase seven-fold with the next 25 years, contributing even more to climate change.

Professor Bauquis, former Head of Strategy at, and later special adviser to, French oil giant TotalFinaElf, sums up the problems faced by the oil sands industry and the uncertainty surrounding its continued growth:

> A key to the full realization of the production potential of these ultra heavy oil reserves will be technology, and more precisely how to find methods … to improve recovery rates at acceptable costs and without excessive energy consumption, which would go against worldwide efforts to control the emissions of carbon dioxide.[27]

ZED design implications

To round off this discussion of our dwindling energy resources, it is appropriate to reflect on the salient points, many of which are picked up later in the book:

- The economics of fossil fuel use is already changing, with costs likely to rise still further in the future. Energy-saving designs, which may appear to be a costly investment now, will reap generous returns later.
- It will be far more cost effective to reduce energy use than to use it.
- Fossil fuels are not going to disappear but they are likely to be in short supply or rationed. Priority will undoubtedly be given to maintaining essential services – (currently) routine uses of fossil fuels, where alternatives are readily available, will become extremely expensive or will cease.
- Energy accounting is likely to develop to the point that joules and kWh are monitored as keenly as pounds and pence.

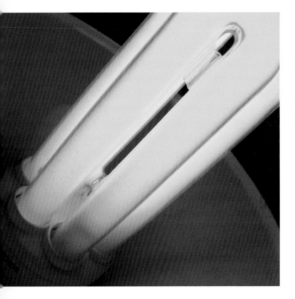

1.2.3
According to the International Energy Agency, a global switch to energy efficient lighting systems would reduce world electricity consumption by 10%.

ZEDfact

World oil supplies are set to run out faster than expected, warn scientists

'Scientists have criticised a major review of the world's remaining oil reserves, warning that the end of oil is coming sooner than governments and oil companies are prepared to admit.

BP's Statistical Review of World Energy, published yesterday, appears to show that the world still has enough "proven" reserves to provide 40 years of consumption at current rates. The assessment, based on officially reported figures, has once again pushed back the estimate of when the world will run dry.

However, scientists led by the London-based Oil Depletion Analysis Centre, say that global production of oil is set to peak in the next four years before entering a steepening decline which will have massive consequences for the world economy and the way that we live our lives.'

The Independent, 14 June 2007

ZED Principle 3

The energy demands of modern, urban lifestyles need to be reduced by at least 80 per cent by 2050 to ensure that the residual demand can be met from renewable energy sources

1.3 Reduce Demand –
Run on Native Renewables

Can the world run on renewables?

The simple answer to this question is a qualified 'yes'. But as with fossil and nuclear fuels, the issue is not so much about the size of the resource but its accessibility and viability. Theoretically, there is enough solar energy hitting the earth's land masses every day to replace – many, many times over – our current use of fossil fuels.

The average amount of insolation (solar radiation) reaching the earth's surface is approximately 2.5 kWh/m^2/day taking into account day- and night-time variations.

Assuming that this energy was captured using photovoltaic (PV) solar cells at an efficiency of 12 per cent (a conservative figure) then covering just three-quarters of one percent (0.75 per cent) of the earth's surface with PV panels would meet all world energy needs (coal, gas, nuclear, oil and so on).

This would mean covering an area about five times the size of the United Kingdom, or 13 per cent of the Sahara desert, with solar panels.

Solar is not the only renewable energy source. In addition to solar energy there is also lunar energy (the gravitational pull from the moon which governs our tides) and geothermal energy (heat originating from deep inside the earth). The former has been estimated as 26.3×10^{12} kWh/yr and the latter as 280×10^{12} kWh/yr. These sources are unevenly distributed globally and have much less potential than solar energy. Nonetheless they could make an important contribution to any future renewable energy strategy. By comparison, world energy consumption is about 100×10^{12} kWh/yr – less than half the potential of tidal power alone although, as illustrated by the solar cells example, accessing renewable resources can be problematic and there are inevitably efficiency losses.

National energy strategies

In practice, future energy strategies are likely to be nationally or regionally formulated to make best use of the most readily available renewable resources and matched to meet local demands for heating, cooling, lighting, appliances and so on.

The national demands for fossil energy vary widely (see Figure 1.3.1) but as globalisation takes hold the distinction is less national and more to do with lifestyle.

To illustrate this, Figure 1.3.2 compares the impact from modern living in Europe with Beijing in China. Though the vast majority of China's population is

Opposite
Delabole wind farm in Cornwall – the first in the UK was commissioned in 1991. Replacement of the turbines with more modern, higher output designs is currently being considered. This will allow fewer, larger turbines to generate three times as much power

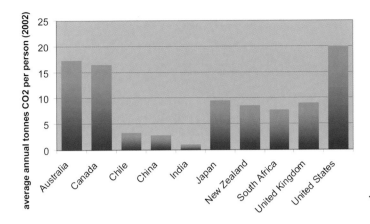

1.3.1

Average annual tonnes of CO_2 per person for selected countries

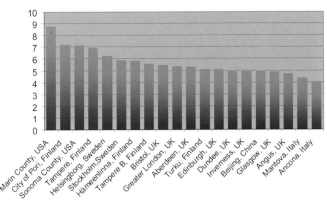

1.3.2

Average ecological footprints (in global hectares per capita) for selected cities

living very low carbon lifestyles, many of the inhabitants of Beijing, a modern international metropolis, are responsible for a footprint similar to the average European.

Notwithstanding this need to address lifestyles, a national approach to energy production still makes sense from both an economic and an energy security perspective.

Maintaining a diversity of supply, and providing energy storage, becomes more important in an economy run primarily on renewables. In this way it is possible to overcome the intermittent nature of some sources. The wind doesn't blow all the time, the sun doesn't always shine and the ebb and flow of tidal streams limits generating capacity.

A forward-thinking Government would assess the potential of different renewables within their boundaries, create a coherent low carbon vision, and then focus on first developing those renewable supplies which made most economic sense. They would also develop the most cost-effective local forms of energy storage to provide energy when renewable resources are in short supply.

Effective and efficient energy storage obviates the need for continued fossil fuel use. Many low- and high-tech solutions already exist. For example, energy can be stored chemically (in batteries), electrostatically (in capacitors), thermally (for example, by heating up water or even the well-insulated structure of a building), kinetically (in a flywheel), pneumatically (by compressing air, for example) or hydraulically (in elevated reservoirs).

Hydrogen is widely touted as the storage medium of the future with much talk about converting our economy from running on hydrocarbons to hydrogen. There are already vehicles running on hydrogen fuel cells with the only 'pollution' being water. However hydrogen is often loosely talked about as a renewable energy source – it is not. Hydrogen has to be generated – usually by splitting water molecules using electrolysis. This is an efficient process but can only really be considered as renewable if the energy source used to generate the hydrogen is itself renewable.

Box 1.3.1: Nuclear power is not the answer

Desperate times call for desperate measures and nuclear power is considered, by its reluctant proponents at least, to be very much an option of last resort. If demand reduction and renewables could deliver sufficient, affordable energy as part of a low carbon supply system (as the authors believe) then there would be absolutely no reason to back nuclear power. On the contrary, there are many sound reasons to resist it:

- *Cost.* There is, as yet, no safe means of disposing of nuclear waste, and the costs of decommissioning and storage are truly astronomical. In the United Kingdom alone, liabilities from the civil nuclear programme are officially estimated to exceed £45 billion, with a clean up timetable extending beyond 2140.[1] Far from being 'too cheap to meter', as the architect of the United Kingdom's nuclear programme, Walter Marshall, is alleged to have promised in the 1950s, nuclear power has consistently been demonstrated to be one of the least cost-effective ways of cutting CO_2 emissions.[2]
- *CO_2 emissions.* Although nuclear power plants generate little CO_2 themselves they are responsible – over their long lifecycle – for 15–40 per cent of the CO_2 per kilowatt-hour (kWh) of a gas-fired system.[3] Energy is used to construct the power station, to extract and refine the uranium, and during decommissioning. Other highly damaging greenhouse gases are also involved in the uranium refining process and these could potentially leak out. In fact, no one really knows exactly how much energy is required over the lifetime of a power plant, as no long term solution for nuclear waste disposal has yet been found – let alone had its energy implications analysed.
- *Uranium supplies.* If the world decided to go nuclear, there could be as little as 10 years' supply of uranium remaining. According to experts Jan Willem Storm van Leeuwen and Philip Smith, 'even if the uranium reserves were found to be much larger than now estimated ...[they would] only satisfy global demand for several decades'.[4] As the uranium ores get leaner, the energy required to recover the fissile material increases exponentially, casting further doubt on the nuclear industry's ability to deliver genuine lifecycle CO_2 savings.
- *Nuclear waste.* Spent nuclear fuel is a hazardous cocktail of radioactive isotopes which must be kept secure for hundreds of years. No system is perfect and accidents happen. Power plants and fuel processing facilities also make allowable discharges under license.[5] There is increasing evidence that these pernicious emissions, even at low levels, are having serious health impacts. One European report estimates that, to date, nuclear emissions could be responsible for more than 61 million deaths from cancer. To reduce ambient radioactivity to safe levels would, they concluded, 'severely curtail the operation of nuclear power stations and reprocessing plants'.[6]

Despite the clear need to plan for the future, few Governments have acknowledged the impending shortage of fossil fuels to the extent that they are mapping out how they might run their entire economies on renewables.

One notable exception is Iceland. With a population of just 300,000, this small country has committed to becoming the world's first hydrogen economy by 2050. This is to be achieved using the island's ample supply of geothermal and hydroelectric energy combined with hydrogen storage.

A smaller example still, though one which is operating successfully at present, is to be found on the remote Norwegian island of Utsira. Here a project is underway to provide the island's power from wind turbines, with flywheels and hydrogen fuel cells – charged when there is excess wind – providing the backup supply. At the time of writing an autonomous system is in operation meeting about 10 per cent of the island's energy needs.

Case study, UK
Reducing demand – running on native renewables

1.3.3
6 to 8 No. 185 Watt PV panels provide enough annual electricity to run an urban electric vehicle for most households:
– a Nice electric car uses about 0.3 KWh/mile
– a 185 Watt monocrystalline photovoltaic panel produces 145 kWh/annum in London, allowing approximately 480 miles of motoring/panel (www.nicecarcompany.co.uk)

Although the emphasis in this chapter is on quantifying the amount of renewable resources and adapting our lifestyles to run on renewables, the role of energy efficiency – the 'fifth fuel', as it is sometimes called – is central to creating a renewables based economy that works. It is generally far cheaper to reduce the use of energy than to generate it.

The crucial questions remain. Is it possible for larger, more populous countries to provide all their energy needs from renewable resources? What energy efficiency improvements are required?

Here we take the example of the United Kingdom, a densely populated, relatively wealthy country of 60 million inhabitants with a diversity of renewable resources. Our aim here is not to design a new UK energy supply system but to catalogue the accessible renewable resources that could potentially meet the country's demands for energy. We have avoided talking in detail about energy infrastructure but recognise the need for change. As others before us have acknowledged, the current centralised systems of power generation and distribution are unlikely to be able to deliver the efficiencies which are required within a scarce energy market. As Paul Mobbs puts it:

> The easiest way to tackle the largest area of energy loss from the UK economy would be to reform the greatest source of loss – our current system of large scale power generation that feeds the national grid.

The losses incurred by our current centralised power are highly significant and inexcusable. This is most apparent in the electricity supply network. Coal-fired power stations are just 30–35 per cent efficient (65–70 per cent of the energy generated is lost to the environment as waste heat). Modern combined cycle gas turbines are 50 per cent efficient – slightly better – but this still means that half of all energy is wasted. There are also losses incurred when transmitting the electricity over cabling and through substations. Another 5–7 per cent is lost in this way.

Microgeneration has the potential to operate far more efficiently. The efficiency of a combined heat and power plant (CHP) can exceed 80 per cent (less than 20 per cent lost as heat to the environment) and transmission losses are low.[7] Renewable technologies such as solar thermal (commonly used for water and space heating), PV (photovoltaic) and wind are actually capturing 'free' energy from the environment so produce no waste heat at all, though the efficiency with which they are able to capture ambient energy does, of course, vary.

Renewable sources integrated into large grid networks, though far more efficient at generating electricity, suffer the same distribution losses as centralised power generators. Cabling losses from offshore wind turbines, for example, can be high.

Although the focus here has been on the electricity network, the possible knock-on effect to the gas supply network is significant. If smaller, de-centralised CHP plants are the most efficient means of providing heat (as well as power) then the importance of a national gas system is diminished. District heating systems – common in many countries – can effectively displace gas networks or work alongside them to provide a more direct source of heat.

Of course, as the insulation of buildings is improved the need for space heating is dramatically reduced and this must be factored in to any future plans for renewing our energy infrastructure. New 'zero heating' specification buildings – which require no dedicated space heating (or cooling) plant at all – are entirely possible and are core to ZEDliving.

All the evidence presented here emphasises the need for a wholesale overhaul of our centralised energy production and distribution systems. Given the wastage inherent in the current infrastructure, any attempt to reduce energy use and associated CO_2 emissions will be far more difficult if this is not part of the solution.

What renewables does the United Kingdom have?

Few attempts have been made to catalogue the United Kingdom's renewable resources. Still fewer have looked at how these might be integrated and combined with energy efficiency and policy measures to produce a viable future energy strategy. Given the huge scale of the challenge, the immediacy of threats such as peak oil, and the economic and social importance of maintaining a secure, reliable energy supply, the UK Government's apparent lack of interest in this topic is difficult to understand.

In essence, the question we are trying to answer here is:

In a world where fossil fuels are scarce, prohibitively expensive and/or restricted due to their damaging influence on the climate, what benign, sustainable energy resources can be relied upon and what demand reduction targets does this indicate?

To place some practical constraints on this, we are assuming a target date for implementing a renewables based energy supply system of 2050 with no export or import of renewable supplies. We have not eliminated oil and gas entirely but assumed that energy from fossils fuels will be reduced by at least 80 per cent in line with stated CO_2 reduction targets.[8]

The Royal Commission on Environmental Pollution (RCEP) has produced arguably the most authoritative analysis of the United Kingdom's renewable resources.[9] Published in 2000, this study would benefit from an update to reflect both the recent dramatic changes in energy prices and recent research, such as that being conducted by Oxford University's Environmental Change Institute,[10] on solutions to the intermittency challenge presented by incorporating high percentages of renewables into the supply mix.

The RCEP assume some continued use of fossil fuels until 2050, but other studies have examined the potential for individual renewable resources. Most notable is a forward-looking study by the DTI which attempts to estimate both economic and accessible renewable resources in 2025 as well as the theoretical maximum.[11]

Not surprisingly, estimates of renewable resource availability vary widely depending on whether the assessment is based on economic viability (which in turn depends on future energy price predictions) or environmental constraints, what

1.3.4
A mixed-use regeneration scheme combining a company headquarters, retail, a hotel and residential apartments complete with building integrated biomass CHP and carpool. Reconciles high density with high land values while staying within the national biomass quota and achieving overall carbon neutrality

assumptions are made about the efficiency of various technologies and how these may interact. Such studies are also influenced by prevailing public attitudes and the political climate.

To clarify the key assumptions made here, each of the main energy sources is briefly introduced. To set the scene, the United Kingdom's current use of energy is explored.

The United Kingdom's current energy supply

The United Kingdom uses the current energy resources set out in Table 1.3.1. These are expressed in million tonnes of oil equivalent (Mtoe).[12] Of the 243.5 Mtoes, 35 per cent is 'lost' before it ever reaches the consumer due to inefficiencies in conversion or distribution. In other words, the current energy supply system is only 65 per cent efficient at converting fuels into usable energy. The residual energy is divided between sectors as indicated in Table 1.3.2.[13] Data here is given in both Mtoes and Petajoules (PJ).

So, allowing for any efficiency losses, renewable sources would have to deliver around 7200 PJ (about 2000 TWh/yr) to meet current UK energy needs.

Describing the various sources below, output is mainly expressed in TWh/yr, rather than installed capacity, using officially recognised load factors. Unless otherwise stated, the estimates are for delivered energy (including all conversion and distribution losses). The issue of energy storage is dealt with separately.

Wind, wave and tidal

Offshore energy sources (wind and wave) offer the greatest potential of all renewables as the United Kingdom is blessed with a shallow coastline and windy weather. Offshore sources have the added benefit of being more reliable than other intermittent renewables.

Offshore wind alone could potentially generate 1500 TWh/yr if turbines were built in all territorial waters to a depth of 50 m.[14] Extending to shallow waters beyond

Table 1.3.1: United Kingdom energy sources

	Consumption (Mtoe)
Coal	38.9
Petroleum	88.0
Natural gas	97.0
Primary electricity (mainly nuclear, hydro, wind)	19.6
Total	243.5

Table 1.3.2: Energy consumption by sector (figures rounded)

	%	Mtoe	PJ
Industry	20	34	1417
Transport	33	57	2397
Domestic	28	49	2034
Services and agric	12	21	872
Non-energy uses	7	12	509
Total	100	173	7228

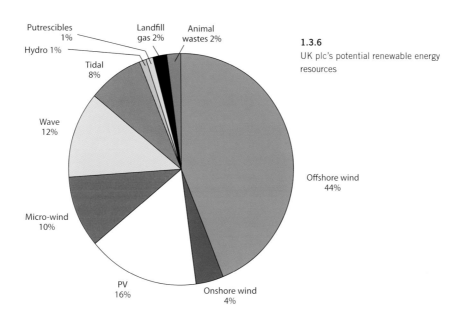

1.3.6
UK plc's potential renewable energy resources

Putrescibles 1%
Landfill gas 2%
Animal wastes 2%
Hydro 1%
Tidal 8%
Wave 12%
Micro-wind 10%
PV 16%
Onshore wind 4%
Offshore wind 44%

1.3.5 (opposite)
Jubilee Wharf in Cornwall is designed to maximise the energy harvested from both the south-westerly prevailing wind and solar gain

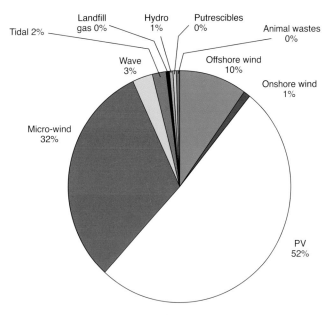

1.3.7
The renewable energy sources available to the housing sector

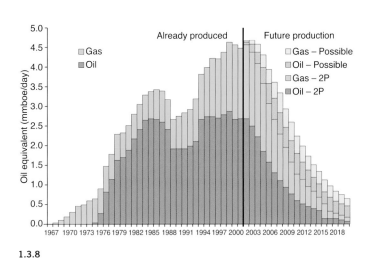

1.3.8
New fossil fuel reserves are not being discovered fast enough to satisfy increasing demand from developing nations

territorial boundaries would more than double this to 3200 TWh/yr (one-and-a-half times the United Kingdom's entire current energy demands). However, cost constraints and the simple practicalities of building, installing and connecting the thousands of turbines that would be required, reduce the maximum 2050 potential considerably.

Considering only the less costly, shallower offshore sites (less than 30 m deep) within territorial waters reduces the maximum potential to 700 TWh/yr. The DTI have suggested that 100 TWh/yr of this might be commercially viable by 2025. Optimistically doubling this figure – assuming growth remains steady – would give a 2050 production figure of 200 TWh/yr. Only about 2 TWh/yr is currently generated by wind energy (both onshore and offshore) in the United Kingdom.[15] By way of comparison, European leader Germany currently generates around 15 TWh/yr from wind.

Large scale onshore wind production is well established and more cost effective than offshore. It currently contributes far more power to the national grid than offshore wind. However the maximum technical potential is lower, estimated at 317 TWh/yr, with possibly 58 TWh/yr economically viable by 2025. Given the planning constraints and public resistance to large turbines, it is highly unlikely that this potential will ever be realised (the DTI expect just 8 TWh/yr to be installed by 2025). The assumption made here is that 16 TWh/yr could be generated by 2050.

Wave energy, though less developed than wind, is also a significant resource. The DTI state that the technical potential is in excess of 600 TWh/yr though just over one-fifth of this could, in their view, be exploited by 2025. Again, let us optimistically assume that this target is met and output doubled by 2050. This gives a figure of 66 TWh/yr.

In addition, the United Kingdom has around 40 sites where tidal streams are rapid enough to make energy generation viable.[16] The DTI estimate a maximum potential of 36 TWh/yr, excluding large barrages, with a possibility of generating about 2 TWh/yr by 2025. Given the relatively benign nature of tidal stream generators and the likely rapid uptake of this technology once established, it is here assumed that the maximum potential could be exploited by 2050.

Biomass

Here we distinguish only between wood fuel, waste vegetable oil, crop residues (straw) and other energy crops. The high population density in the United Kingdom means that land is one of the scarcest resources and would be largely required, in a sustainable world, for the production of food and animal feed, for grazing livestock and for growing crops which have other uses (for example, paper production, fibre, oil crops and timber for construction). Space also needs to be set aside to preserve biodiversity.

The United Kingdom has a land area of 24.3 million hectares (Mha). Of this, around 4.6 Mha is arable cropland, 12.4 Mha grasses and rough grazing, 2.9 Mha forest and 4.3 Mha categorised as urban land, other agricultural land, set aside and other unspecified uses.[17]

It has been suggested that a *maximum* of 4 Mha could be spared for energy crops.[18] Planting out this entire area with lignocellulosic crops could, theoretically, yield 60 million oven dried tonnes (odt) or 240 TWh per year (used at 80 per cent efficiency).[19] Practically, the figure would be much lower. Using the 4 Mha instead for transport biofuels would yield around 1,000 litres per hectare, or 3,200 million litres per annum (at 80 per cent efficiency).[20] Clearly there is a tension between the production of crops for heat and power and for transport. Furthermore, optimum yields are unlikely to be achieved as the best quality land will inevitably be given over to food production – a more basic need.

To try and resolve these conflicts over land use, we have here assumed that the demand for heating and power is less elastic than the need for transport. Keeping warm and dry is certainly a more basic human need. We have therefore prioritised use of the 4 Mha accordingly.

Experience with zero space heating developments has shown that around 200–500 oven dried kilogrammes of biomass per person is required to provide hot water, occasional top-up heating and power. The higher figure is less typical but would be needed when the constraints of the building (for example a high dwelling density) means that the opportunities for on site renewable energy generation are limited and the biomass is therefore also needed for power generation. For older, upgraded legacy properties biomass use will be greater – about 800 kg per person. This figure is highly dependent on occupancy rates, property type and future climate. Warmer weather would, somewhat ironically, ease the strain on the United Kingdom's limited biomass resources. The biomass that needs to be set aside for legacy properties is also dependent on housing replacement rates and the allocation of the reduced supply of fossil fuels to domestic properties. For the purposes of estimating the available resource in 2050 we will here assume an average requirement (for both new and old properties) of 600 kg. It could be argued that this figure is optimistically low as it effectively assumes an ambitious replacement programme of new ZEDstandards build and the refurbishment of all remaining older properties to

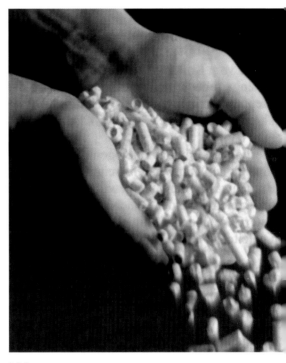

1.3.9
Wood pellets – the ultimate convenient biomass fuel?

the high standards set out in the '40 per cent house'.[21] Certainly, we do not claim to have provided a definitive answer – but it serves the purpose of highlighting the finite nature of our biomass resources and illustrates one possible scenario.

For energy crops to provide 600 kg per capita almost all the 4 Mha of 'free' land would be required, leaving very little for biofuel production.[22] However one study estimates that up to 7.5 million odt of crop residues – primarily straw – (not included in the 4 Mha) could be diverted for energy generation by 2050.[23] This is equivalent to an additional 125 odkg per person. If these residues are included in the equation then some land (about 1.15 Mha) is reclaimed for transport fuel production. This amounts to just 22 litres per person – taking into account the energy needed to cultivate and refine the crop.

Another possible source of transport fuel is waste vegetable oil. Its use as a fuel is well established in the United Kingdom. Though there is relatively little of this resource, no more than 200,000 tonnes a year or 2.2 TWh/yr, it is easily accessible. If used as a vehicle fuel it would equate to around 176 million litres per year or 3 litres per person.

Total available biofuel for transport is therefore less than 30 litres. At an efficient 3 litres per 100 km this will transport you a modest 1,000 km per year.

Table 1.3.3 summarises the figures for biomass production and land use.

Table 1.3.2: Summary of biomass production and land use in proposed scenario based on an available land area of 4 Mha

	Land use (Mha)	Usable yield per hectare (estimates take into account efficiency losses)	Total yield	Resource availability per capita
		odt/ha/yr	Mt	odkg/person/yr
Straw	0 (is waste product of agriculture)	–	7.5	125
Forestry	0.25	10	2.5	42
Other energy crops	2.6	10	26	433
Sub-total (fuels for heating and power)	2.85		36	600
		litres/ha/yr	Ml	litres/person/yr
Biofuel (based on oil seed rape)	1.15	1139	1310	22
Waste vegetable oil	0 (is waste product)	–	176	3
Sub-total (transport fuels)	1.15		1486	25

Micro wind, solar and hydroelectric

Here we include small wind turbines, photovoltaics (PV) and small hydro. Though these are currently costly, the first two – in particular – have the potential to become inexpensive mass market products. The amount of energy these technologies could generate is limited only by uptake and is therefore highly price sensitive.

The Energy Savings Trust predicts that micro wind and solar will become financially competitive well before 2050.[24]

To estimate the potential for micro wind we assume that one-quarter of the 20 million dwellings in the United Kingdom could accommodate a 1.5 kW turbine with a modest load factor of 15 per cent.[25] This would generate 44 TWh/yr. Small commercial and industrial installations could increase this further.

For PV, it is estimated that 50 per cent of dwellings could accommodate a rooftop 2 kW array, each generating 1,800 kWh/yr. In total this would provide 20 TWh/yr. Clearly the potential on commercial buildings is much higher than this – with the price of PVs already cost competitive with some commercial and industrial cladding materials. The DTI estimate a technical potential of more than 600 TWh/yr with 37 TWh/yr commercially viable by 2025. Here we assume linear growth beyond this generating 74 TWh/yr by 2050. This is the equivalent of covering about one-quarter of one percent (0.25 per cent) of the United Kingdom with solar panels.[26]

The potential for small hydro is limited by the number of suitable sites. The DTI estimate a maximum technical potential of 40 TWh/yr with a slow uptake. They expect no more than 3 TWh/yr to be practically accessible by 2025. Here we assume linear growth beyond this delivering 6 TWh/yr by 2050.

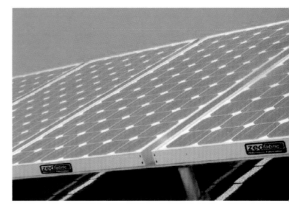

1.3.10
Photovoltaic pay off their embodied CO_2 within three to three and a half years, and should last between 25 and 50 years with a 5% to 8% reduction in electrical output towards the end of their useful life

Waste technologies

> If all municipal solid waste [in the United Kingdom] was incinerated then it could provide 5% of the UK electricity demand. This would be good if the incineration of waste produced less carbon dioxide per kilowatt-hour than the combustion of gas, oil or coal, but it does not.[27]

There is a range of 'energy from waste' options for generating energy from material that would usually be sent to landfill.

With certain exceptions, these technologies have no place in a sustainable future, because far more energy can be saved by reclaiming most materials (metals, plastics, paper, glass, cardboard) than can be yielded by destroying them.[28] The exceptions are technologies which efficiently extract energy from raw, biotic materials such as food and garden waste (often referred to as putrescibles).[29] Human and animal wastes are similarly suited for energy generation.

Trying to run an economy on energy derived from waste is simply chasing your own tail. It is impossible to generate enough waste to provide more than a fraction of the power the economy requires without increasing the throughput of materials. This uses considerably more energy to create the materials, so overall, carbon emissions are increased.

1.3.11
Can we design out our waste stream rather than rely on it as a fuel source?

ZEDfact

After sectoral allocation of national renewable reserves – assuming phased out nuclear and fossil fuel use reduced by 70 per cent – our fair share of resource is about:

- 600 oven dry kg of biomass per capita per year

- 1,300 oven dry kg of biomass per household per year

- 1,400 kWh of electricity per capita per year

- 3,100 kWh of electricity per household per year

- 300 litres of diesel equivalent per household, allowing 4,400 vehicle km per capita, dropping to 2,000 km per year as fossil fuels are phased out.

We could run the United Kingdom on renewables by 2050 if we achieved a 1.7 per cent annual reduction in their use.

Planned Powerdown is essential, but long-term strategies must not be jeopardised by the quick wins – so phased future proofing options become important.

Energy from waste technologies also detracts from recycling and reuse initiatives, encouraging linear supply chains rather than more sustainable 'closed loop' economies. Generating energy from general waste is neither truly renewable nor secure.

For our 2050 calculations, we have therefore estimated only the likely energy generation from putrescibles, human and animal wastes and landfill gas (itself a declining resource as fewer and fewer biodegradable materials are buried).

About 20 per cent of municipal solid waste is made up of putrescibles – this amounts to about 6 TWh/yr (assuming no conversion losses).[30]

Landfill gas is unlikely to provide more than 7 TWh/yr and will decline as the burying of biodegradeable waste decreases. Animal wastes could generate around 10 TWh/yr – enough in itself to power the entire agricultural sector.[31]

Summarising the United Kingdom's available renewable resource

Very little of this generating capacity is in place – only 2 per cent of the United Kingdom's total energy demand is currently met from renewable sources.[32] To ensure that the United Kingdom's economy is able to thrive in an energy constrained world, a co-ordinated, Government-led programme is needed to plan and implement the Renewable Generation programme outlined here.

There is an added incentive to move quickly. As has been noted above, the United Kingdom's offshore energy resources are potentially vast. If the United Kingdom's needs can be met and additional resources harvested, this could form the kernel of a new energy export industry. This would go some way to making up the gaping hole in the country's trade balance left by the demise of North Sea oil.

The efficiency with which the United Kingdom's renewable resources can be exploited relies on matching supply with demand, optimising conversion efficiencies, minimising distribution losses and integrating sufficient back up storage.

Estimating the total losses in the supply system depends, at least partly, on the use to which a resource is put and the technologies adopted to yield the energy. Burn wood efficiently and perhaps 90 per cent of the energy is usable as heat. Gasify wood to produce electricity in an inefficient power plant and efficiencies can be as low as 25 per cent.

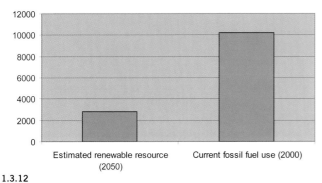

1.3.12
Petajoules of energy (all fuels) current fossil fuel use compared with accessible renewable resources. Neither figure takes into account conversion or distribution losses

In arriving at the sectoral allocations, we have made the following key assumptions:

Fossil fuel use is reduced by 70 per cent (if 10 per cent of the reduction comes from conversion and distribution efficiency improvements, this meets the first ZEDstandards principle by reducing CO_2 emissions per capita to 2.1 tonnes CO_2 by 2050).

Industry has been allocated 40 per cent of all renewable grid electricity (the large scale sources) and 15 per cent of the available fossil fuels.

The transport sector has also been allocated 40 per cent of all large scale renewable grid sources, 48 per cent of available fossil fuels and all available biofuels.

The agriculture and services sectors have been allocated the remaining 20 per cent of renewable grid electricity, 6 per cent of the fossil fuels, all the animal wastes and 50 per cent of the solar PV supply.

Thirty-five per cent of the fossil fuels have been allocated to non-energy uses (chemicals, lubricants, plastics and so on).

Finally, the domestic sector has been allocated all of the micro wind, 50 per cent of the solar supply, 6 per cent of the fossil fuels and all the remaining biomass.

This debateable, but logical, allocation of the available resources results in the following sector energy reduction targets:

- Industry 62%
- Transport 69%
- Domestic 79%
- Services & Agriculture 51%
- Non-energy uses 68%

Another significant factor is how much energy needs to be stored for later use (a necessary consideration where there is a high percentage of intermittent renewables in the supply mix) and the efficiency of the storage technology.

Though there are many variables to play with and, inevitably, no single correct answer, the scale of reductions needed to run the United Kingdom entirely on native renewable energy is clear. Energy savings in the order of 75 per cent would be required by 2050.

For reasons of energy security, it should be a goal of every economy to live within the limits imposed by its native, natural energy yield. The urgency of climate change, peak oil and peak gas warrants that the necessary reductions in energy demand are implemented as rapidly as possible.

For the United Kingdom to run largely on renewables by 2050 would mean reducing its overall energy use by about 1.7 per cent each year. This is a challenge which the United Kingdom has so far been unable to meet. Over the last 20 years primary energy use has been steadily increasing at about 1 per cent each year.[33]

Allocating limited energy resources

This limited supply of renewables must be shared out between sectors of the United Kingdom economy: domestic, transport, industrial and commercial. Decisions over sharing and priorities will dictate where reductions in demand must be made.

There are many reasons why one might want to favour certain sectors, for example to protect health care facilities or keep public transport systems running reliably. As circumstances unfold then priorities will become clearer. However if Governments are serious about moving their energy supply systems on to a more sustainable footing, planning for specific reduction targets is essential.

Here we suggest one allocation which reflects our opinion on where reductions would be easiest to make, and what economic and social priorities a Government would most likely follow. We have also taken into account the best practicable use of renewables, and pragmatically assume a continued, but much reduced, level of fossil fuel use based on the carbon reduction targets set out earlier in this book combined with some efficiency improvements in the supply system.

For those wishing to enter their own assumptions, the interactive model upon which this analysis is based has been posted at www.zedstandards.com.

Using the allocations described (see Box 1.3.3) we have derived the following indicative personal and household targets for annual residential energy use (both new build and legacy properties):

- 600 oven dried kilogrammes of biomass per capita (1,300 odkg per typical dwelling)
- 1,400 kWh/yr of electricity per capita (3,100 kWh/yr per household)
- It is suggested that the fossil fuel energy allocated to the domestic sector, amounting to 2,300 kWh per capita (5,400 kWh per household) is set aside for those historic buildings and hard-to-heat homes which cannot be quickly, easily or simply upgraded. Given the United Kingdom's low housing replacement rate, less than 1 per cent, this top-up supply will provide an essential safety net to 2050.

As we shall see in later in this book, meeting these tight targets requires thoughtful and holistic thinking, super energy-efficient building fabric and appliances, the widespread use of passive solar measures (sunspaces, solar thermal water heating) and an attention to detail.

Turning to personal transport, we have here assumed that 80 per cent of the national transport fuels are allocated for essential freight and public transport with the remainder, plus all the biodiesel, for private use.

This gives the equivalent of 300 litres of diesel per household, enough for each person to travel solo 4,400 vehicle kilometres (vkm) per year (further if journey sharing) by efficient car (85 km per week). About half of this motive power still comes from fossil fuels (albeit used much more efficiently). As fossil fuels are progressively phased out this allocation would drop to about 2,000 vkm/yr (40 km per week).

Any energy that can be generated on site (for example electricity from PVs to charge electric cars) would be in addition to the above allocation of national resources.

1.3.13
Farmers' markets provide easy access to local produce – zero carbon zero waste is easy if you cycle to your nearest farmer's market and are happy with brown paper bags in place of elaborate packaging

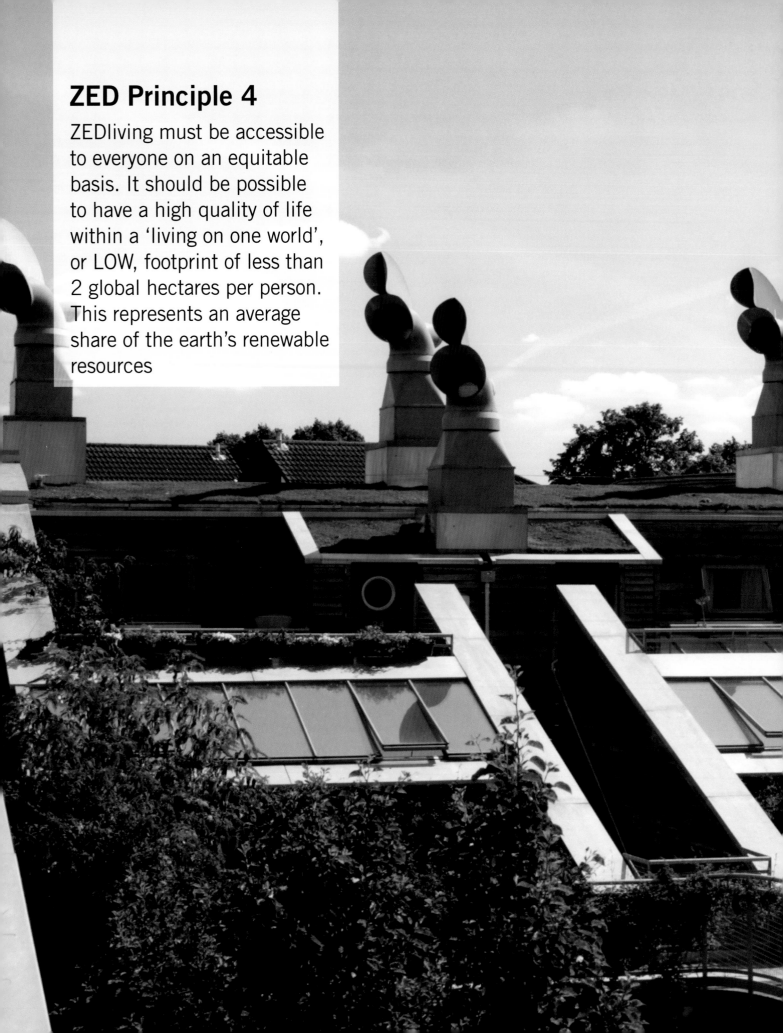

ZED Principle 4

ZEDliving must be accessible to everyone on an equitable basis. It should be possible to have a high quality of life within a 'living on one world', or LOW, footprint of less than 2 global hectares per person. This represents an average share of the earth's renewable resources

1.4 Enable a High Quality of Life on a LOW Footprint

Living on one world

The global economy is currently in overshoot. About 30 per cent more resources are being consumed each year than can be sustainably provided. In other words, we need 1.3 planets each year to support the lifestyles of the world's 6.5 billion citizens.

The richer countries (with a combined population of about 1 billion) use disproportionately more resources per head than the rest of the world. For example, if everyone on the planet adopted the lifestyle of the average European we would need almost three earths to support global resource consumption.

Here we make the case for *living on one world* – what we refer to as a LOW footprint lifestyle. This sets ZEDliving within a global context promoting the equitable use of resources.

Our ecological footprint

The consequences of overusing resources are all too apparent. One after another, ecosystems are being degraded as more and more resources are extracted or harvested for human use. The forests are shrinking, soils are eroding, grain harvests are failing to keep up with demand and potable water is in short supply.

Oil and gas are not the only resources under pressure. Nor is renewable energy the only bottleneck to comfortable, sustainable living. Clearly, we also need to feed ourselves and have access to whatever other resources we need to maintain a high quality of life.

The ecological footprint is an environmental indicator which compares the demand for natural, renewable resources (the footprint) with the regenerative capacity of the planet (the biocapacity). Where the biocapacity exceeds the footprint then the economy can be said to be operating within ecological limits. That is, no more is being harvested or extracted from the planet than can be provided without degrading ecosystem services. It can be said that – under these circumstances – we are *living on one world* rather than borrowing from future generations or drawing down supplies of existing, renewable resources. On the other hand, if the footprint is larger than the biocapacity – as all the evidence suggests it is now – then the economy is in overshoot.

The New Economics Foundation, together with the Global Footprint Network and Best Foot Forward, have started to commemorate 'World Overshoot Day', the

Opposite
BedZED north elevation with sky gardens and north lights

The benefits of a ZED and low carbon lifestyle

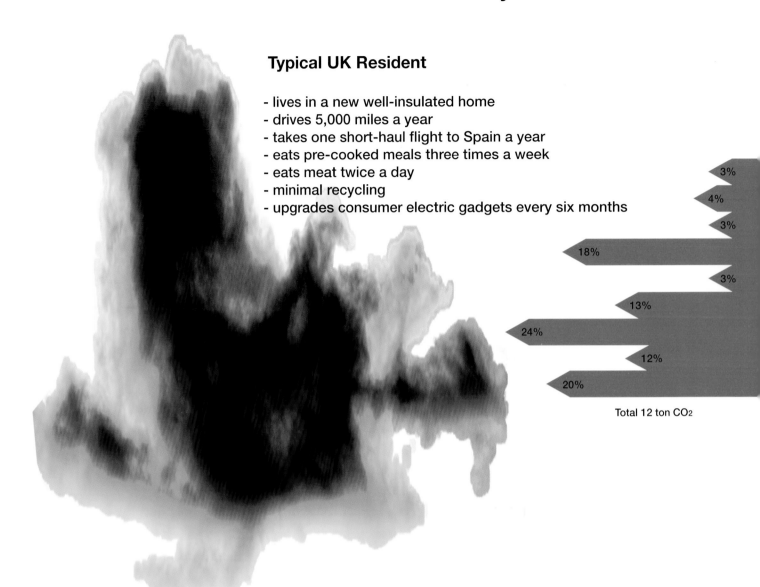

Typical UK Resident

- lives in a new well-insulated home
- drives 5,000 miles a year
- takes one short-haul flight to Spain a year
- eats pre-cooked meals three times a week
- eats meat twice a day
- minimal recycling
- upgrades consumer electric gadgets every six months

3%
4%
3%
18%
3%
13%
24%
12%
20%

Total 12 ton CO2

12 ton CO$_2$/yr

Typical UK volume house builders product

Typical ZED Resident

PV and solar thermal upgrades fitted -
drives veg oil car -
holidays in UK or takes ecofriendly transport option abroad -
cycles to work/train station daily -
cycles to local market -
receives deliveries from zero fossil energy farm -
opposes war for fossil fuel -
keeps fit by cycling -
uses ethical financial services -
campaigns for low carbon infrastructure -
low motor way use -

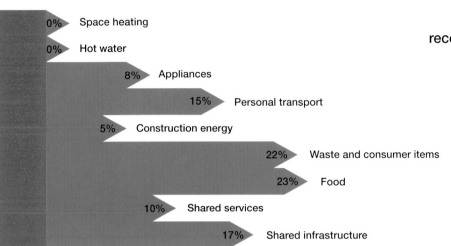

0% Space heating

0% Hot water

8% Appliances

15% Personal transport

5% Construction energy

22% Waste and consumer items

23% Food

10% Shared services

17% Shared infrastructure

Total 3.5 ton CO_2

If all renewable energy sources were to be developed
they could only meet 30% of our current demand

In our current energy-hungry society there will never
be enough green grid energy to go round

The only way of living in a low carbon future is to reduce
our current demand by 80% and then microgenerate the
remaining 20% with building integrated renewable technologies.

This leaves scarce green grid electricity for public
transport heritage buildings, industry and food
production/distribution

3.5 ton CO_2/yr

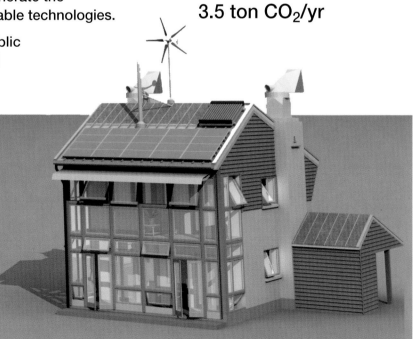

Fully specified Zero fossil Energy Development house

point in the year when consumption exceeds the sustainable supply of resources. In 2006, we silently crept into overshoot on 9 October. If consumption continues to increase then Overshoot Day will arrive ever earlier each year – at current rates approximately one month earlier each decade. This simple explanation ignores the fact that the very existence of overshoot is damaging the regenerative capacity of the planet. So, not only is Overshoot Day occurring earlier, but also the year is getting shorter.

At what point life on earth might become untenable for the bulk of the global population is a matter of conjecture. One conservative estimate suggests that planetary ecosystems could be totally exhausted within 50 years as the rising ecological debt progressively degrades planetary productive capacity.[1]

The ecological footprint measures environmental impact by estimating the surface area of the earth that would be required to provide the resources used to support a particular activity, lifestyle or population. For example, what size of field would be required to grow the grain necessary to provide a year's supply of breakfast cereal? What size of forest would be needed to meet a region's demand for wood fuel? How much built up area does a city need to house its population?

As we only have a finite area of land and sea, the earth is limited in the amount of food, timber and renewable energy that it can provide. It can only absorb a certain amount of waste before pollution starts to accumulate and damage natural systems.

The footprint is usually expressed in hectares (one hectare is equivalent to 10,000 m^2). As land quality varies the world over – a hectare in Europe will generally be more productive than a hectare in Africa – all areas are converted to world average bioproductive hectares. These are termed 'global hectares' (abbreviated to gha) to avoid confusion. Using global hectares allows direct comparisons to be made between countries and regions the world over.

Fair shares

Using the ecological footprint, it is possible to derive various sustainability benchmarks. At the global level it is possible to calculate whether the total use of resources exceeds planetary carrying capacity. At the country level it is useful for policy-makers to determine whether the national economy is operating within local ecological limits. At the organisational level an understanding of environmental performance can help target efficiency improvements. At the personal level, it is useful to guide individuals as to the sustainability of their lifestyles.

To understand the design constraints for ZEDliving we focus here on the latter.

The earth consists of approximatey 12 billion hectares of usefully productive land and sea – crop land, pasture, forest and the coastal margins – the rest is relatively low yielding, for example, desert, ice cap, high altitude mountains or deep ocean. Dividing the productive area by the global population (6.5 billion) gives the current available biocapacity per person – an equitable, fair footprint for sustainable living on one world.

LOW footprint = 12 billion productive hectares/6.5 billion people = *c.* 2 gha

To be sustainable, ZEDs should therefore enable LOW footprint living on less than 2 global hectares per person per year.

Note that no account has been taken of the area required by the millions of other species that exist on this planet. Many of these survive only through the maintenance of pristine natural habitats. At least 12 per cent of the productive area of the planet should be allocated for biodiversity protection.[2]

Currently, the footprint of the average Western European is just under 5 gha. The typical North American has a personal footprint of more than 9 gha.[3] Modern lifestyles therefore require reductions of between 65 and 80 per cent to achieve the LOW footprint target.

Though this is undoubtedly challenging, the majority of the world's population, typically those in the world's poorer countries, are already subsisting on a footprint of less than 1.8 gha. Many would argue that this is at the expense of a diminished quality of life. So, is it possible to have a high quality of life on a LOW footprint?

Box 1.4.1: Millennium Ecosystem Assessment
www.millenniumassessment.org/

From: 'Living Beyond Our Means: Natural assets and human well-being'. Statement from the Board.

The Millennium Ecosystem Assessment (MA) was called for by UN Secretary-General Kofi Annan in 2000. The objective of the MA was to assess the consequences of ecosystem change for human well-being and the scientific basis for actions needed to enhance the conservation and sustainable use of those systems and their contribution to human wellbeing. The key messages of the MA include:

- Everyone in the world depends on nature and ecosystem services to provide the conditions for a decent, healthy and secure life.
- Humans have made unprecedented changes to ecosystems in recent decades to meet growing demands for food, fresh water, fibre and energy.
- These changes have helped to improve the lives of billions, but at the same time they weakened nature's ability to deliver other key services such as purification of air and water, protection from disasters, and the provision of medicines.
- Among the outstanding problems identified by this assessment are the dire state of many of the world's fish stocks; the intense vulnerability of the 2 billion people living in dry regions to the loss of ecosystem services, including water supply; and the growing threat to ecosystems from climate change and nutrient pollution.
- Human activities have taken the planet to the edge of a massive wave of species extinctions, further threatening our own well-being.
- The loss of services derived from ecosystems is a significant barrier to the achievement of the Millennium Development Goals to reduce poverty, hunger and disease.
- The pressures on ecosystems will increase globally in coming decades unless human attitudes and actions change.
- Better protection of natural assets will require co-ordinated efforts across all sections of governments, businesses and international institutions. The productivity of ecosystems depends on policy choices on investment, trade, subsidy, taxation and regulation, among others.

1.4.1
Living a LOW footprint lifestyle is easier in BedZED (bottom photo) than typical suburban developments (top photo)

Not much need for an alarm clock nowadays since I gave up the morning commute. I now walk to work at one of the ZEDquarter small business units, dropping off my daughter at the nursery on the way.

My wife is not so lucky. She is one of the 50 per cent who live here but work elsewhere. However, her commute is shorter than it used to be – only 30 minutes by public transport. We found we didn't need the family car any more and recently sold it – we borrow from the car pool when necessary. This has saved us a lot of money – and adds to the spare carbon credits we have to sell.

Conveniently, our ZEDquarter has its own organic bakery (powered by the waste heat from the combined heat and power (CHP) plant). We have a few large greenhouses which also make use of the waste heat. This extends the growing season and means we don't need to import so much produce. The local wine is extremely popular.

A few residents are also involved in an interesting experiment using the CHP waste heat to dry the fruit we grow for use year round – the apple rings are certainly a hit with the children.

The ZEDquarter school uses the greenhouse as an educational resource, they have their own plot and, what with the café, community hall and bar right next door, it has become a real social hub.

Nothing is wasted here. All food scraps and leftovers eventually end up in the greenhouses – or on one of the outdoor growing areas – after first going through the 'digester'. This produces a useful bit of extra energy as well as nice sterile compost.

Food shopping is hardly a chore. You can either order home delivery online or go to the weekly farmer's market. Either way all packaging is recycled or reused.

The Council resource collection service (they used to call it 'waste') only visits fortnightly now. All this helps keep the Council Tax bill down – freeing up funding for improvements to cycle routes.

When we first moved in two years ago, we didn't know what to expect. We hadn't thought of living here as a particularly long-term commitment. But we really enjoy life here and definitely have more time together as a family. We have also made many friends and are generally happier and more relaxed.

1.4.2
The bar at BedZED provided a social focus and helped build a strong community in the first few years

The importance of happiness

Unless those of us planning, designing and engineering low impact developments acknowledge the full role that social aspirations play in deciding how we live, then truly sustainable and satisfying lifestyles will never be realised.

Our aim here is to show that leading a fulfilling life is not incompatible with living within natural, environmental limits. Far from it. We believe that those lifestyle choices which improve quality of life are also those which underpin ZEDliving.

By way of introduction, Box 1.4.2 provides a diary account of what it might be like living in a large sustainable community. Although fictional, the text draws heavily on the experience of BedZED.

This tale of a 'day in the life of' a typical 'ZEDquarter' resident helps highlight some of the perceived benefits of sustainable living.

You can't buy happiness

> In the long run neither an ice cream cone nor a new car nor becoming rich and famous produces the same feelings of delight that it initially did ... Happiness is not the result of being rich, but a temporary consequence of having recently become richer. (Ronald Inglehart)[4]

Our modern society promotes the creation of financial wealth as the predominant means of achieving happiness. Conventional wisdom has it that increasing personal wealth will in turn improve the general 'standard of living'. As the economy grows, so the argument goes, the benefits of increasing material consumption will improve our well-being and, in turn, our satisfaction and happiness.

The 'trickle down' effect, central to conservative economic theory, states that in a liberalised economy any wealth that is created, wherever it is generated, will eventually benefit everyone.

Hence expanding the economy – with its ever increasing appetite for resources – is generally seen as a desirable goal.

Increasingly, however, policy-makers are realising that the relationship between the happiness of individuals and the state of the economy is more complex. The influential British Economist, Professor Richard Layard, has even argued that improving happiness should be the primary goal of public policy.[5]

The story of the Smiths and the Johnsons (Box 1.4.3), while somewhat blunt, serves to underline the point that higher consumption does not guarantee a higher quality of life. On the contrary, as we shall see, being more frugal with natural resources may even result in a more satisfying and fulfilling life as well as being a sound investment in the future.

Box 1.4.3: A tale of two families

Consider two families.

In the Smith family the father works 60 hours per week and has recently had heart bypass surgery. He smokes 20 cigarettes a day. The mother works 55 hours per week and has regular counselling to combat stress-related illness and alcoholism. They employ a child minder to look after their pre-school child 5 days a week and have an older child who goes to an after school club. The older child has regular hospital appointments concerning her recurrent asthma, thought to be brought on by the poor air quality in the industrial town in which the family live. The children spend most of their leisure time watching cable TV or playing with computer games. The family uses a lot of gas and electricity, produces mountains of waste each week and finds that their hectic life necessitates running two cars. The family have recently fitted a range of security devices and alarms to their house following a burglary four months ago. The mother is currently seeking legal advice on how to go about divorce proceedings.

The Johnsons live in a modest house in the suburbs. Both mother and father have found local jobs working part time. They share the parenting of their two children and no longer employ any outside childcare. They do not smoke and have no health problems. The children spend most of their time, when they are not at school, playing with neighbours or out with their parents. They try to eat as much local food as possible, they are moderate energy users, produce relatively little waste, and run a small, economical car. Crime is rare in the area. The family has a good network of friends and family members living nearby.

In terms of their relative contribution to the wider economy, the Smiths are a model of prosperity and success since all of the activities described involve significant financial transactions. For example, the Smiths are indirectly responsible for payments to lawyers, police, health practitioners and a wide range of other public and private organisations which manufacture goods or provide services. This increased consumption and economic activity is likely to have a substantial footprint. It seems unlikely, though, that they are happy.

The Johnsons, by contrast, are economic misfits. They don't earn as much, they don't buy as many consumer goods, they don't consume as much energy or travel as much, they don't employ childcare, they don't make extensive use of medical care facilities, legal or policing services. They pay for little of their entertainment and have no costly addictions. Yet their lifestyle choices have undoubtedly made them happier than the Smiths *and* they tread more lightly on the planet.

1.4.3
Bed-deck in a BedZED live/work unit

Consuming passions

> Materialism is not only bad for the environment, it also undermines our well-being.
>
> New Economics Foundation[6]

All the evidence suggests that above a basic subsistence level of income there is little correlation between financial wealth and happiness. As part of the World Values Survey residents of different nationalities were asked to rate their happiness.[7]

Far from showing a consistent relationship, the happiness of respondents levelled off as wealth increased. Above about US $15,000 per head, higher income is no guarantee of greater happiness. Some countries, particularly those in Latin America,

1.4.4
Live/work at BedZED –ground floor with kitchen in a cupboard

1.4.5
Happiness on a LOW footprint – can we integrate
the values of a small holding permaculture
community into higher-density urban regeneration?

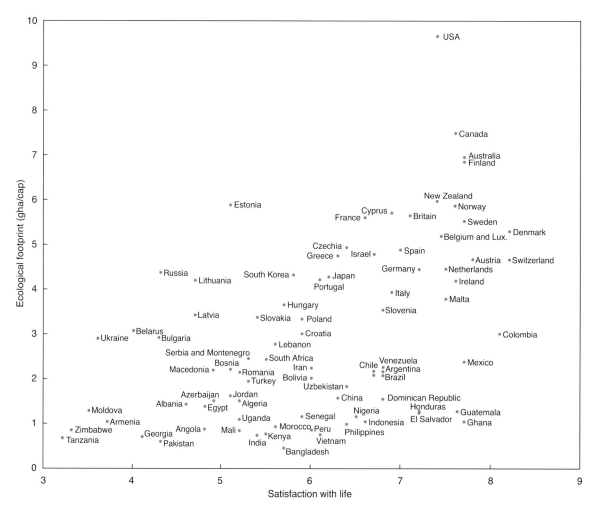

1.4.6
Ecological footprint and
happiness

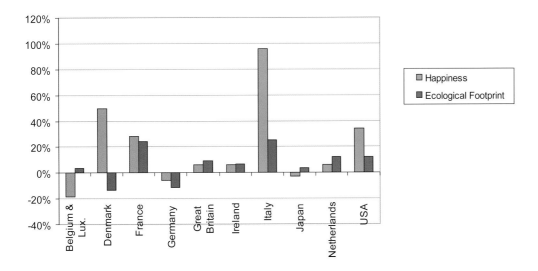

1.4.7
Ecological footprint and happiness, 1973–2004

actually show similar levels of happiness to those countries with three times the wealth. Compare, for example, Mexico with Switzerland.

Comparing national happiness – in this case determined by levels of satisfaction – with the average ecological footprint tells a similar story (see Figure 1.4.3).

Although happiness does seem to be weakly related to consumption, increasing consumption of energy and materials is certainly no guarantee of higher levels of satisfaction. For example, Americans would seem to be less satisfied than Columbians despite having an environmental impact three times as large.

Of course it can be argued that comparing average satisfaction levels in different countries is prone to error. Cultural reference points vary, as does the gulf between the 'haves' and 'have nots'. Certainly there is evidence to suggest that how you perceive yourself relative to others is significant in determining happiness. One survey of US students showed that they would prefer a salary of US $50,000, if they knew others were getting half that, over and above a salary of US $100,000 if they thought others would get US $200,000. Happiness at receiving a generous pay rise can quickly turn sour when you discover that your colleagues are being awarded even more.[8]

Looking at historical changes in satisfaction and consumption within a single country can provide a clearer picture.

Figure 1.4.7 shows the relative changes in satisfaction and footprint indexes between 1974 and 2004 for a subset of countries.[9] Whereas all countries except Denmark and Germany have increased their footprint between these dates, satisfaction in Belgium, Germany and Japan is in decline. The scale of change is also very different even in those countries where the trends in satisfaction and footprint are going in the same direction. There appears to be no clear, consistent relationship between ecological footprint and 'satisfaction'.

ZEDfact

What makes people happy?

Try this out with a group of friends, as part of a class-based exercise or in a workshop.

Divide people into pairs. Ask each pair to decide which one of them has the highest footprint. Record the results. A little later ask the same paired groups to try and judge which person is the happiest. Again, record the results.

In how many groups was the person with the highest footprint also the happiest? In most cases there is no correlation. There seems to be no consistent link between a high footprint lifestyle and happiness.

This is just one game you can play with the Global Steps cards (see www.bestfootforward.com/globalsteps.html).

1.4.8
Reclaimed materials used to create a new architectural
language at the Earth Centre, Doncaster

1.4.9
A US housing development has a large footprint

American dream or American depression?

New generations, whilst aspiring to the 'American lifestyle', may also disagree with their policies. This factor is unlikely to make a dent on the domination of American brands across the world as consumers rarely have a conscience and this will obviously be to the detriment of indigenous offerings.

Abbe Paul, Consultant, Origin Brand Consultants, UK[10]

The USA makes an interesting case study. It is well known for its conspicuous consumption and correspondingly high footprint, and it has been tracking levels of happiness since 1974.

Whereas the footprint has risen steadily, those reporting that they are 'very happy' has actually decreased slightly (see Figure 1.4.10).

Ask Americans what would make them more satisfied and they are about three times more likely to ask for some improvement in their health or social well-being than they are for more consumer goods (see Figure 1.4.11).

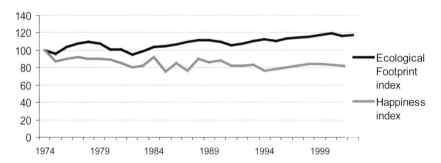

1.4.10
Indices of happiness and ecological footprint: USA 1974–2002

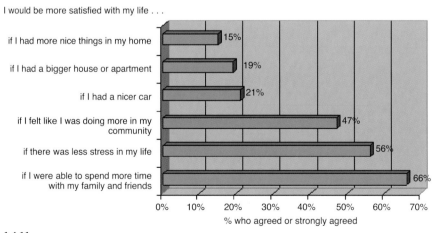

1.4.11
What Americans say would make them more satisfied with their life

An opinion survey commissioned by the US-based Merck Family Fund has revealed a deep seated dissatisfaction of citizens with the 'American Dream'.[11, 12] People of all ethnic backgrounds are convinced that 'materialism, greed, and selfishness increasingly dominate American public life and the private lives of individuals. These forces are crowding out a more meaningful set of values centred on family, responsibility, and community.'

More than 85 per cent of those surveyed say that 'today's youth are too focused on buying and consuming things', and 58 per cent describe most American children as 'very materialistic'. More than 80 per cent of Americans agree that 'most of us buy and consume far more than we need'.

America's 'super-rich' hold similar views. The Forbes' 100 wealthiest list were surveyed by researchers at the University of Illinois to ascertain their levels of happiness. They appear to be only marginally happier than the US average despite having net worths all exceeding US $100 million. Around 80 per cent also agreed with the statement that 'Money can increase OR decrease happiness, depending on how it is used.'[13]

Worryingly, the personal doubts expressed by Americans about the lack of balance in their own lives do not appear to have influenced the direction of their economy, or of the economies of those other countries who are seeking to emulate the 'American Dream'.

The desire to live a happier, less encumbered life is, of course, not new. The benefits of simple living have been promoted for millennia by religious groups, such as the Buddhists, who seek to emphasise the spiritual merit of such a lifestyle choice. American Henry David Thoreau, writing in the 1850s, is largely credited with broadening the appeal of simple living to a more general audience. In the influential *Walden* (1854) he wrote:

> 'In short, I am convinced, both by faith and experience, that to maintain one's self on this earth is not a hardship but a pastime, if we will live simply and wisely; as the pursuits of the simpler nations are still the sports of the more artificial.'[14]

Thoreau was not evangelical in his promotion of simpler living. His point was merely to prove the viability, feasibility and benefits of such a lifestyle. He went to great pains to document all aspects, financial, social and ecological, to guide others wishing to follow his lead.

Of course, Thoreau lived in a different era and his solutions are not all appropriate to modern times. The central tenets of his work, though, remain unimpeachable. It is possible to live a happy, fulfilling life on less.

More than 150 years on from Thoreau, there is now broad consensus on the pressing need to reduce society's impact on the environment. In the rush to tackle the ecological crises looming before us, we must not forget an equally important goal: the pursuit of happiness.

Box 1.4.4 Suggestions for a happier life

David G. Myers, Professor of Psychology at Hope College, USA and author of *The Pursuit of Happiness* has 9 suggestions for a happier life:

1. Realize that enduring happiness doesn't come from success. Wealth is like health: its utter absence breeds misery, but having it doesn't guarantee happiness.

2. Take control of your time. Happy people are masters of their own time. Don't over-estimate what you can accomplish in a day – instead plan over longer timescales and break down goals into simple daily and weekly tasks.

3. Seek work and leisure that engages your skills. Happy people often are absorbed in a task that challenges them without overwhelming them. The most expensive forms of leisure (sitting on a yacht) often provide less flow experience than gardening, socialising or craft work.

4. Join the 'movement' movement. Exercise not only promotes health and energy, it also is an antidote for mild depression and anxiety. Sound minds reside in sound bodies.

5. Give your body the sleep it wants. Happy people live active vigorous lives yet reserve time for renewing sleep and solitude. Many people suffer from a sleep debt, with resulting fatigue, diminished alertness and gloomy moods.

6. Give priority to close relationships. Intimate friendships with those who care deeply about you can help you weather difficult times. Confiding is good for soul and body. Resolve to nurture your closest relationships: to not take those closest to you for granted, to display to them the sort of kindness that you display to others, to affirm them, to play together and share together. To rejuvenate your affections, resolve in such ways to act lovingly.

7. Focus beyond the self. Reach out to those in need. Doing good also makes one feel good.

8. Keep a gratitude journal. Those who pause each day to reflect on some positive aspect of their lives (their health, friends, family, freedom, education, senses, natural surroundings and so on) experience heightened well-being.

9. Nurture your spiritual self. For many people, faith (in all its various forms) provides a support community, a reason to focus beyond self, and a sense of purpose and hope.

Adapted from David G. Myers, *The Pursuit of Happiness* (Avon Books, 1993).

1.5 The ZEDstandards:
A Checklist for ZEDliving

As we have seen in previous chapters, to be truly environmentally sustainable, building developments must adhere to certain basic ZEDliving principles which we have summarised as follows:

- Make Carbon History
- Design Out Fossil Fuels
- Reduce Demand – Run on Native Renewables
- Enable a High Quality of Life on a LOW Footprint.

Each principle is associated with specific goals and targets but no attempt has been made to link these to specific design decisions or discuss the infrastructure, buildings or behaviours needed to make them a reality. The subsequent sections of this book do just that.

However before delving into the technical details and cases studies we will provide – for the reader wishing to venture no further – a simple template to help determine compliance with ZEDliving principles. We call this the ZEDstandards Sustainable Building Code.[1] The aim of the Code is to assist in the assessment of planned developments, renovations and the associated infrastructure. Like all such guides it should be used with caution as it cannot cover all eventualities or in any way substitute for the experience of a skilled practitioner. Nonetheless, time and time again we have been convinced of the value of providing a simplified means of evaluation. In the busy world of planners, policy-makers and engineers, a checklist may be the only thing standing between an energy-hungry abomination and a planet-friendly eco-development.

Here we provide examples of six different density developments and show the characteristics (food, housing, transport, materials and waste, services spending and so on) that would be needed in each case to achieve compliance with the Standards.

The ZEDstandards take a whole-life approach recognising that all construction and regeneration undertaken today will have to be economically viable, and provide comfortable living, in a very different low carbon future. The team that put together the original ZEDstandards – ARUP, Best Foot Forward, Bill Dunster Architects/ZED-factory and Bioregional Reclaimed – were motivated by the need to establish a simple roadmap for affordable homes, workspaces, public buildings and their associated infrastructure to document what standards and design approaches must be adopted now to make the future work for the next generation. ZEDstandards offers a way forward which is of assistance for volume builders, masterplanners, agents of community regeneration, Agenda 21 groups, policy-making and all those with an interest in creating more sustainable communities.

1.5.1
A house in Christiania – a self-governing eco-community situated in the heart of Copenhagen

Any development compliant with ZEDstandards can be sustained by the limited national renewable energy resource that we expect to be available in 2050. As we shall see, this is achieved by combining state of the art energy-efficient passive heating and cooling techniques while maximising the opportunities for renewable energy harvesting within a site's boundaries. This step-change reduction in ecological footprint and carbon emissions can be achieved today, at the same time as improving overall quality of life. This is important as, if presented with a choice, the ZEDliving option must be at least as attractive as the conventional offerings.

However the economic, social and environmental pressures to comply with the ZEDstandards extend beyond the core principles set out in the ZEDliving principles.

The Kyoto Protocol commits countries to, albeit modest, CO_2 reduction targets (8 per cent cut from 1990 levels by 2012 across the European Union). Even these are proving a challenge. For example, Europe looks likely to achieve this reduction (if it indeed does) only by using the 'loophole' in the Kyoto Protocol to invest in overseas offset projects rather than actually reduce its own emissions. Some countries have formally acknowledged the inadequacy of Kyoto and are setting longer term targets. Germany has expressed its willingness to reduce its own emissions by 40 per cent below 1990 levels by 2020.[2] In the United Kingdom, the Royal Commission on Environmental Pollution has proposed reducing CO_2 levels by 60 per cent before 2050 – a goal confirmed and formalised within the Energy White Paper.[3]

Energy security is now a key concern for many industrialised and industrialising countries. To protect the domestic economy it makes sense to develop a diverse energy portfolio, including making best use of native renewable energy sources. Abundant supplies of oil, gas, coal and uranium are only found in relatively few countries. Transporting them around the world involves complex supply chains which are prone to interruption for myriad reasons. Fuel imports into North America have been disrupted due to hurricane damage, gas supplies to Europe have been reduced due to domestic disputes within Russia and the Ukraine, warlords and strikers have restricted exports from Nigeria and Venezuela respectively.

Despite the best efforts of Governments to build their way out of the problem, many countries (from China to the USA) are now facing supply shortages as first generation nuclear stations are decommissioned, 'dirty' coal or oil power plants are phased out or simply because demand is increasing faster than generating capacity.[4]

Carbon taxes are beginning to bite. At the time of writing, CO_2 was trading at €17 per tonne in the EU Emissions Trading Scheme and some have predicted that it could rise by up to €10/tonne each year. By 2020 it is could therefore be €170.[5]

Fuel poverty is a serious problem now and will only get worse as energy costs rise. Due to the impacts of climate change we are already seeing the problem of 'winter deaths' from insufficient heating being added to by 'summer deaths' as extreme heatwaves become ever more frequent. Vulnerable persons in poorly insulated and badly designed homes will need to pay for the upkeep and maintenance of both heating and cooling systems.

Increasing population numbers and modern lifestyles mean more homes, but fewer people per dwelling. The world's population is expected to increase by 50 per cent from 6 to 9 billion by 2050[6] and, if the trends seen in Europe are replicated elsewhere, then the average number of occupants per house could dip to below 2.3.[7]

Even if new developments were built to the best current Government standards they would still prove to be obsolete before the end of their design life due to their energy inefficient design – the equivalent of modern 'shanty towns' unfit for comfortable living. No current standards require new buildings to be future proofed against energy price rises or the consequences of climate change. Retrofitting obsolete buildings would be costly and complex.

Having a clear set of standards helps to establish reliable supply chains – pushing down prices, creating economics of scale and capacity-building design expertise.

Solutions matching scale

The ZEDstandards are target based – the solutions will inevitably change according to scale and location. In urban areas, where higher densities are demanded, it may be difficult to achieve the necessary solar access to provide PVs or hot water solar collectors for all units. Wind turbines can provide an alternative or complementary solution. On the other hand, in urban areas there is generally better access to public transport, so it is easier to implement a green transport plan, and there is less need for private vehicles.

In rural areas, solar access is much easier to achieve. Paradoxically, lower density ZEDs can actually be more resource self-sufficient than higher density, because less resource from outside the project's site boundaries is needed to achieve low carbon living and a significant proportion of food can be grown in private or community gardens. With poorer access to public transport, live/work communities and electric vehicles can provide an answer.

Development density is one of the most important criteria for choosing which low carbon strategies to prioritise in both urban and rural regeneration and new infra-structure construction.

There is considerable confusion in the industry about which technologies are appropriate for a specific location. For example, is solar access for passive solar gain more or less important than maximising development density around a good public transport node? Is building on a greenfield site, at the cost of increased food miles, a sensible strategy? The answers are not simple, and require a careful analysis of each context, with planning constraints and local community consultation often setting the maximum permitted densities for any development site.

To help simplify this complex decision matrix the ZEDstandards propose a simple set of guidelines based on the following ZED density options.

- RuralZED (detached) 1 to 15 homes/ha
- RuralZED (semi-detached) 15 to 35 homes/ha
- RuralZED (terrace) 35 to 75 homes/ha
- Live/workZED 75 to 120 homes/ha
- UrbanZED (below 6 storeys) 120 to 240 homes/ha
- CityZED (SkyZED) 120 to 240 homes/ha

Zero carbon multi-generation solar
cooled home in Shenzen, China

Sharing responsibility

The ZEDstandards recognise that change is a shared responsibility: individuals, business and Government all must play their part to bring about a sustainable world. As the UK energy calculations in Chapter 1.3 demonstrated, all sectors of the economy must tighten their belts and reduce their footprint. In Table 1.5.1 we implicitly allocate resource savings to the farmers, manufacturers and service providers who feed, clothe, furnish and otherwise design, manufacture and deliver the other 'external' services that ZED residents and workers rely upon. Indicative figures are used here (based on the calculations presented in the earlier chapter) but with larger developments which include significant commercial activity these could be calculated more accurately.

The ZEDstandards also recognise that while some efficiency savings are design-related others require behaviour change. Old habits die hard but at least they can, and do, wither. The ZEDstandards do assume some behaviour change, though to an extent this can be traded off against other possible lifestyle decisions.

1.5.2
Thermal imaging shows how standard houses glow with emitted heat compared with ZED designs

New developments and renovations

The ZEDstandards are intended to be used both pre- and post-occupancy to assist in developing planning briefs and assessing outline designs as well as to guide conversions and renovations. As the Standards are target based and expressed per capita they can be more flexibly applied than straightforward design checklists.

Note that all the example developments listed comply with the ZEDstandards:

- Fossil fuels have been designed out – the housing requires no fossil fuel use and renewably powered transport options have been integrated into all the developments.
- Residents can live comfortably on an ecological footprint of less than 2 gha per person.
- Residents are responsible for CO_2 emissions of 2.1 tonnes – or less – per person.
- The developments use no more energy than could be provided from native renewable sources (in this case based on availability within the United Kingdom).[8]

Ensuring compliance with ZEDstandards

With a little effort, most developments or development proposals can be assessed against the ZEDstandards. Ecological footprint analysis is becoming a widely accepted and standardised assessment procedure with the Global Footprint Network taking an international lead with partner organisations in many countries. Baseline data for more than 150 countries is available covering most of the globe. Many lifestyle footprint calculators exist which can be used to verify compliance with the ZEDstandards and a purpose-built one is freely available on the ZEDstandards website (www.zedstandards.com).

Table 1.5.1: Guideline figures for six different density developments (homes/hectare) – all are ZEDstandards compliant

	RuralZED (<15/ha)	RuralZED (15–35/ha)	RuralZED (35–75/ha)	Live/workZED (75–120/ha)	UrbanZED (120–240/ha)	SkyZED/ CityZED (150–250/ha)
Food supply						
% of diet which is animal-based	20	20	20	20	20	20
% of food which is fresh, unprocessed & local	100	100	60	50	21	21
Reduction in food waste (%)	50	25	10	5	1	1
% efficiency savings in food supply chain [1]	80	80	80	80	80	80
Mobility						
Biofuel vehicle (vkm/person/yr)	2,700	2,250	750	260	260	300
Ultra-efficient petrol car (vkm/person/yr)	0	0	3,000	1,300	780	600
Electric car (vkm/person/yr)	2,700	2,250	750	780	300	300
Public transport (pass. km/year)	600	1,500	1,500	2,600	4,160	4,800
Buildings						
Fossil fuel consumption kWh/yr	0	0	0	0	0	0
Consumption of renewables (excl. wood) kWh/yr	1,500	1,500	1,500	425	375	1,500
Of which Renewable electricity – wind	750	750	1,125	375	225	1,350
Renewable electricity – PV	750	750	375	150	150	150
Wood fuel consumption kg/yr	200	200	200	500	500	500
Living space (m^2 per person)	290	174	79	43	24	43
Area left managed for wildlife/food production (m^2 per person)	247	131	36	0	0	0
Materials & waste						
Municipal waste (kg/person/year)	260	260	260	260	260	260
… to landfill	39	39	39	39	39	39
… to recycling	156	156	156	156	156	156
… to composting	65	65	65	65	65	65
% efficiency savings in industrial sector [2]	60	60	60	60	60	60
Services						
Spending £/year	2,400.00	2,400.00	2,400.00	2,400.00	2,400.00	2,400.00
% efficiency savings in services sector [3]	60	60	60	60	60	60
Footprint gha/capita/yr	1.56	1.65	1.66	1.68	1.72	1.77
CO_2 t/capita/yr	2	1.7	1.7	1.5	1.5	1.60
Number of worlds	0.82	0.87	0.87	0.88	0.91	0.93

Notes [1], [2], [3] These can be considered as either efficiency savings, reductions in consumption or the consequences of extending the ZEDstandards to these other sectors. The case study in the next section of a Zero Emission Farm (or ZEF) suggests how to adapt the concept to the food supply chain.

Carbon emissions calculators are similarly widespread – though, at the time of writing, relatively few have a sufficiently broad lifestyle focus. The ZEDstandards website again contains a suitable estimator which will assist.

Being target based there are many ways to comply with the ZEDstandards. Hence they do not prescribe certain construction materials, specific electrical appliances, transport infrastructure, food supply chains and so on. In fact, such prescriptions can constrain progress and can actually mitigate against innovation.

For example many building standards recommend installing A-rated white goods such as fridges. This is certainly better than recommending B-rated devices but, to reduce energy use, it is much more cost effective to specify the latest A++ fridges. These use less than half the energy of A-rated devices and it is far cheaper to reduce energy than try to generate it from renewables. If the ZEDstandards were drafted to specify A++ devices we may well – eventually – fall into the same trap. A more energy-efficient alternative may become available or other solutions might be preferable. One ecological development we know of incorporates a 'passive fridge' – a modern interpretation of an old fashioned larder which stays cool year round, negating the need for any electrical refrigeration. In our wired up world it is easy to forget that refrigeration is just one preservation method – many societies survive from harvest to harvest without relying on electricity. We have much to learn – or re-learn – about the efficient way of feeding ourselves.

It is certainly not the case that the ZEDstandards are easy to achieve. Compliance requires careful thought and planning. To help structure the compliance process, it is here recommended that a Plan is drafted which clearly sets out those actions necessary to achieve the ZEDstandards targets.

A ZEDstandards Plan

Such a Plan should address all the individual ZEDstandards components:

- Food Supply
- Personal Mobility
- Buildings
- Materials and Waste
- Services

Under each sub-heading, the specific measures needed to achieve the ZEDstandard targets should be described and analysed for their potential role in delivering energy or footprint reductions.

For example, the section on Food Supply would include descriptions of the following:

- Space provided for, and likely yields from, on site food and drink production (allotments, greenhouses, private gardens, roof gardens, window boxes, orchards and other communal spaces).
- Opportunities to accommodate on site 'zero carbon' secondary food producers or suppliers; perhaps brewing or bottling facilities, a bakery, a convenience store which offers to re-use packaging, a wholefood shop, bar, café, communal kitchen and so on.

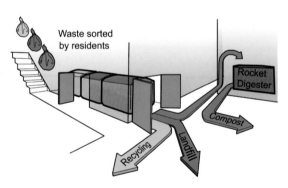

Waste sorted by residents

Rocket Digester

Compost

Recycling

Landfill

1.5.3
Design to encourage effective recycling – waste segregation at source

- Provision for community-supported agriculture off site (community farms, local allotments, seed banks and so on).
- Access to local food (farmers and community markets, box schemes and other supply chain links to local food and drink producers).
- Facilities for the sustainable management of food waste (a defined means of segregation, recycling and composting).
- Educational advice offered covering, for example, guidance on the sourcing and preparation of fresh organic food, healthy eating, the avoidance of waste and food cultivation.

Each measure needs to be quantified to demonstrate how the ZEDstandards can be met. It is also important to state how each measure will be managed and monitored. Options include one or more of the following:

- Enforcement through planning agreements written in when the development received planning permission. On-going monitoring would then rest with the local planning authority.
- Partnership agreements with local stakeholders. For example, in the case of food supplies, this might take the form of an agreement between the developers and a local dairy farm for the on-going supply of milk and cheese. Alternatively, it might be a broader agreement with a local sustainable food partnership to provide on-going education and advice to residents.
- Local management by residents, tenants or a suitably constituted trust. This form of management is already widespread where premises are leasehold and/or there is a common interest in facilities (gardens, lifts, car parks and so on). This remit can easily be extended to include the management and monitoring of those elements needed to deliver the ZEDstandards.

At www.zedstandards.com we have included a template ZEDstandards Plan to assist in securing compliance. The solutions will necessarily vary according to the type of development, location and density. As time passes new technologies will be developed or become commercially viable. However, the ZEDstandards Plan structure need not change.

In the next section we will provide more detailed case studies of ZEDstandard developments.

Applications of the ZEDstandards to non-residential uses
ZEDfarming

Agriculture accounts for a relatively small proportion of the global CO_2 emissions. It is estimated that about 9 per cent of all emissions attributable to fossil fuel burning are related to the production, processing and packaging of food and drink.[9]

Many campaigns have focused on reducing 'food miles' – the distance food travels from farm gate to plate – but this is only part of the story. Though food is well travelled by the time it lands in your shopping basket (a study of London calculated an average

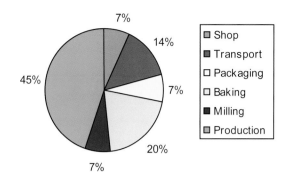

1.5.4
Energy required to produce a 1 kg loaf of bread.[11] Note that food miles accounts for only 14 per cent of the total

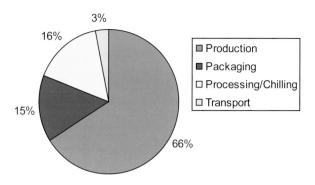

1.5.5
Carbon emissions embodied in a typical weekly shop[12]

journey length of 640 km by road alone),[10] for the most part the carbon footprint of transportation is dwarfed by the emissions from production, processing and packaging (see Figures 1.5.4 and 1.5.5). It is certainly true that processing and packaging is often only required *because* food is increasingly being stored and freighted over long distances, but to merely cut down on food miles without tackling the rest of the supply chain is to miss an important opportunity to reduce overall carbon emissions.

It is self-evidently crucial that any economy can maintain adequate food supplies and guarantee food security into the future. This alone is sufficient justification for closer scrutiny of this sector of the carbon economy. How might fossil fuel-free farming be realised?

Again, the ZEDstandards principles provide a useful framework. Improving the efficiency of the food supply chain and making best use of local energy resources is key to the creation of zero emission farms (or ZEFs) that can provide secure and reliable nourishment into the future.

Farms vary widely in their production methods and the scope of their activities. Some farms are involved in food processing and distribution as well as cultivation, others are engaged in education. Some specialise in organic agriculture, others have developed an expertise in growing rare or 'gourmet' crops. It is important to tailor the application of the ZEDstandards principles on a case by case basis.

Here we relate our experiences of collaborating with Commonwork farm in Kent.

The Commonwork case study

Commonwork Land Trust is part of the Commonwork Group, a group of organisations, enterprises and charitable trusts set up in 1977. It is based on an organic farm at Bore Place in Kent which incorporates a study centre.

The Trust is working to deliver sustainable solutions in farming, the environment and education. The centre at Bore Place creates opportunities for learning for people of all ages through education, environment, food and farming programmes. The buildings include a conference and study centre.

An integral part of Commonwork's educational and enterprise activities is a mixed organic dairy farm based on the heavy Wealden clay soil of Bore Place. The dairy unit was first constructed in 1977. The organic conversion of the farm was started in 1995 and completed by 2001.

Three hundred and fifty hectares are farmed in total, including 155 owned and the rest rented from neighbouring farms to increase self-reliance in terms of feed stuff and to allow stock numbers to be kept up to around 270 cows. Land is made up as follows:[13]

- 53 ha cereal
- 47 ha mixed forage for silage
- 21.5 ha winter beans
- remainder grass.

The dairy herd consists of Friesian Holstein milking cows (which make up about 90 per cent of EU herds – the ubiquitous black and white cow), which due to high quality forage, good rationing and excellent management are reported to be in fine condition. Milking is done twice a day.

During the winter the cows are housed in timber-framed, elm-clad sheds. Hygiene is carefully planned with dairy and slurry treatment at opposite ends of the large cow-cubicle building. All slurry and manure is used on the land to recycle fertility to the growing crops and add organic matter to the soil.

The herd has been managed to organic standards from July 1999, and were fed organically for 12 weeks prior to obtaining organic status on 1 April 2000. With organic conversion there is less mastitis, foot trouble and fewer metabolic problems, and in general the herd appears happier and more content.

All milk is sold via the Organic Milk Suppliers Co-operative.

It will already have become apparent to the reader that Commonwork is not a typical dairy farm. In line with ZEDstandards principles, it has already made substantial efforts to reduce the energy intensity of its production systems. For example, it has:

- *Lowered its stocking rate*. Stocking rates have fallen from 2.1 cows per hectare to 1.5 as a result of discontinuing inorganic fertiliser applications.[14] Grass leys have been replaced with white or red clover and grass leys, which are able to affix atmospheric nitrogen. However due to the renting of extra hectares total numbers will remain the same.
- *Eliminated chemical sprays*. This means maize will cease to be grown for forage and be replaced with cereal crops cut for silage. Also weeds, particularly docks, can be a problem so a topper has been purchased to stop them seeding and spreading.
- *Reduced the use of antibiotics*. The farm is now using homeopathic remedies and does not now routinely antibiotic tube all cows at drying off. However if a cow is seriously infected, antibiotics are still used with the vet's advice.
- *Fewer veterinary fertility treatments*. During the 4 months' breeding season the vet used to come each week, but last year only twice. This has greatly reduced veterinary bills but only marginally increased the farm's calving index (average days/cows/calf).
- *Increased time on milk for calves*. Calves now stay on milk for a minimum of 12 weeks (previously 6 weeks). Wormers are no longer used, with reliance placed on grazing 'clean' (no stock for at least one year) pastures.

Local woodlands

Local rapeseed fields

Universities

Schools

MSW

Vegoline

'University of Organics' Education / Outreach programme

Veg oil fuel

Laverstoke Park

Waste wood

Wood chipper

Rapeseed cake

Rapeseed press

Pelletiser

Transport fuel

Veg oil farm vehicles

Runoff from buildings and land

Laverstock rape crop

Compost

Happy soil

Farm lab

Reservoir

H_2O

Pyrolysis or biogas

'H' reformer

Fuels cells

Absorbtion chiller from heat provides cooling to abatoir

Buildings off heat main use pellet boilers

District heat main from fuel cell waste heat

Farm Micro Grid

Laverstoke Park
– zero carbon production
– zero waste production
– zero carbon delivery to the urban community

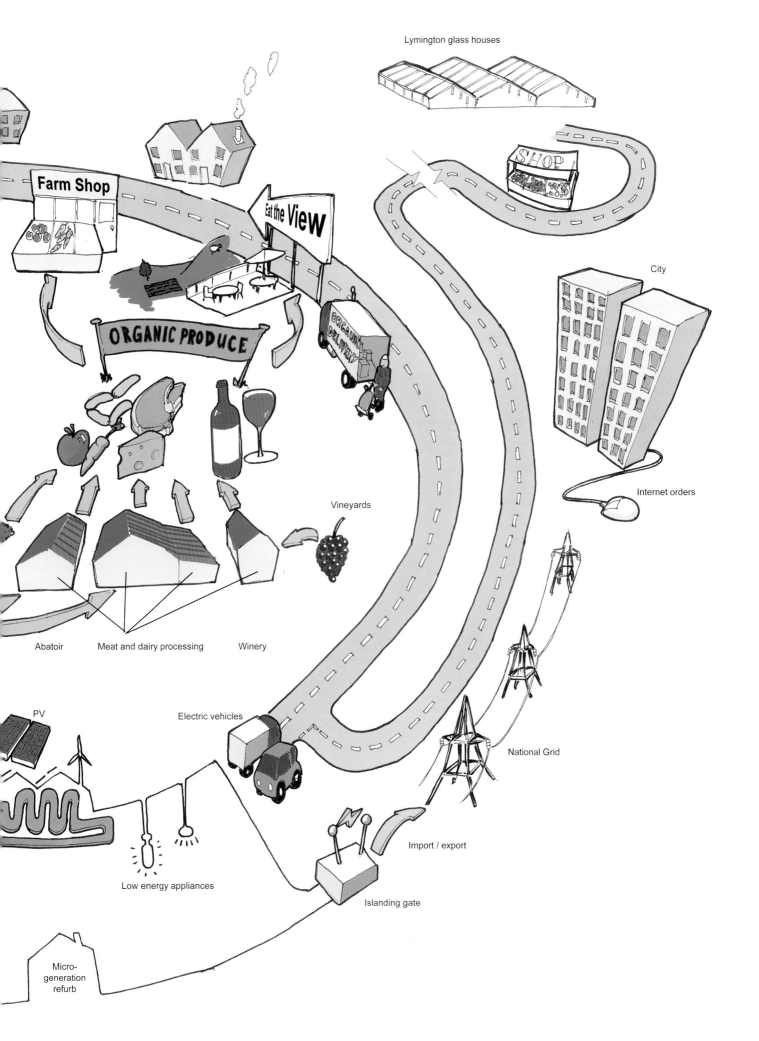

Lymington glass houses

SHOP

Farm Shop

Eat the View

City

ORGANIC PRODUCE

Internet orders

Vineyards

Abatoir   Meat and dairy processing   Winery

PV

Electric vehicles

National Grid

Import / export

Low energy appliances

Islanding gate

Micro-generation refurb

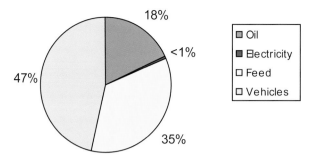

1.5.6
Summary of the amount and source of all known CO_2 emissions at Commonwork
which relate to milk production (tCO_2 per year)

- *Eliminated the routine use of chemicals.* For example fly control no longer
  involves spraying the cows with insecticide but instead relies on a fan in the
  milking parlour and a water mist over the door to prevent the flies coming
  into it.
- *Changed the feed content.* The biggest change has come as a result of needing high quality organic forage, which must make up at least 60 per cent of
  the cow's ration, which means:
  - no protein feeds with genetically modified organisms
  - no animal proteins
  - no general mineral and vitamin supplements
  - no (chemically) extracted protein feeds.
- *Switched to renewable electricity.* In 2004, the farm started to source all its
  electricity from off site renewable resources – primarily from wind turbines.

As a result of all these efforts, the carbon emissions attributable to the farm were
already well below those that would be expected from a conventional dairy farm (see
Figure 1.5.6). The switch to renewable electricity alone (the most easily quantifiable
change) reduced CO_2 emissions by one-third across the entire farm and educational
complex.

Studies of existing diary farms led to an expectation that emissions from milk
production would equate to around 0.6 to 0.7 kg CO_2 per litre of milk produced.[15]
The data collected at Commonwork indicated that the figure was already below
0.2 kg CO_2 per litre – a saving of more than 70 per cent.

The fact that Commonwork has already made substantial efficiency gains is to be
applauded. They have already demonstrated what can be achieved by following the
mantra at the heart of the ZEDstandards: research, reduce, reclaim, renewables.

The challenge was to build on this success and see whether CO_2 emissions could
be reduced still further – ideally to zero.

With its emphasis on education and dissemination, Commonwork is ideally placed
to promote zero emissions farming but – to really do this effectively – it was felt that
the energy use of the educational facilities on the Bore Place site would have to be
addressed along with the farm operations.

Total CO_2 emissions were estimated to be just over 260 tonnes per annum (see
Table 1.5.2).

Table 1.5.2: CO_2 emissions from different farm and educational centre activities[16]

	Value	Units	kg CO_2	Comments
Diesel	34,783	litres/year	92,201	Farm vehicles
Car travel – petrol	8,458	vkm/year	1,573	Education/farm/admin
Public transport (train)	3,996	passkm/yr	240	Education
Feed concentrate – molasses/seaweed/minerals	30,000	kg/year	13,949	Imported feed
Feed concentrate – rape	120,000	kg/year	55,795	Imported feed
Wood	4,212	kg/year	0	Centre
Renewable electricity – wind	49,336	kWh/year	320	Centre
Renewable electricity – wind	1,143	kWh/year	7	Environment
Renewable electricity – wind	1,143	kWh/year	7	Gardens
Renewable electricity – wind	10,459	kWh/year	68	Education
Renewable electricity – wind	4,906	kWh/year	32	Office
Renewable electricity – wind	390	kWh/year	3	Maintenance
Renewable electricity – wind	144,681	kWh/year	938	Farm
Renewable electricity – wind	684	kWh/year	4	KWW
Oil	18,472	litres/year	49,445	Centre
Oil	13,488	litres/year	36,105	Farm
LPG	2,909	litres/year	4,796	Centre
LPG	1,746	litres/year	2,878	Office
LPG	1,164	litres/year	1,918	Education
Total			260,286	

Applying the ZEDstandards principles, five specific actions were identified, as follows.

Complete a comprehensive energy and water audit of the dairy supply chain
The aim being to consider both the more local and the wider opportunities for further influencing and reducing the overall impacts of delivering dairy products to consumers. In this way it is possible to relate the CO_2 emissions and ecological footprint to the per capita ZEDstandards targets. *What proportion of the overall footprint is milk responsible for?* Careful research is also necessary to avoid 'rebound effects' where savings in one part of the supply chain adversely impact on another, reducing the overall benefit. An initial energy audit provided the justification for, and quantification of, the remaining measures set out here.

Further efficiency savings
Even with an organisation as committed as Commonwork to energy efficiency it was possible to identify further opportunities for savings. The range of possibilities included:

- more energy-efficient lighting
- up-rating energy efficiency of appliances
- draught proofing
- improvements to glazing
- additional buildings insulation.

Although the potential carbon savings for these measures were not quantified in detail – due to the numerous permutations possible – it is anticipated that the main benefit would be from changes to the lighting and the reductions in heating load from the glazing/draught proofing/insulation.

A conservative estimate of savings is 10 per cent of electrical demand in the offices and educational buildings (6500 kWh/year) and 20 per cent of heating load in the office and educational buildings (saving about $12tCO_2$).

Run farm machinery on biofuel
This has the potential to reduce the net carbon impact from the use of diesel – the largest source of CO_2 emissions at Commonwork. Assuming all diesel is displaced by biofuel grown in an energy-efficient manner (a limited amount of fossil fuel energy is required to produce the biofuel),[17] then this has the potential to reduce emissions by more than 80 tCO_2 or 30 per cent.

Biodiesel could either be grown on site, bought in, or derived from used vegetable oil. The latter is the most environmentally friendly option as used oil is otherwise treated as a waste product. Growing biodiesel requires a significant area of arable land. Around 30 hectares of land would be required to produce sufficient renewable fuel to displace all current diesel use. This, again, emphasises the benefits of recycling used vegetable oils and the need to upgrade to more fuel-efficient vehicles.

Derive energy from existing animal wastes
When manure is stored without proper aeration it fails to decompose fully to CO_2 and, instead, releases CH_4 (methane) a more potent greenhouse gas.[18]

The methane emissions from slurry are difficult to quantify as they vary according to storage method, length of storage, by season and even the type of feed. To get an idea of the scale of methane emissions from cattle, one particular study (of a 150-strong dairy herd) measured the annual CH_4 emissions from waste as equal to approximately 5 tCO_2 per head of cattle per year.[19] With around 270 cows (equivalent to approximately 1,500 tCO_2 per year) at Commonwork, it can be seen that the emissions from animal waste could potentially swamp any direct CO_2 emissions from fossil fuel use.

Installation of a biodigester – a device which captures the gas produced as organic materials decompose and uses this to generate energy – has the potential to massively reduce greenhouse gas emissions both by displacing fossil fuels and reducing methane emissions. Such 'Cow Power' plants, as they have been called, are a safe, proven method of energy production.[20] Studies have shown that the manure from a single cow can provide anything up to 5,150 kWh per year.[21]

Assuming a modest 1,400 kWh usable output per cow, a combined heat and power plant (CHP) could be coaxed to produce about 155,000 kWh of electricity per annum and 230,000 kWh of energy as heat.[22] This is equal to about 70 per cent of

Commonwork's electrical demand and about 60 per cent of its heat demand (as estimated from oil and LPG consumption data).[23] Installation of a biodigester therefore has the potential to reduce the overall CO_2 emissions from fossil fuels by around 60 tCO_2 or 23 per cent. This excludes any savings from the avoidance of methane emissions which are potentially, in terms of their global warming equivalence, very much larger.[24]

Meet remaining electrical and heat demand with on site wind, solar and biomass
Two modestly sized 15 kW wind turbines (blade span of 10 m, hub height of around 15 m) would provide sufficient output to meet the residual electrical demand following the installation of a biodigester. Even these might not be required if the biodigester were proven to be more efficient than expected or further energy savings could be identified.

Estimated CO_2 savings are set out in Table 1.5.3 below.

The current high capital cost per kW of installed solar photovoltaic panels would make them a second choice to wind – where the latter is practical. Nonetheless, with grant funding or where panels would be replacing other cladding materials, their use may be cost effective.[25]

Several other options for meeting the demand for heat are listed in Table 1.5.4: wood stove, boiler and solar thermal system. Indicative figures are given for output, fuel use and CO_2 savings. Based on the availability of wood fuel and insolation levels, these may form a useful seasonal adjunct to other systems. At a conservative estimate, these could reduce heat load by a further 20 per cent (19 tCO_2).

Table 1.5.3: CO_2 emissions and savings from wind turbines

Turbine	Estimated output per year (kWh)	kg CO_2/yr emissions (based on manufacture & maintenance)	kg CO_2/yr (if electricity had been standard grid supply)
Proven 15 kw x 2	60,000	388	28,222

Table 1.5.4: Alternative means of meeting the demand for heat

Technology	Fuel	Efficiency	kWh/tonne fuel	kg CO_2 savings per tonne fuel
Ceramic kacheloven stove	wood or wood chip (moisture content 30%)	85%	3,000	670
Wood pellet boiler	wood pellets (moisture content 5%)	85%	4,000	890
			kWh/system	kg CO_2 savings per system
Solar thermal tubes	solar		2,000	450

Summary

The measures described present a logical progression – looking first at further opportunities for energy reduction before engaging with the local renewable resources. This case study has certainly not exhaustively explored all options – for example no effort has been made to address the energy embodied in the animal feed procured by the farm (though it is counted in the final carbon footprint). Nor has the issue of improved vehicle efficiency been considered (though savings would no doubt be possible).

What the reductions outlined here mean in terms of the $kgCO_2$ per litre of milk produced can be seen in Figure 1.5.7. Here this potential is compared with both current and conventional emissions. The measures presented here would reduce CO_2 emissions by a *further* 65 per cent over and above the reduction already achieved by Commonwork. The combination of existing Commonwork initiatives and those suggested here would lead to a massive 92 per cent reduction in CO_2 emissions from a conventional dairy farm. It is worth remembering that we have also included here the emissions from the educational facilities on the site, which makes the savings all the more impressive.

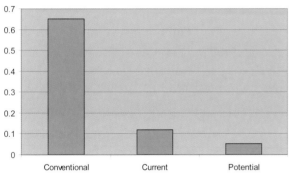

1.5.7
kg CO_2 per litre of milk

1.5.8
A computer image of two 15 kW Proven wind turbines

1.5.9
RuralZED homes for visitors to the education centre or farmworkers

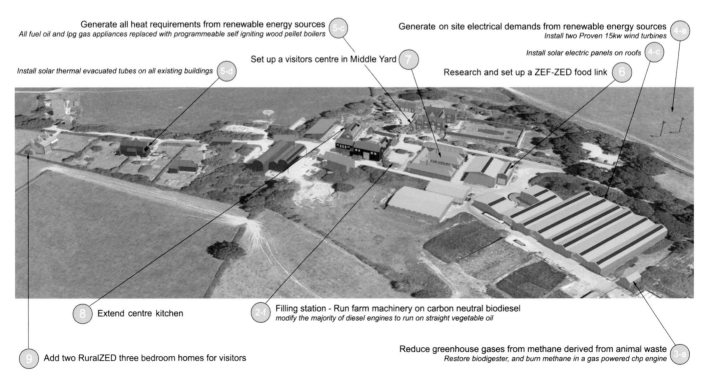

Generate all heat requirements from renewable energy sources　(5-c)
All fuel oil and lpg gas appliances replaced with programmeable self igniting wood pellet boilers

Generate on site electrical demands from renewable energy sources　(4-a)
Install two Proven 15kw wind turbines

Set up a visitors centre in Middle Yard　(7)

Install solar electric panels on roofs　(4-c)

Install solar thermal evacuated tubes on all existing buildings　(5-d)

Research and set up a ZEF-ZED food link　(6)

(8) Extend centre kitchen

(2-f) Filling station - Run farm machinery on carbon neutral biodiesel
modify the majority of diesel engines to run on straight vegetable oil

Reduce greenhouse gases from methane derived from animal waste
Restore biodigester, and burn methane in a gas powered chp engine　(3-a)

(9) Add two RuralZED three bedroom homes for visitors

1.5.10
The common work farm – 'ZEF' strategy

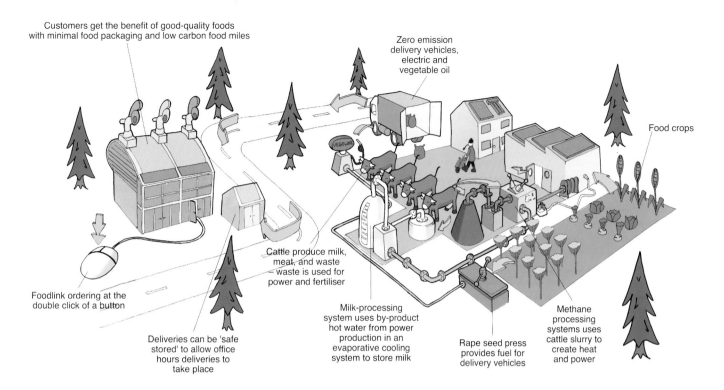

Customers get the benefit of good-quality foods with minimal food packaging and low carbon food miles

Zero emission delivery vehicles, electric and vegetable oil

Food crops

Foodlink ordering at the double click of a button

Deliveries can be 'safe stored' to allow office hours deliveries to take place

Cattle produce milk, meat, and waste – waste is used for power and fertiliser

Milk-processing system uses by-product hot water from power production in an evaporative cooling system to store milk

Rape seed press provides fuel for delivery vehicles

Methane processing systems uses cattle slurry to create heat and power

1.5.11
Possible links that could be developed between housing developments such as BedZED and Commonwork

ZED infrastructure: transportation

To support zero emission developments it is necessary to provide integrated transport solutions which meet the basic need for mobility.

Globally about one-third of all CO_2 emissions are transport related. Around three-quarters of these are due to road transport.[26] Vehicle emissions in countries classified as 'Developed' are higher – both in absolute terms and proportionately – than those in so called 'Developing' countries. Transport accounts for 28 per cent of emissions in the former and 19 per cent in the latter. Air and car travel are by far the most polluting means of moving people around (see Figure 1.5.14), with the latter responsible for the bulk of passenger transport emissions due to the high ownership and usage levels.

Making goods and people mobile is a vital part of a global economic system. Localisation – making goods and services more locally accessible – is a necessary precursor to any sustainable transport solution.[27] As we have seen with the UK example earlier, renewable resources alone cannot support the high levels of freight or personal mobility that are associated with modern industrialised living.

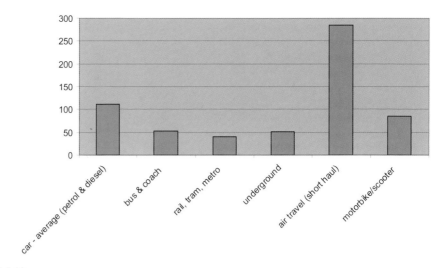

1.5.12
kg CO$_2$ per 1000 passenger kilometres by mode

The ZEDliving principles apply here as elsewhere: it is vital to design out fossil fuels, lower CO$_2$ emissions and reduce demand so that the residual need for travel can be met from native renewable resources.

In a resource-constrained world, the transport infrastructure will most likely draw its energy needs from diverse sources. The calculations for the United Kingdom in 2050 envisage a roughly equal mix of biodiesel, renewable electricity and fossil fuels for personal vehicle use. This might manifest itself in the form of hybrid, multi-fuel vehicles or in a range of models tailored to specific purposes. For example, electric vehicles might be used for short distances and biodiesel for longer hauls.

1.5.13
The ZEDfactory electric pool car charging at BedZED

1.5.14
EV1 electric car

Renewable electricity as a fuel

Electric vehicle technology is well-established and energy efficient. EVs have set land speed records, crossed continents and won races. A century ago there were more electric cars on the road than gasoline powered vehicles. The EV1, an electric car first produced by motor giants GM in 1996 – and the subject of the controversial film *Who Killed the Electric Car* – was a popular response to California's Zero Emission Vehicle (ZEV) Mandate which set targets for the introduction of zero emission (zero at the point of use) cars.[28] The EV1 was leased to users for a modest US $400–500 a month. However after industry lobbying the ZEV Mandate was watered down with the result that the EV1 was withdrawn and the vehicles tragically crushed (or 'recycled' as one GM spokesperson claimed).

Data on the EV1's performance is readily available, proving what a major car manufacturer could, in future, provide. The later model (1999) EV1 could travel 9 km on a 1 kWh charge.[29] This is impressive when compared to an efficient petrol vehicle, which would manage less than half that distance on the same input.[30]

The small and inexpensive G-Wiz, currently available in the United Kingdom, does a reported 8 km per kWh. Not quite as impressive as the EV1 but still much better than its petrol-powered cousin.

Charging electric vehicles from small-scale photovoltaics or micro wind turbines is a realistic prospect. A 2 kW PV array or 1 kW turbine (both of which would fit on a typical domestic rooftop) would provide enough electricity for a worthwhile 12,000 vehicle kilometres per year. As electric vehicles are run off batteries, they are also useful for soaking up surplus energy when demand is low. This feature can be used to great advantage with both local and national grid supplies. One can imagine an intelligent charging system which would use the battery capacity in millions of grid-connected electric vehicles to help manage the intermittency inherent in renewable resources.

Of course, electric vehicles have their drawbacks. The battery technology required to provide for long range travel is in its infancy and therefore costly. The Tesla Roadster (which is being built in the United Kingdom for the US market) is a taste of things to come.[31] With the performance of a sports car and a range of 400 km, the Tesla returns about the same efficiency as the G-Wiz (8 km per kWh) but gains its advantage through the use of high capacity, lightweight lithium ion batteries of a kind familiar to users of laptop computers.

1.5.15
The next generation of electric cars will be practical and fun for urban runarounds

Plant oils as a fuel

Another proven technology is the use of pure plant oils as fuel. Rudolf Diesel, inventor of the ubiquitous diesel engine, tested plant oils in his engines and even recommended the use of such biofuels. However the low cost of mineral oil-derived diesel fuel overwhelmed the market with the result that today's diesel engines are optimised for the burning of the fossil-derived product.

The main benefit of using plant oils as fuel is that instead of digging up carbon from underground and pumping it into the air as CO_2, the gas released from burning plant oils is reabsorbed by the plants when the next crop grows, thus negating its effect on the environment.

Following spikes in fuel prices in the 1970s, interest was rekindled in using plant oils for fuel, but the cheap price of fossil fuels during the 1980s dampened the demand.

1.5.16
A 'Blooming Futures' plant oil conversion kit suitable for most European diesel engines (www.bloomingfutures.com)

Meanwhile research into the use of plant oils followed two paths. First, work has progressed on means of modifying plant oils so that they can be utilised in unmodified diesel engines. This has lead to the growing use of a chemically-modified plant oil widely known as biodiesel. Biodiesel is produced through a process known as transesterification, which results in a thinner oil more suitable for use in conventional diesel engines. Transesterification generally uses about 20 per cent methanol, by volume, which is produced from fossil fuels.

The alternative research path, led by several small companies based in Germany, has focused on modifying diesel engines so that they operate reliably on simple plant oil (known as pure plant oil – PPO – or straight vegetable oil – SVO). The favoured oil is oilseed rape (or Canola as it is known in the USA). Modified engines can also be fuelled with ordinary diesel.

PPO is preferable as it avoids the use of methanol and is generally easier to produce.

To advance the use of oilseed rape as a fuel, a partnership of academics, plant oil press operators and engine conversion companies collaborated and, in 2000, published a fuel standard for rapeseed oil to guarantee its quality. The DIN (German Institute for Standardisation) has taken an interest in this fuel and is now working on an official German DIN standard for rapeseed oil fuel. This standard, E DIN 51 605, was expected to be released during 2006. Parallel to this the German Federal Association of Vegetable Oils (BVP) is acting to ensure a quality service from the rapidly growing number of companies now offering these conversions, now in their hundreds. Within the last decade, facilitated largely by the growing use of the Internet, interest in the use of PPO has grown worldwide. This uptake has been led by individuals and small companies but largely ignored by Governments and the existing vehicle and fuels industries.

A number of smaller engine/vehicle retailers have now offered appliances for which they approve the use of PPO as an alternative fuel. This has been largely due to the fact that the engines that they offer happen to be of a design that is particularly suitable for the use of PPO. There are a few companies that have developed engines designed specially to run on vegetable oil – but production has been limited.

Many other standard production engines are being converted by a growing army of DIY enthusiasts and small companies. Some of the latest conversions have achieved compliance with the strict 'Euro 4' exhaust emissions standards and have proven reliability.

The production of PPO is relatively easy and can be carried out on a small scale. It is possible, for example, for individual farms to produce a quality biodiesel for direct sale. This is becoming a common means of distribution in Germany and, to a lesser extent, elsewhere in Europe with several hundred small oil mills. Local production brings with it the benefits of local employment, fuel security and a reduced need to transport the finished product. These advantages are recognised in the European Union Transportation Biofuels Directive 2003/30/EC.

The use of PPO undoubtedly presents fewer technical and economic barriers than the use of electricity as a vehicle fuel. The process of converting a diesel engine to run on PPO can be easily performed by mechanics familiar with this engine type. Vehicle conversions are either dual fuel or multi-fuel.

With a dual fuel, or twin tank, conversion, a second fuel tank is fitted along with fuel heating and fuel supply control. The vehicle is started on diesel fuel and when the engine and fuel are at a suitable temperature the supply is switched to PPO. This is necessary because before it is warmed up, PPO is too viscous to use in the engine. Before the engine is shut down for extended periods the fuel supply is switched back to diesel and the engine is purged of PPO ready to restart, cold, on diesel fuel. In the more sophisticated systems fuel switching is largely automated. With a multi-fuel, or single tank conversion, a number of engine components are changed and fuel heating equipment is added to allow the vehicle to be fuelled with either PPO or diesel fuel, or a mixture of both.

Given the right economic conditions the use of PPO fuel across Europe could follow the German example, with many operators taking advantage of fuel cost savings and converting fleets of lorries and buses to run on PPO.

Uptake of national or international fuel standards for plant oils would inspire confidence in these fuels. The number of vehicles being converted would increase, showing sufficient demand for vehicle manufacturers to consider bringing PPO-ready or multi-fuel vehicles onto the market. The European Union Transportation Biofuels

1.5.17
It is now possible to increase local vegetable oil production without competing with agricultural food production by companion cropping using 'camilina sativa' in-between wheat, barley and pea crops. This effectively produces two crops at the same time, reduces weeds and pesticide use, and uses conventional mechanical sieve grain separation at harvest

Directive, which has set rolling targets for the introduction of biofuels, will further stimulate demand.

However biofuels are not without their problems. The wisdom of promoting a massive increase in the growth of plant-based fuels has been rightfully questioned. They compete with other land uses, most notably food production, encourage mono-cropping and the availability of suitable land is, in many cases, limited. Certainly, replacing more than about 8 per cent of the diesel currently used in the United Kingdom with oilseed rape-derived fuel (equivalent to an area of about 4 million hectares) would be difficult and environmentally counterproductive. The use of PPO does however offer a renewable transportation option which, in combination with efficiency savings, demand reduction and the greater use of other alternative fuels, could provide some essential mobility while society tackles the longer term goal of achieving a truly sustainable transportation system. In 2005 it is estimated the United Kingdom grew 1.9 million tonnes of rape, exporting 160,000 tonnes of this production. These exports could be advantageously diverted quite rapidly into domestic fuel production along with, perhaps, some of the produce which is currently used domestically. A small proportion of diesel could also be replaced with used cooking oil (<1 per cent).

To mitigate some of the problems associated with biofuel production it is imperative to make best use of the harvest. Oilseed rape crops, for example, produce useful straw and seed cake, both economic products, as well as the fuel oil (see Figure 1.5.18). The former has several uses, including energy generation, while the latter can be used as animal feed. A complete carbon balance of rape oil (see Figure 1.5.19) illustrates that using these other 'by-products' can further offset and reduce

1.5.18
VW Lupo 87 mpg – conversion to run off straight vegetable oil, £1,350

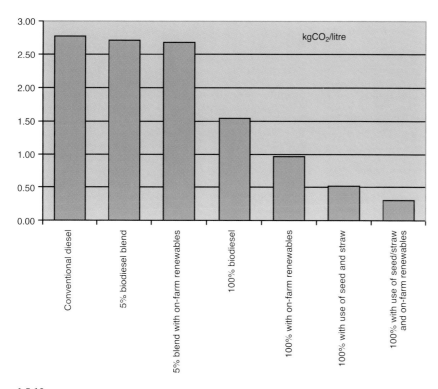

1.5.19
CO_2 reductions possible from use of entire harvest (seed cakes, straw and oil). Various options compared with emissions from conventional diesel

the carbon emission associated with cultivation and fuel production. More than 88 per cent CO_2 savings are possible.

This section would not be complete without a brief discussion of the options for continued use of fossil-fuelled transportation. The scale of CO_2 reductions required would equate to cuts of more than 80 per cent in the use of conventional oil-based transport fuels. This sounds dramatic, and is certainly daunting, but consider this quick thought experiment:

Take a medium-sized car with fuel consumption of 10 litres per 100 km. Newer, fuel-efficient cars can run on half this amount of fuel.

Now consider the distance and mode of travel. Cutting unnecessary journeys by half or switching a significant proportion to more efficient forms of transport could easily half fuel use again.

Finally, consider the occupancy of vehicles. The majority of journeys are made with just the driver. Car share and the effect is to reduce fuel use by half again.

The combined effect of these simple measures would reduce fuel use by well over 80 per cent (100% * 50% * 50% * 50%). Add in the possible contribution from other alternate fuel sources and the future looks a little less bleak.

1.5.20
Although the focus here has been on motorised transport, pedal-power remains hugely under-exploited as this new rickshaw service in Oxford demonstrates

Part two

Designing ZEDs

Zero carbon mixed-use urban regeneration including hotel, office, retail and residential uses

Designing ZEDs:
Realising ZEDstandards Projects

Introduction

This chapter considers how a zero carbon–zero waste development can be achieved using local skills and training initiatives. It should be read in conjunction with 'A guide to ZEDstandards' which describes the principles of ZEDstandard construction.

There are four ingredients to delivering zero carbon–zero waste urban regeneration:

1. a client that wants to realise a zero carbon–zero waste project
2. a design team capable of delivering one
3. a low cost component supply chain with pre-negotiated volume discounts
4. well-trained local contractors confident enough to avoid risk pricing.

ZEDfactory always recommend that reasonable scale projects carefully plan their delivery strategy before reverting to normal industry practice.

Once the brief has been agreed, and performance targets set by the client, we believe the following strategy is consistently capable of delivering high quality results.

Strategy for achieving ZEDstandards

Agree a masterplan with the wider community – possibly using 'Enquiry by Design' principles

Allocate the public open space, pedestrian and vehicle desire lines, active commercial frontage, family residential locations, leisure and sports allocation – all with reference to enhancing the overall quality of life for existing residents and businesses. It is always worth trying to find out which services, accommodation or social facilities are missing from an existing community before finalising any large-scale regeneration brief.

Take care to incorporate the following unusual physical criteria in addition to all the usual concerns inherent in urban design best practice:

*   solar access for winter passive solar gain
*   avoid overshadowing or loss of daylight to existing residents or commerce
*   summer shading to avoid overheating in both buildings and public realm
*   solar access for solar thermal collection
*   solar access for photovoltaic generation and future installation
*   aerodynamic performance to maximise wind driven ventilation all year

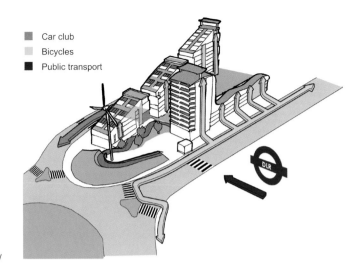

Car club
Bicycles
Public transport

Transport strategy

- windspeeds at street level to maximise human comfort at all times of year
- summer through ventilation to avoid stagnating air and urban heat island
- winter windspeeds to maximise building-integrated wind turbine output
- winter sunlight in public realm
- high daylight levels in all principal habitable rooms in all seasons
- maximise green horizontal surfaces to increase transpiration/summer cooling.

Add the social hubs

Integrate food delivery, public transport, local taxi service, car pool, bike hire, sales and repair, community café / bar, childcare, children's play and shared IT telecommuting equipment.

Finalise the energy masterplan and building physics model

Allocate microgeneration targets to each building, choosing optimal locations for centralised boiler plants and CHP installations, taking care with flue locations, bulky biomass storage, maintenance and access, heat main distribution and fuel delivery logistics. The building physics model can be cost checked to ensure it provides

Eco Transport hub includes bike repair, bike hire, car pool, vegetable oil pump and electric car charge

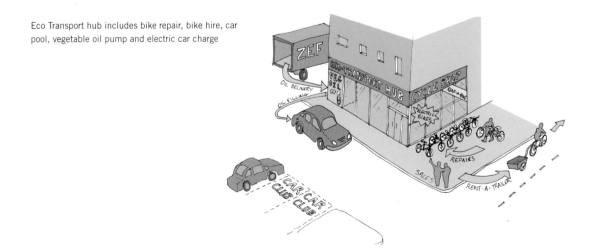

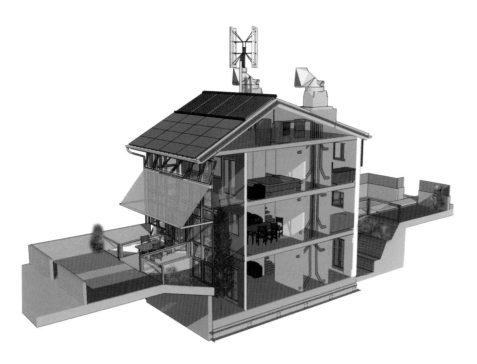

Cross-section through a ZEDstandards house

best value for local climatic conditions, and its principles simply communicated to subsequent design teams of later phases in an instruction code book.

Once the design team and client have finalised the masterplan and environmental performance targets have been allocated to each building – providing ZEDstandard construction and the local supply chain are used – it should be possible to provide considerable freedom of architectural expression, texture and materials. The variety of new urban regeneration almost relies on different artistic visions.

Agree the generic local materials and supply chain

The idea here is to fix the price for both labour and components for generic construction products and works packages that are likely to be common to the majority of the new buildings – whatever the final design. This enables the procurement of local labour, initiating training programmes for low energy construction and renewable energy systems, and the bulk buying of local materials such as precast concrete, in situ concrete, reclaimed steelwork fabrication, brick and block, and finally renewable energy systems. The energy masterplan will provide a shopping list of renewable energy microgeneration components enabling bulk buying initatives to save up to 50 per cent of the capital cost for many components and services. ZEDfactory have already started negotiating with many international manufacturers, and have found that organised volume procurement – pooling economies of scale available from a number of projects – is the only satisfactory way of reducing out turn construction costs. We believe that on a 600- to 1,000-home project it should be possible to limit the increased overall cost of a zero carbon specification to between 5 and 7.5 per cent of the Building Regulations minimum

Ken Livingston, Trudie Styler and Sebastian Coe change to low-energy lightbulbs at the Future London ZEDfactory exhibition installation

Superinsulated masonry wall construction exhibit

School children visit the Future London ZEDfactory exhibition

standards. This increased cost is often paid back by the UK stamp duty relief legislation for zero carbon homes, initiated in summer 2007. On larger projects of between 2,000 and 5,000 units there should be no additional cost due to savings in site-wide infrastructure provision and increased buying power.

Demonstration of the design, buildability and renewable energy systems

We propose including an early demonstration project designed to:

- demonstrate the added sales value for open market sale or commercial rental
- start on site construction and training courses for local people
- demonstrate the visual appearance to the local planning authorities
- demonstrate the renewable energy systems in operation
- provide an exhibition and sales centre for local people wanting information
- provide an on site project office for design team and contracting staff.

When the construction works are complete, this building can be partially handed over to the new community, and could possibly contain the social hub and shared communal facilities.

2.1 A Guide to ZEDstandards

ZEDfactory have always tried to describe ZEDstandards as 'the new ordinary'. It was a conscious decision when the office was formed to address the mass market and not hide away in the world of high spec, high design architecture. This involved a culture change for the Architects and consultants that were brought to work on the first ZEDfactory projects, all of whom had previously worked in this world with its high consultancy budgets and high levels of specialist design. At the time (late 1990s), the majority of new homes built in the UK were not designed by architects, but copied from contractors pattern books.

To engage with this culture, but apply the lessons learnt from the projects the consultant team had previously been used to, involved a steep learning curve. No longer could you rely on performance specification and expect a contractor to design an intelligent solution. The margins allowed by contractors in the housing market were so low that design time was not allowed for, and most new homes were simply taken out of a file of standard house and flat types.

What became clear was that in order to produce a competitive housing product, the culture of house builders had to be engaged with and subtly modified. An alternative range of standard typologies also had to be developed that could be sensibly delivered within the low fees paid within this sector.

Hence high performance details were developed that built on the existing industry skills base. Mechanical and electrical systems were developed that could be built entirely by the local plumber, electrician, carpenter and bricklayer. It is this spirit that ZEDstandards tries to foster, while limiting the number of specially developed components to a achieve production economies of scale as soon as quickly as possible.

ZEDstandard construction

ZEDstandard construction produces buildings that, when occupied and with correct solar orientation, can operate without conventional space heating. To achieve this, they are built to be thermally massive, superinsulated and airtight.

The heat loss of ZEDstandard construction is so small that heat loss can be replaced by a combination of the waste heat given off by appliances such as fridges and TVs, heat from people, heat from cooking, hot water use and solar gain through south-facing windows. Large south-facing windows that allow winter sunshine into the main spaces can provide between 10 and 20 per cent of annual space heating requirements.

Building Regulations currently produce buildings with a heating requirement of around 78 W/m^2. Zero heating construction specification requires the building fabric

2.1.1
ZEDstandard superinsulated masonry construction using existing trades easily found within the construction industry

to reduce this to 42 W/m². Passive heat exchange ventilation can reduce this further to 22 W/m². This is the ZED zero heating specification.

Thermal mass

Thermal mass is important because thermally massive buildings have the ability to absorb heat from times of high gain that can then be re-emitted at times of heat demand. This ability to absorb heat also keeps thermally massive buildings 4–6°C cooler than peak summer daytime temperature, reducing the need for carbon intensive electrical air-conditioning.

Without thermal mass a building has to closely control the temperature of its internal environment. This tends to lead to technologically complex control systems and powerful heating and cooling plant. Without thermal mass any heat loss or gain has to be replaced or removed by actively supplying heating or cooling. If an external door or window is opened, a thermally lightweight building will quickly reach the same temperature as the outside. Likewise if a thermally lightweight building has a large south-facing window through which the sun is shining, internal temperatures can quickly become uncomfortably high. This ends up in energy being used to heat the building on when there is no sun, and then cool it after a couple of hours of sunshine.

Thermally massive ZEDstandard construction can absorb heat from solar gain through a south-facing window without the internal temperature of the space increasing uncomfortably, and then release the warmth to the room later in the day after sunset. ZEDstandard construction has about 5 days worth of thermal storage. This means that if all heat gains were removed from a ZEDstandard building, it would take 5 days for that building to cool down to uncomfortable levels. No sophisticated control system is therefore needed and hence no 'peak output' heating and cooling systems are required. As heating and cooling are avoided the interiors benefit from a pleasant, healthy, stable internal environment without any of the scorched air and dryness problems that can be experienced in a traditionally heated house. Excess humidity is also absorbed within the massive masonry construction.

2.1.2
Exposed precast soffits are a low-cost method of achieving a large exposed radiant massive internal surface. The public reaction to the interior quality of finish has been favourable at BedZED and later projects

Superinsulation and typical construction

The ZEDstandards approach of superinsulating the whole internal envelope requires an attention to detail to avoid thermal bridges and achieve higher levels of airtightness, but the actual construction process is conventional masonry standard practice with only the sequence of operations slightly modified. There is no call for specialist works contractors, and all site skills are well within the scope of a local jobbing builder and labourers. This opens up the range of contractors capable of building ZEDstandards construction to all competent builders with experience of reasonable quality masonry construction.

ZEDstandard typical wall, floor and roof construction has a U-value of 0.1 W/m²K. This means that if it is freezing outside and a normal room temperature of 20°C inside, a square metre of wall, floor or roof will only loose 2 W of heat to the outside. (A typical adult male gives off 106 W of heat, a woman 92 W and a cat 16 W!)

ZEDstandard masonry wall construction is typically (from inside to outside) 13 mm of traditional dense wet applied plaster, 140 mm dense concrete block (minimum density 1,400 kg/m³), 300 mm of mineral fibre insulation and an external skin of either masonry such as brick, block, facing block or even stone, or a timber frame and timber cladding such as weather boarding. There is no vapour barrier as the wall is a 'breathing' construction.

The most important three elements are the wet applied plaster, the thermally massive inner skin and the insulation.

One of the best ways of preventing heat losses from uncontrolled air leakage (draughts) is by covering block work with a wet applied plaster. By using dense rather than lightweight plaster, the thermal mass of the concrete block behind is conducted to the air of the room.

On no account should construction ever be dry lined. Dry lining effectively isolates the air of the room from the thermal mass of the construction giving the effect of a thermally lightweight building. Not only does this make the space prone to over heating and chilling, it also wastes the embodied energy that has gone into the concrete blocks. Concrete can be a polluting, high embodied energy material and must be used carefully, where the thermal performance benefits are an order of magnitude higher than the embodied CO_2 of the material.

Brick layers when questioned have said that they actually find working on ZED-standard wall construction easier than current Building Regulation construction. The wide cavity gives easy access to both sides of the wall being built, allowing easier positioning of bricks and blocks and much easier cleaning and pointing. They also like the robust 'wallness' of the construction that makes the most of their trade.

If someone can lay blocks, they can build ZEDstandard walls. Brick and block laying is one of the most common British building trades and local builders will naturally be the most cost effective as they have fewer travelling expenses. They are also used to working closely with and training up labourers as they work, as the latter are essential to their working methods. (Someone is needed to fetch more bricks and carry a steady supply of mortar to where a layer is working.) It is normal for people who start on a site labouring to leave the site on completion as brick and block layers – creating a skill base capable of delivering the highest quality low carbon construction.

There are new ranges of low and even zero OPC dense concrete blocks, enabling a durable low embodied carbon masonry solution. If the outer skin is predominantly reclaimed brick, local stone or self-firing bricks, rockwool cavity fill and stainless steel wall ties are specified – it is possible to provide extremely durable walls more than capable of meeting the BRE definition of a long life building with a structural integrity and skin capable of lasting in excess of 125 years. As the cost of carbon intensive construction materials rises over the next few years, it will become increasingly difficult to replace short-term modern construction systems with life expectancies of less than 60 years. We have to use the last days of cheap carbon wisely to create a legacy that will work well without maintenance in the low carbon society of 2050.

Local timber rain skin cladding can provide a cost effective and simple way of building a protective outer skin to a superinsulated construction. However this depends on local labour conditions. The ZEDstandards detail is to simply place a sole plate on top of a 300 mm brick splashblack plinth, allowing simple reclaimed softwood timber framing studs to replace the masonry rainscreen outer leaf.

On small projects, the ease of installation can make this technique much cheaper than masonry alternatives as it can be significantly faster to build than facing brickwork. However on bigger projects, retaining enough site-based carpentry labour can be difficult and ultimately expensive. Here, the risk of labour supply can cause timber cladding to be risk priced at a rate higher than masonry. However every project should be looked at on a case by case / contract by contract basis.

The skills involved are again not specialist, and the labour problems tend to stem from most carpenters actually being over qualified for the job, so preferring to take on internal joinery work instead of external (wet and cold) carpentry work. This, however, presents an opportunity for local training programmes of dedicated local teams for individual projects. Someone with no previous skills can be trained to build timber cladding within a fortnight given adequate personal motivation. This can both get over the problem of professional carpenters not wanting to take on this work (or overpricing it) and provide a useful local training programme.

Floor and roof construction

'How much thermal mass is needed?'

Studies have been carried out that show that a space the size of a typical house will remain at a constant temperature if all surfaces surrounding that space are made from a thermally massive material 1 m thick. The temperature of that space will be the average of all the temperatures it is exposed to over the year.

Of course building a house with this much thermal mass would be impractical. The temperature would also be difficult to control and it would be hard to heat or cool the space if the average temperature was not what was required.

The level of thermal mass chosen for ZEDstandard construction is based on what can be realistically achieved using the spatial constraints of standard urban building practices to achieve a useful amount of thermal mass. Higher levels of thermal mass could be appropriate where land values are lower in rural locations, and where locally sourced bulk materials such as stone quarry waste are easily available. Bonding low cost thermally massive reclaimed aggregates or masonry blocks with lime-based mortars can also significantly reduce the embodied CO_2.

The place where thermal mass has its greatest effect is on the ceiling. The upper layer of air in any space will be the warmest and by having thermal mass on the ceiling, any thermal gains in a space will be easily absorbed. People radiate most of their heat from their heads, making the surface ceiling temperature visible to the top of their heads have the greatest effect on perceived comfort. A one degree change in the surface temperature of a radiant thermally massive surface has the same effect on the comfort of a room's occupant as a three degree rise in the air temperature of the room. Low energy heating and cooling will normally seek to provide economical comfort by very slightly changing the temperature of large massive surfaces, rather than relying on high temperature convective radiators.

For this reason, the most important construction elements are the visible radiant thermally massive ceiling and floor surfaces. In masonry ZEDstandard

2.1.3
Reclaimed steel and precast concrete floor planks

construction this is normally a precast concrete hollow core plank with a direct decoration quality underside. The top of the slab is finished with an acoustic isolating layer of 30 mm of Rockwool Rockfloor, if the floor is party between two households, or 5 mm of isolation foam if not, then 75 mm of sand cement screed or gypsum alternative. *Again on no account should the underside of the slab be dry lined.* This would effectively isolate the radiant thermal mass from the room interior. The construction build up outlined above will meet the requirements of the Building Regulations for acoustic performance without the need for a so called 'Part E Robust Detail'.

While not high tech in any way, precast slabs are a prefabricated element that comes with a specialist team. However this is a tiny part of the build process that normally takes less than an hour per dwelling. Slabs come from a number of manufacturers around the country, complete with laying team. The crane and driver are normally hired locally. It is always preferable to source the slabs as close to the site as possible, possibly using low cement concrete or GGBS – however alternative, more environmentally benign, concrete mixes do take longer to cure, so can increase the costs of prefabricated concrete components.

As the slab is performing a thermal / energy function on the space below it as well as supporting the floor above, it is important to retain a thermally massive ceiling construction on the top floor. Omitting mass on the uppermost ceiling is always tempting, as the structural support can normally be achieved by lightweight roof trusses. However this strategy virtually guarantees overheating, as thermally buoyant hot air tends to rise to the top of any building, and aggravates the effects of the high exposure to sunlight inevitably experienced by the uppermost floor. Moreover this massive 'roof slab' provides a very good stable surface upon which to build a durable roof finish and a strong base for resisting the wind loads encountered when fixing microgeneration technologies such as photovoltaics and micro wind turbines.

The standard roof build-up is hollow core concrete planks with a spacer supporting an aluminium standing seam zip roof, with 300 mm of Rockwool insulation filling a cavity between the planks and roof.

Green roofs

The detailing strategy for both sedum- and soil-based green roofs is simple, and generally overrated by the construction industry. It is often straightforward to source local sedum mats pregrown into a woven polyester matrix from local farmers or horticulturists, providing a large enough order is placed to justify setting aside the land for a year or two. If the order is placed 18 months before being required on site, local sourcing will both be cheaper and create significant seasonal employment, avoiding imports from the continent and creating a valuable new industry that can easily be supported by a local garden centre with minimal investment. Green roofs requiring foot traffic have a minimum soil depth of 300 mm, and can be built by local existing flat roof contractors providing some of the specialist drainage products and slabs are bought in.

2.1.4
Sedum mat in late spring

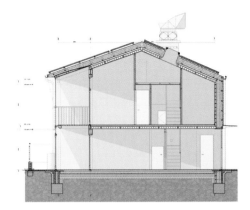

2.1.5
Cross-section through a ZEDstandards masonry house in
Northampton

Foundation detail – meeting the ground

There has been debate over the years as to the benefit of insulating to the ground.
The desire to make use of the thermal mass of the earth has led some low energy
builders to not insulate at all, and others to compromise insulation specification as
this is the place where least heat is lost.

Following research, the ZEDstandard detail is designed to insulate from the
ground to the same level as the walls and roof. The construction fabric of a ZED-
standard building already provides adequate and controllable levels of thermal mass
and reports from low energy houses with un-insulated ground floor slabs suggest
excellent summer cooling from the thermal mass of the ground, but increased heat
loss in the winter. If the UK climate was to change to give us milder winters, this
detail might be re-examined, but for the time being the ZEDstandards building physics models says the ground floor slab must be insulated.

Ground works differ from what a builder would normally do only in the addition of
300 mm of expanded polystyrene (EPS) under the structural slab and in the cavity
walls. Normally a builder would expect to either suspend a slab straight over the
ground or just cast an oversite slab on the ground. Cavities would normally be filled
with concrete below ground level. Insulation is normally seen as something you put
on top of the slab under a floor finish.

Given ground conditions are suitable for a load bearing slab, the typical ZED-
standard foundation detail is a simple mass concrete footing. From this is built two
skins of block work with 300 mm of 70kPa expanded polystyrene (EPS) insulation between and the two part wall ties at the same spacing as the main walls. The
ground under the slab is reduced to allow for 300 mm of the same EPS and this
is returned down the inside of the inner leaf of sub ground block work down to the
foundation. This ensures that the inevitable cold bridge of the sub ground block work
from the foundation to the slab is long enough to make conductive heat loss of low
significance.

The slab construction itself is dependant on the size of project and the contractor's preference. On single house projects, a lightly reinforced oversite slab may be
preferred, on larger projects beam and block or simple hollowcore plank floors may
be the most economic solution. The ideal is the hollow core plank floor as these use
the least amount of cement and steel reinforcement. With each floor construction
care must be taken to make sure there is no void between the insulation and the
floor slab.

If beam and block or plank floors are used, the damp proof membrane (DPM)
is best placed between the two layers of EPS. This protects it from damage while
the floor is laid. The DPM dresses over the inner skin where it is joined to a vertical
DPM that is dressed in to the inner skin with the cavity tray. All insulation below the
cavity tray is EPS as it retains its insulation value when wet. All insulation above is
Rockwool cavity batts that perform better in a breathing wall construction and are
more cost effective. The cavity tray is preformed in polypropylene. Care must be
taken to ensure that insulation is fitted right into the taper created by the cavity tray
to prevent a partial cold air bridge.

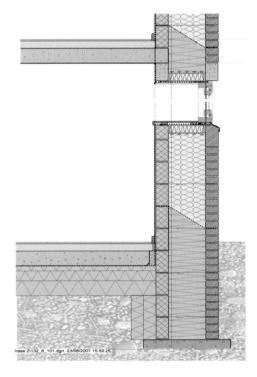

2.1.6
Section through ground floor – insulation at the edge of
the floor slab is essential to minimise heat leakage and
can maximise storage of heat in the ground

High performance glazing

The British high performance window industry has been almost non-existent until recently and the market dominated by Scandinavian companies. The British industry has measured itself against the PVC window industry which can be built very cheaply by unskilled labour out of a standard kit of parts designed for ease of assembly rather than performance or looks. Hence the only timber windows traditionally found in the United Kingdom are either poor quality softwood windows or high spec custom-made hardwood windows.

The high performance timber windows required for ZEDstandards are becoming available from UK manufacturers, but they struggle to compete with established Scandinavian suppliers and now with the new Eastern European manufacturers.

ZEDfactory have been working with at least one major manufacturer in the West Country and are confident that local sourcing is possible, but only if sufficiently large volumes can be promised to justify investment in a dedicated production run.

Financial realities change for every project and the best value window manufacturer will be chosen in each particular instance. What will need to happen locally of course is installation. The ZEDstandard detail has been developed over a number of projects working closely with building physicists and window installer (and once with all parties installing a window together). The eventual detail allows for ease of installation by first installing a sheet of plywood at the bottom of the opening to allow the window foot to be slid out across the cavity, and then fixing galvanised straps from the window frame, back to the inner skin. All are non-specialist skills easily undertaken by a carpenter and labourer working as a team.

Even the highest performance window you can buy has a U-value ten times worse that ZEDstandard wall construction. Early superinsulated houses had the tendency to reduce window sizes to reduce energy losses. However the interiors became dark and depressing, requiring artificial light throughout the day. This both decreased desirability in marketability terms and increased CO_2 production, as although heat energy was being saved, much more carbon-intensive electrical energy was being used to light spaces.

Architectural elevation design must therefore be optimised to maximise daylight, visual contact with the outside world and winter passive solar gain. By having a south-facing sunspace / conservatory with both screens double glazed, the building effectively has quadruple glazing with a very large number three airspace. This configuration means that the overall flow of heat energy in the winter is from the outside to the inside, with a south-facing window harvesting more heat over the winter season than it loses.

ZEDstandard windows to the north, east and west must be designed carefully to provide maximum daylight to spaces that otherwise would have little, provide visual connection between inside and outside, and finally and very importantly, positioned to produce a pleasing elevation to the building. The compromise between energy loss and the three concerns above must be carefully balanced so on one hand, the building is not oppressive, and on the other, it does not lose excessive amounts of energy.

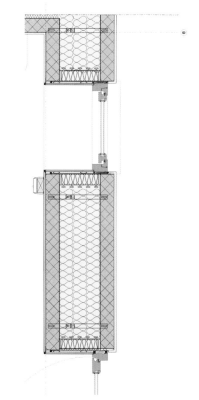

2.1.7
Horizontal section through masonry wall – the best glazing will still have much lower insulation values than a ZED wall but provide visual connection with the outside

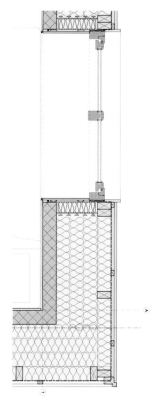

2.1.8
Horizontal section through hybrid masonry timber clad wall

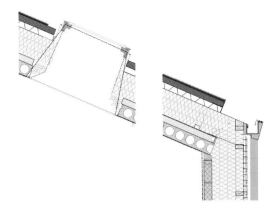

2.1.9
ZEDstandard roof construction – insulation details

ZEDstandard specification for windows are double glazed, soft low E coated, argon filled sealed units with a minimum overall U-value of 1.4 W/m²K. Due to recent advances in double glazing technology, triple glazing is no longer as important as it used to be. However triple glazing should be considered if particularly large windows are used. Small panes, mullions and transoms should also be avoided as a window loses most of its heat through its edges. Use of 'warm edge' spacers should be considered although not all window manufacturers yet offer this technology. High performance softwood frames should be used which should be finished in a factory applied high build stain. If aluminium clad systems are required for increased weather exposure in high rise or marine locations, choose the system using the lowest weight aluminium sections.

Shading to prevent summer overheating

Large areas of south-facing glazing of course have the tendency to promote overheating of the room behind in the summer. This can be controlled easily by providing enough opening windows in the outer glazed sunscreen for it to behave as open veranda on hot summer days. Providing that the inner glazed screen windows are shut, any warm air is vented externally without actually reaching the habitable room areas. This is important, as in peak summer external air temperature during the day is significantly higher than the internal room temperatures. Problems only occur with sunspaces if the doors and windows to the living room are left open on hot days, or the occupants have forgotten to leave the external windows open. At BedZED regrettable cost savings were made by the client to omit opening rooflights on the top floor sunspaces, making it harder to ventilate warm air build up. This problem is not experienced at all on the lower maisonettes, where a combination of low level windows and doors and high level tilt turn windows provide good sectional ventilation. Internal slatted balconies and the floor of the unit above also help shade the internal glazed screen from direct sunlight. Care must be taken to allow sunspace ventilation without creating security problems if occupants are absent. On rooms without sunspaces, external retractable canopy shades are required.

2.1.10
Sunspaces provide both insulation and warmth on sunny winter days

Airtightness – preventing uncontrolled draughts

Once superinsulated, approximately 50 per cent of winter heat demand is typically lost by natural ventilation using industry standard trickle vents. Ventilation is required for breathing, moisture control and odour control. Again early superinsulated houses attempted to control energy losses due to ventilation by just reducing ventilation. However the air quality they experienced meant you had to be 'committed' to live in them.

ZEDstandard houses control energy losses due to ventilation with airtight construction that then means all incoming and outgoing air can be controlled and passed through a flat plate heat exchanger allowing up to 70 per cent heat from the stale exhaust air to be transferred to the incoming fresh air. In this way, the interior space receives the necessary fresh air for breathing without bringing large amounts

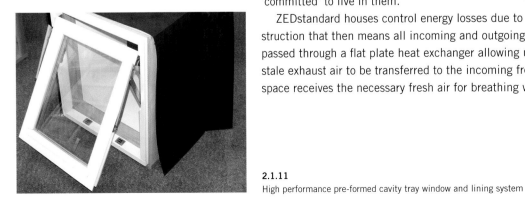

2.1.11
High performance pre-formed cavity tray window and lining system

of cold external air into the room. A 3 mm gap around one metre long with external air temperature around 0°C will require about 1 kW of installed heating capacity to offset the heat loss from infiltration. There seems little point in building highly insulated draught proofed buildings without using heat recovery ventilation systems. The downside is that many fan driven mechanical heat recovery units (MVHR units) can use between 250 and 500 kWh of carbon intensive electricity a year.

ZEDstandards fit out is no different to standard fit out. Wet plaster provides one of the best ways to ensure an airtight envelope, plasterers are just asked to plaster right down to the screed rather than leave the wall exposed at the bottom as they normally do. Window boards are fully bedded in silicon to ensure an airtight seal between the wall and the window assembly, and all junctions between plaster and frames are covered with architraves (as would be done traditionally to hide cracks).

Reclaimed timber can be supplied for internal studwork. For the joiner, this makes no difference except that the timber will be well seasoned and they are less likely to be called back to shave problematic sticking doors and frames.

Decorators are encouraged to make full use of flexible acrylic decorator caulk (painter's mate) to seal and fill between walls, skirting and architraves. Not only does this produce a high quality finish, it also reliably produces the airtightness specification of 1.5 air changes per hour at 50 pascals as required by the zero heating building physics model.

Wind-assisted passive stack heat recovery ventilation

The Wind Cowl is a natural ventilation system that offers passive ventilation with heat recovery without using electrically powered fan motors. It has been developed to harness natural wind currents to create air pressure sufficient to provide a healthy fresh air supply to buildings with no running energy cost. Saving an annual electric load of around 500 kWh/yr is equivalent to the annual power output of a small wind turbine, or four 80 W PV panels. It is so much easier to achieve zero carbon status if electrical loads are reduced. This is why the ZEDstandards will always prioritise passive energy efficiency techniques over electrically intensive mechanical technologies with large numbers of moving parts, and associated high maintenance costs. As a general rule we have found that the more complex a technology, the higher the capital cost, the higher the embodied CO_2 and the quicker the installation breaks down in use.

The system also uses passive stack ventilation principles, and can operate in near windless conditions, although the main period of use is in winter when there is normally more wind. The heat exchangers in the Wind Cowls recover up to 70 per cent of heat that would normally be lost with the outgoing air from a building.

Currently this product is manufactured in Chippenham, Wiltshire. Significant cost reductions could be achieved by scaling up production. Installation training is hardly required, as conventional galvanised steel air distribution ductwork is used. This product is now well tested and ready for volume production. We are currently working with a university to develop a modified horizontal version for high-rise buildings.

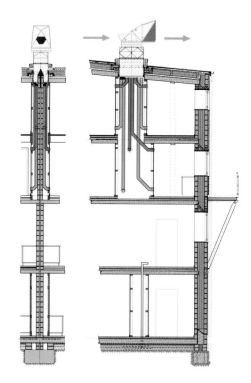

2.1.12
Wind cowl passive heat recovery ventilation at Jubilee Wharf – note workspaces use small mechanical heat recovery units to match different occupant's requirements

2.1.13
The latest generation ZEDfabric wind cowl with easy access heat exchanger units

The ZEDstandards payback study

Why did we chose the technologies we did?

To decide on the ZED M & E strategy we undertook a detailed building physics and financial payback study. This looked at how CO_2 emissions could be reduced based against the zero point of a 2002 Building Regulation house with a gas condensing boiler. The aim being to reach zero energy status.

The technologies were tested against projected lifecycle costs, additional running costs and income. (The assumptions made are stated below.) The additional cost of the technology was then divided by the percentage reduction in CO_2 realised over the 2002 house. The cost per percentage point improvement can then be seen (the so called 'bangs per buck').

Factoring in the rising cost of fossil fuel

By projecting fuel costs for the next 45 years, payback can be worked out, both in cost per percentage CO_2 reduction and in overall cost / income experienced. If you just lived in a 2002 Building Regulation house, your CO_2 reduction would be zero and the cost / income experienced would be zero.

Saving fuel leaves more pounds in your pocket and so is treated as income

Energy generators of course have a straight income stream that improves as energy prices increase, tempered by the need to replace them. Saving energy is also treated as an income as it puts more pounds in your pocket than you would have had living in the 2002 house.

Technologies that use energy to save CO_2 are costed at the cost of the energy used at the grade it is used, less the cost of the energy saved at the grade it is saved.

2.1.14
Graph showing increase in fuel costs with an 8 per cent annual gas price escalator and electricity pegged to four times the cost of gas

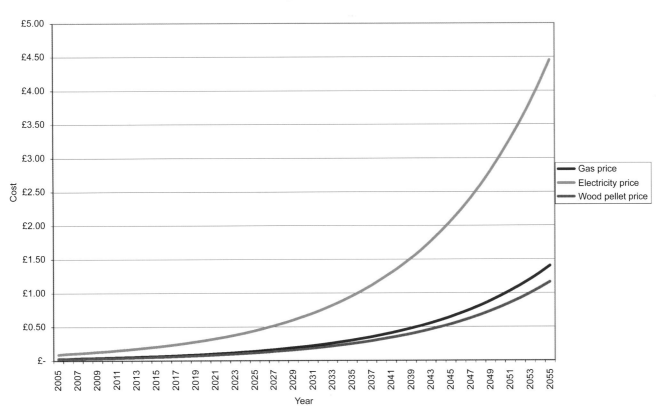

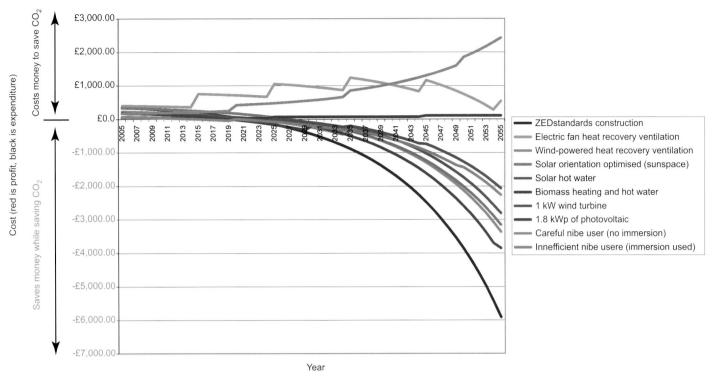

2.1.15
Lifecycle cost CO_2 analysis of different energy saving and microgeneration techniques

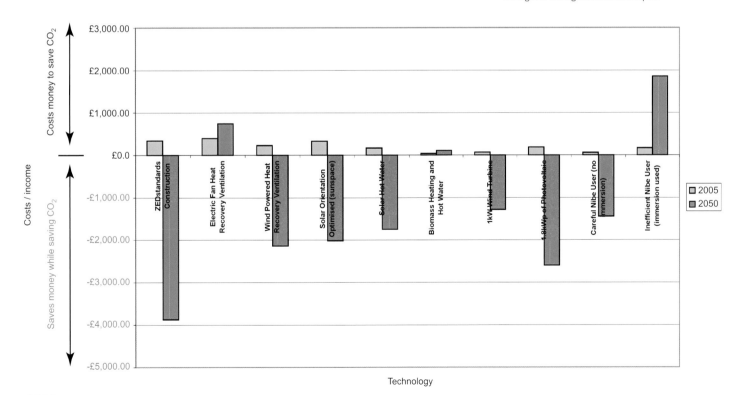

2.1.16
Cost/income per unit CO_2 reduction for both 2005 and 2050
– ZEDstandards construction is an excellent investment

Hence fan or heat pump heat recovery ventilation powered by electricity saves heat energy powered by gas.

Income and running cost are then run for the number of years of the projection and added to the original cost of the technology. The total cost of the technology over the building's life can then be seen as well as the total cost per percentage point reduction of CO_2.

Summary of findings

Don't use electricity

The first finding is that any technology that uses electricity becomes a very expensive way to save carbon. Within 5 years all the technologies that use electricity end up costing more per percentage point reduction of CO_2 than any of the other technologies. This is because for every unit of cost saved, other more expensive units are used. Mechanical whole house ventilation, while making a 5 per cent reduction in carbon and saving 2,435 kWhr of gas, uses 657 kWhr of electricity to do so. Although this is an apparent saving of 1,778 kWhr, when the study was first run at the end of 2005 and the value of the gas saved was £56.05, the cost of the electricity required to do this was £65.70. So saving the energy and the associated 5 per cent CO_2 reduction costs you £10 a year! The price of gas in comparison with electricity has since moved such that there is a slight advantage in favour of such technologies (gas prices have gone up 19 per cent whereas electricity has only gone up 8 per cent). However we suspect electricity prices will soon increase again to track the gas price rise.

Heat pump technology costs more to run than it would to burn gas

The use of air to water heat pumps is similar to fan driven heat exchangers. Their greater efficiency and low additional capital cost (only £1,000 more than the gas

2.1.17
Simple financial payback chart covering the first 20 years of installation

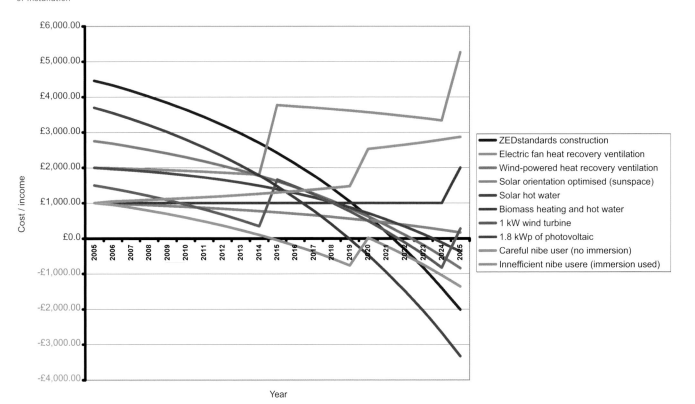

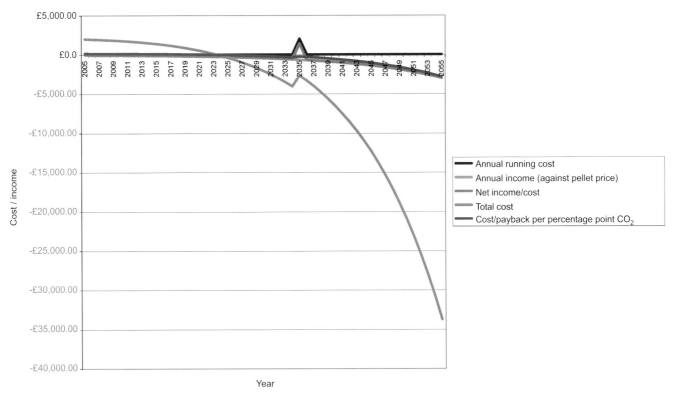

2.1.18
Solar thermal payback chart

boiler they replace) buffers the cost for the first few years until the projected cost of electricity, and the large amounts of energy involved, pushes their cost right up towards the end of the projection. Again, while they are saving 9,317 kWhr of gas heat a year, they are using between 2,214 and 3,115 kWhr of electricity to do this. So the cost (at 2005 prices) of the gas saved is £209.17, while the cost of the electricity used is between £220.21 and £309.82. This time saving the gas energy and associated 6–17 per cent CO_2 reduction costs you between £11 and £100 a year. At the end of the projection these devices cost you between £65 and £590 more a year to run than it would have cost you to just burn the gas.

The winners
The winning technologies, surprisingly, are those traditionally thought to have long payback times, that is, photovoltaics and wind turbines.

This is partly to do with the lower prices these can now be bought for, the grants available for PV and the fact that they are generating high value electricity. Technologies that save gas heat energy take longer to pay back as the gas heat energy is of a lower financial value, especially when compared with the 2002 Building Regulations, which is a reasonably energy efficient starting point.

Solar thermal panels produce a surprising result and this has been rechecked a number of times. Solar thermal has always been reported as the number one payback renewable technology, yet our figures show payback at about 20 years. The sense check comes by looking at typical summer gas usage. All the solar thermal panels are doing is displacing this fuel use. To be useful into the autumn and the spring they tend to be oversized, so in the summer they may be able to provide 150–200 per cent of what you would normally need. Great if you have a hot tub, but all we are comparing against in this study is normal use.

However – and this is a big however – one of the main concerns of shift towards a biomass-based economy is the availability of biomass. The conversion of food growing land to biomass production is retrogressive for carbon dioxide as the carbon footprint of food is very high. Importing biomass has implications with rainforest destruction. Effective use of solar thermal reduces biomass consumption drastically. If fuelled on biomass, a ZEDstandard house with solar thermal uses a quarter of the biomass of an equivalent 2002 Building Regulation house. Figures from the Forestry Commission on current wood fuel availability show that in the United Kingdom we can be said to have 150 kg of dry wood fuel currently available for each person per year. The three bed, five person house built to ZEDstandards with solar thermal this study is based on requires 650 kg of pellets per year. Less than five persons' share.

Assumptions used in ZEDstandards payback study

- The 2002 Building Regulations house is of standard volume house builder construction and fitted with a basic 85 per cent efficient gas condensing boiler. All heat demands to calculate gas cost are therefore divided by 0.85.
- ZEDstandard construction is assumed to add 5 per cent to the build cost of the 2002 house (thermal mass, superinsulation, high-spec glazing only).
- Electric heat recovery ventilation is assumed to cost £2,000 installed. This is the additional net cost excluding the price of the mechanical extract ventilation that would have already been in the bathrooms and kitchen of the 2002 house.
- The same applies to wind-assisted passive stack, whose additional installed cost is £2,750.
- Solar orientation is assumed to be through the addition of a sun space for £11,000, but this will increase the value of the property by £10,000. The total additional cost is therefore £1,000.
- Solar hot water is assumed to cost an additional £2,000.
- The solar hot water system is assumed to cost its whole price in replacement in 30 years and cost £200 to maintain every 5 years.
- Biomass hot water and space heat is assumed to cost an additional £1,000 as a share of a district (block or terrace) heat system (cost of biomass boiler and system minus cost of the gas boiler now not needed).
- Biomass fuel is assumed to match and track the price of gas over the projection.
- The biomass boiler is assumed to cost its additional price in maintenance/replacement in 15 years.
- Wood pellet power density 5.36 kWhr/kg (dti via Coed Cymru).
- Wood pellet boiler efficiency 92.7 per cent (3g energy).
- The wind turbine is assumed to cost £1,500 installed, generate 900 kWhr a year and cost its whole price in maintenance/replacement in 10 years.
- The PV panels are assumed to cost £3 per Watt and £2,000 for their installation and inverter. A 50 per cent grant is then applied.
- The PV system is assumed to cost its whole price in maintenance/replacement in 25 years.
- The PV system is assumed to generate energy at a rate of 832 kWhr per Kw peak installed.
- The air to water heat pump system is assumed to cost £1,000 more than the equivalent gas boiler system would have done.
- The air to water heat pump system is assumed to cost its additional price in maintenance/replacement in 15 years.

ZED M & E strategy – how to power a ZEDstandards home

Summary

The mechanical and electrical systems of a ZED are intended to:

1. be robust
2. be simple
3. be control-free/light
4. be DIY modifiable
5. be repairable with readily available components
6. be inexpensive
7. minimise electric consumption.

This description is an overall concept strategy and not a detailed specification. It therefore does not list out code requirements or go into detail on standard requirements such a system flush valves, pressure release valves or expansion tanks. This is intentional to allow each system designer / installer to make choices of what equipment to install to suit the precise requirements of each project.

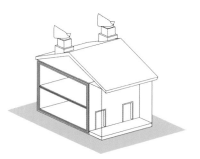

2.1.20
Superinsulated box

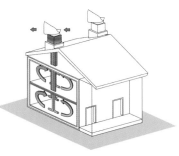

2.1.21
Winter passive heat recovery ventilation

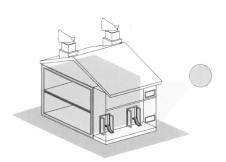

2.1.22
Winter passive solar gain

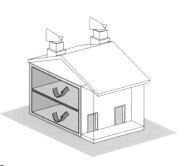

2.1.23
Thermal storage – cosy winter night

2.1.19
Cutaway of level 6 Code for Sustainable Homes RuralZED zero carbon house kit

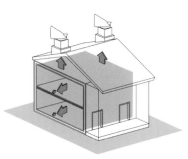

2.1.24
Airtight box with controlled natural ventilation

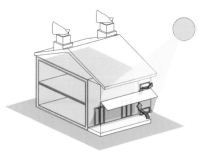

2.1.25
Eaves overhang and shade canopy prevents summer heat

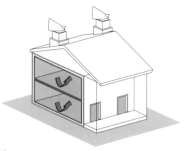

2.1.26
Thermally massive interior surfaces for summer coolth

2.1.27
Sedum roof provides summer evaporative cooling

Heat

A home or office constructed to ZEDstandards in the United Kingdom will require little or no space heating when occupied. However the occupants still require hot water. Hot water can be produced domestically either by solar radiation on a solar thermal array or by biomass combustion. It is almost always possible to supply a minimum of 50 per cent annual domestic or commercial hot water from solar energy in the summer, leaving only a tiny requirement for the 50 per cent annual hot water to be found from another renewable energy source in the winter period. If solar thermal technologies are combined with biomass the boiler can be turned off all summer, with dramatic reductions in fuel consumption. This reduction in fuel load brings the total annual biomass consumption to within a UK citizen's personal biomass quota. Almost any other strategy will exceed this quota – meaning that one individual's carbon neutrality has been achieved by appropriating another citizen's fair share of scarce national resource. Recognition of the limits to communal national renewable resource is the only way any country can set up an equitable and politically stable national energy policy.

Hot water in ZEDstandard homes and workspaces

All ZEDstandards buildings must have an efficient large hot water storage tank, capable of taking input from both solar thermal and possibly a range of alternative biomass boilers – allowing both pellet and log options in future. The hot water storage tank is one of the largest and most expensive plumbing components to replace in future, making it very important that this component is futureproofed to anticipate future microgeneration technologies. For example wood pellet powered CHP or fuel cells will be available long before the tank has ended its useful service life.

To the householder, the hot water system should operate no differently to a traditional indirect system with a hot water cylinder. They will have a cylinder of hot water available to them that will be recharged when emptied. The difference is that the hot water that flows though the heating coil in the cylinder is not heated locally by a gas boiler, but in a combination of a biomass boiler that serves a number of households and, if installed, local solar thermal arrays.

Ideally the hot water tank should use a mains pressure heat exchange loop / thermal store strategy. This avoids the need for a cold water tank in the attic as well as giving good pressure for showers. If a mains pressurised system is not used, a low pressure boost pump should be considered for the hot water circuit. It is hoped that by fitting this pump the future installation of high energy power showers will be avoided.

Back up space heating

The space heating demand of any home built to ZEDstandards is so low that it can normally be met from internal incidental gains (cooking, televisions, fridges, hot water use and people) and solar gain through south-facing windows. When these gains are not present, or less than expected (winter holiday, unoccupied, extended periods with no sunshine), a back up space heating system is required.

Due to the very small amount of top up space heat that would be required in these situations, a single radiator in either the living room or hall easily provides all the heat output required.

ZED M & E strategy alters from traditional heating in that the hot water circuit for the radiators is indirectly heated from a second heat exchange coil in the hot water cylinder or the actual store water inself, enabling the radiator to be heated by the immersion should the central heat source be inoperable.

The radiator is controlled via a simple 'fixed' thermostat in the living space. This controls a low powered circulation pump and a motorised valve on the radiator circuit. The motorised valve is required as it has been found that hot water in the circuit has had the tendency to circulate round the system due to convection even when the pump is not energised.

New generation DC pumps should be considered due to their decreased power consumption, but since under normal operating conditions the pumps will not be activated, the capital cost should be the deciding factor in pump choice.

Heat metering – for district heating

In the street (or corridor in the case of flats) outside the property will be two large diameter pre-insulated heat main pipes, one for supply, the other return. From these will branch smaller diameter pipes to supply the household, again one for supply, the other for return.

Just like any other utility, the amount of energy the household is taking from the heat main is metered. Modern heat meters detect the temperature of the incoming water and compare it with the temperature of the returning water and its flow rate. From this data the meter automatically calculates the amount of heat that is being taken from the main. This is recorded in kWhrs. These meters can either be read manually or automatically via wired networks (mains talk or telecom). New meters are now becoming available that work wirelessly and can be read by a passing meter reading van or by SMS over mobile phone networks.

From experience it has been found that without metering and charging for heat usage, consumption levels increase drastically (up to four times national average has been recorded). If heat is free, or a fixed standing charge within a service charge, occupants have been known to try and extract maximum value from their service charge by taking four baths a day!

A motorised valve on the heat main circuit is controlled by a thermostat mounted low down on the hot water cylinder. When this thermostat detects that tank is full of hot water, it will close the valve.

Heated towel radiator

It is considered desirable to have a heated towel rail at all times of year. For this reason the primary heat main circuit passes through the towel radiator after passing through the hot water cylinder primary coil. A manual valve and bypass gives the option to switch this radiator off during high summer.

The advantage of this circuit configuration is that when no hot water is being demanded from the system, the district main circuit will be closed, so the towel radiator will be off. However, if hot water is used (for a bath or shower) the district main circuit will be opened to replenish the hot water in the tank and the towel radiator will be heated - just in time to dry the wet towels.

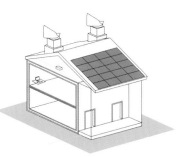

2.1.28
Solar electric generation mainly in summer

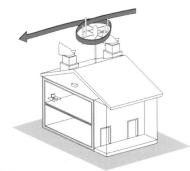

2.1.29
Wind electric generation mainly in winter

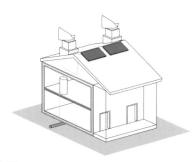

2.1.30
Summer solar thermal hot water, winter communal biomass heat

2.1.31
Rainwater harvesting all year round

The heat main

The heat main supplies water at around 70-80 °C. Typically this water is circulated from a large capacity thermal store (accumulator tank). The amount of heat energy that can be stored in the tank is such that even at times of peak demand (morning and evening) the heat main will always be at the correct temperature. The thermal store is heated indirectly. This is typically from a biomass boiler, though can be from any heat generating source (chp, communal solar array, etc.) The thermal store also enables the boiler to work at full power and therefore to full efficiency. When the tank reaches a preset low temperature, the boiler will automatically ignite, burn at full power till the tank reaches it's upper preset temperature, then switch off.

Without the thermal store the boiler would spend time burning at lower outputs where its efficiency is far lower. The boiler would also have to be sized for peak output rather than average output – as in times of high demand the heat main can draw on both the heat stored in the tank and the direct hot water supply from the boiler.

The water in the heat main is kept within safe temperature limits by blending the return water with fresh water. Variable speed DC pumps can be designed in to the system to reduce the energy consumption of the system at times of low demand and assist with temperature control.

When the boiler is switched off for maintenance or if it breaks down for any reason, the thermal store will continue to supply heat to the main for a reasonable period of time. If the boiler is not running by the time the thermal store is exhausted, and the individual hot water cylinders in the households become cool, traditional immersion heaters will have to be used. They are manually controlled via timed hour 'boost' buttons. This means that the occupiers will be aware that the main is no longer supplying heat and informs them that they should be more sparing with their hot water usage as immersion heaters are very expensive to run.

To avoid misuse of the immersion heater, it is prevented from working if either the hot water cylinder is already up to temperature, (by a thermostat on the tank) or if the heat main is supplying heat (by a pipe stat on the incoming heat main pipe). To make sure the immersion use is minimised the pipe stat monitors the temperature of the incoming heat main pipe. The motorised valve that switches the flow on and off in the heat main supply has a 'trickle past' facility. This means that the supply pipe will always be hot if the main is hot.

Heat source

Choosing a heat source is dependant on the number of homes being heated and the fuel source available. A single home might have a small wood pellet boiler or a wood stove with a back boiler. A small development of less than 50 units would run off a wood pellet boiler. Up to 100 units could either run off a number of wood pellet boilers, or if a reliable fuel source was available, a wood chip boiler. Over 100 units, biomass combined heat and power units become viable.

ZEDfactory recommends choosing a reliable manufacturer at an early stage of the project, and then training interested local plumbers to act as local distributors providing maintenance and commissioning services. The integration of the boiler control system with solar thermal or backup condensing gas boilers will be explained – facilitating the commissioning process that tends to plague the introduction of many of these renewable technologies.

2.1.32
ZEDfabric domestic hot water cylinder plumbed for connection to biomass boiler, solar thermal collectors and gas back-up heat sources. By pre-filling solar-powered pumps, hot water circulation pumps and control systems, what was once a complex installation challenge becomes simplified allowing both local plumber or enthusiastic DIY installation

All sizes benefit from the addition of solar thermal systems, with the possible exception of the combined heat and power plant solution. These reduce wood fuel consumption and allow homes to reduce their consumption down to near the per capita UK wood fuel share.

Individual houses and ZEDupgrades. With both options below a thermal accumulator would be required to allow the boiler to work at optimum efficiency. Heat metering would of course not be required.

A Rikka-type pellet stove in the living room with a pellet store in garage / outbuilding or under the front garden. This is an ideal solution where there is no outbuilding space, or there is the desire for a stove to be the centre piece of a room. This type of pellet stove has a glass fronted combustion chamber designed to be a focal point in a living room. They are completely self-contained and ignite automatically when heat is required. The glazed panel enables sight of the naked flame, yet loses only 15 per cent of the stoves output as heat to the room leaving 85 per cent of the 15 kw output available for water heating. However, in high summer any room heat is unwelcome so this stove should only be considered in conjunction with solar thermal collectors – restricting ignition to the winter months

10 to 15kW pellet boiler (Ashwell or similar) and store in garage / outbuilding. Where outbuilding space is not limited and a room stove is not required, a cost effective solution is to have a straightforward wood pellet boiler in an out building or utility room. Again they are completely automatic and self-feeding from underground or surface pellet stores. If the fuel store is above ground, allow a minimum storage of 6 tonnes, which is half a pellet tankers typical delivery load. Reductions in fuel store size simply increase the fuel delivery costs.

Terraces, apartments blocks or small districts of less than 100 homes. Communal biomass boilers are a simple and reliable heat source. By keeping the boiler size small, the technology can be kept domestic rather than commercial. This allows the boilers and systems to be maintained by local plumbers rather than specialists. It also means that if there is a problem, only a few household are affected rather than a whole district.

A 10kW to 75kW pellet boiler suitably sized to match the number of units with a pellet store sized for annual top up or a serviced delivery round. Ideally this should be a prefabricated unit on the end of a terrace or central point in an urban block. In an apartment block the boiler and pellet store should be as close as possible to the pellet delivery point. The longer the delivery pipe, the more the pellets degrade (turn to sawdust) during delivery. The delivery pipe should be 10 m maximum length.

Developments of over 100 homes with new infrastructure. The smallest biomass CHP system currently on the market has a thermal output of 200 kW. As a rule of thumb, heat demand for a home constructed to ZEDstandards is 2 to 3 kW per home. Therefore biomass CHP only becomes viable in developments of over 100 homes / workspaces. It is important to plan the flue to be at the highest point on site, to avoid contaminating rooftop windcowl air intakes, and to allow sufficient storage for at least two hgv woodchip deliveries beside the biomass plant.

There are currently two differing technologies for biomass CHP that ZEDstandards would consider suitable.

The first is perhaps the best known and was the system originally installed at BedZED. This is gasification CHP. The technology is similar to natural gas CHP in

2.1.33
Communal wood pellet boiler at ZEDstandards scheme in Brixton

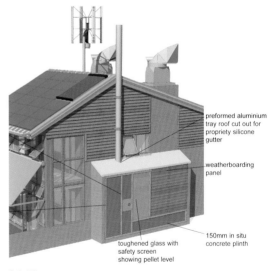

preformed aluminium tray roof cut out for propriety silicone gutter

weatherboarding panel

150mm in situ concrete plinth

toughened glass with safety screen showing pellet level

2.1.34
Prefabricated wood pellet boiler housing

2.1.35
8.5 kWh wood pellet boiler installation at Hope House'

2.1.36
DIY solar thermal installation on a zero carbon new build home for Steve Harris

that gas is used to fuel a large diesel engine that turns a large electrical alternator while the engine's cooling water provides heat for the district heat main. Typically the heat output will be twice the electrical output.

Biomass CHP makes its own gas out of biomass rather than using fossil gas from the main. The gas is made by heating biomass without the presence of oxygen till it releases its volatile gases. This gas is then cleaned and fed into the engine. The whole process works continually with biomass being automatically fed into the gasifier with the CHP plant providing the heat to perform the gasification.

The second technology is a hot air turbine CHP. This system is simpler than gasification as it does not first have to gassify biomass and clean the gas before burning it. It simple burns the biomass in a straightforward combustion process. A stream of hot air is fed into a turbine to create rotational energy to power an electrical generator with a cooling jacket providing hot water.

There is a third technology that turns cellulose plant waste, including biomass into a liquid fuel for diesel engines similar to biodiesel. However this transport grade fuel is not promoted for use in CHPs for the same reasons that locally sourced vegetable oil must be retained for agriculture and transport in a society trying to relieve its addiction to fossil fuels.

The 100 kW of renewable electricity and the 200 kW of renewable heat produced by the system will lead to a carbon dioxide emission reduction of around 600 tonnes per unit each year compared to emissions from conventional fossil fuel fired heat and electricity production..

There is currently only one reliable biomass CHP product supported in the United Kingdom, and this technology would be required if a large-scale zero carbon regeneration is planned.

We would recommend installing this technology in the final phases of the regeneration project, as around 200 to 250 homes and significant workspace is required to achieve sufficient critical mass to avoid having to heat dump. Office space with cooling demand and swimming pools again help to match electric output with thermal demand.

ZEDfactory recommend involving the manufacturer at the earliest stages of masterplan design, and immediately tendering the opportunity for a Water and Energy Services company to administer and run the machinery on behalf of the developer. It is often possible to achieve a reasonable capital contribution towards installing the heat distribution, energy and water treatment services, providing the engineering design facilitates maintenance and plant replacement / servicing.

Solar thermal arrays
The UK's ability to produce biomass is limited if we are to avoid losing agricultural food production. The price of biomass on the open market is likely to be more or less equivalent to heating oil, and will escalate in cost as demand exceeds supply. The best way of avoiding fuel poverty is always matching biomass systems with solar thermal collectors. Solar thermal can provide the household's hot water between April and October and give a contribution for the rest of the year. It has been calculated that by doing this, for a typical three-bed, five-person house, half a tonne of wood pellets can be saved a year.

(Ground source) heat pumps – a warning
Using electricity to produce heat is very carbon intensive, even if using heat pump technologies. Something still has to be burnt at a power station to generate the electricity in the first place. Only 25 per cent of the heat from the powerstation's fuel is turned into heat in the home.

A ground source heat pump (GSHP), if used correctly so that it achieves an average coefficient of performance (COP) of 3 might improve this efficiency to 75 per cent of the original fuel's heat value. However, a typical 3.5 kw thermal output GSHPs requires around 3 MWhr of electricity a year. This is around one and a half times the amount of electricity a household may typically need for all its other electrical needs. So if this is to be generated with building integrated renewable energy systems, approximately double the PV area would be required. Even if the household had sufficient space to mount this additional collector area, it would be unlikely to be affordable.

Electricity

Living in a ZED home will be no different than living in any other home. You will be able to plug into the mains just as you would anywhere else, it's just your bills will be considerably lower. Low and ultra low energy fittings would be fitted as standard. This includes induction cooking hobs, which 25 per cent less electricity than traditional electric hobs.

Requiring less electricity is the most cost effective way to generate it. For example, to lower your demand from the national grid into your home by 75 Watts you can either:

- buy a 75 W solar electric (PV) panel for around £300
- buy a 25 W energy saving light bulb for around £3 to replace a 100 W traditional bulb
- which would you do first?
- very few additional skills are required, possibly only familiarity with the following new components:

LED lighting. With each fitting using around 2 W, it is relatively easy to light a room with 12 W, and a whole home for between 60 and 100 W. Fairly similar in installation to low voltage lights, there should be little trouble adapting existing skills.

Solar electric panels. With ZEDfactory's simple roof-mounted rail system, it is straightforward for any competent electrician to install both the inverter and the more conventional roof-mounted panels. ZEDfactory are nervous about closer building integration, as re-radiation from the back of the panels – and reduced electric output with increasing temperature – suggests rainscreen-type applications are both the simplest and the most efficient. Single-glazed glass / glass-laminated PV panels can be used within patent glazing in sunspace roofs, providing there is 30 to 50 per cent opening ventilation-free area. No premium should be payable for PV installation, as this technology has now become plug and play. A large-scale regeneration project could open up a local market for this technology – particularly for upgrading existing buildings.

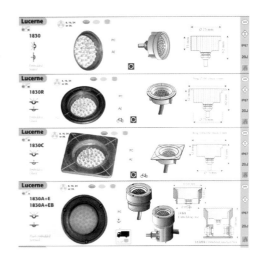

2.1.37
Every month more and better LED fittings come onto the market

2.1.38
Micro wind turbines can provide significant amounts of
electricity but must be mounted to work with building
aerodynamics

2.1.39
The Talbots biomass CHP

2.1.40
3 kW electric and 10.5 kW thermal pellet
powered CHP (www.sunmachine.fr)

Micro wind turbines. Providing careful consideration is given to building surface aerodynamics – and turbulent airflow is avoided where possible – it is possible to provide a significant contribution to the overall annual electric demand of most buildings. The small-scale domestic turbines need very careful examination – however they are useful providing the building surfaces manage to achieve an increase in ambient velocity of 1.5 ms⁻¹ (easily measurable with hand or stick held anemometers). ZEDfactory, working with leading manufacturers, would set up training / briefing courses covering structural stability, vibration isolation, fixing and maintenance checks, and electronics / grid connection.

All of the above technologies can then be carefully specified and designed by the design team and procured on a sitewide basis. The energy design codes, the bulk purchasing initiative, the local training courses, the reclaimed and locally-sourced materials, and the creation of local business opportunities for energy saving and microgeneration using renewable energy all combine to produce an optimistic offer to the local community. As much cash as possible is recycled locally, new skills are provided to the wider workforce and an optimistic future perspective is launched. Regeneration schemes launched in this way become much easier for local people to support, and it is often easier to obtain planning permissions. The buildings are designed to maximise both amenity and quality of life, and reduce environmental impact. The advantages of a zero carbon urban quarter can then be demonstrated to the wider city – enabling the concept to be adopted because it offers genuine advantages, and a higher quality of urban life for most people.

Electricity generation

Import and export. Due to the fossil fuel based centralised generation supplying the majority of the energy supply market in the UK, the feed in tariff (money you receive for energy you generate and export back to the grid) is less than the supply tariff (price you pay the electricity company for electricity they supply to you). It is hoped that this will change soon as in Germany, France and Spain where a high price is guaranteed for any renewable electricity that can be generated. In the UK this has led to 'guerilla' tactics. Traditional mechanical meters (the type with a spinning disk and numbers on rollers) will run backwards when exporting back to the grid. This means net metering is achieved and the same price is paid for electricity consumed as electricity generated. During any metered period, the meter may run forwards fast at times of high demand, run forwards slowly at times of high demand and moderate generation, and then run backwards at times of low demand and high generation.

Modern digital meters cannot run backwards therefore an additional export meter is required in the circuit or a specialised import export meter. With such a meter fitted the import and export readings will be separated on the utility bill with a debit amount for one and a credit for the other. Older meters approved by the electric utilities in the past – often have the ability to run backwards, and represent the easiest, if not strictly legal way of obtaining a fair price for your surplus electricity generated from renewable energy generated on site. Finding one may be difficult. A lobby should be started to campaign for the right for every customer to install simple reversible meters.

Methods of generation

Photovoltaics. Photovoltaic panels are generally fixed to the south-facing part of a roof although they can be mounted in south facing/sloping conservatory glazing or balustrades as bespoke 'glass–glass' laminates. In the basic system, these are wired together and feed back to a grid inverter. This device converts the raw DC the panels produce to pure sine wave 50hz AC at 240V in phase with the mains supply. The output of the inverter is then fed via a meter to record the kWhrs that have been harvested and an isolator, into the domestic fuse board. The lowest cost PV panels are not translucent, and are contained within simple aluminium frames that bolt to horizontal fixing rails supported proud of the waterproof roof surface. More expensive panels interlock like roof tiles, and allow the photovoltaic cells to blend with the surface texture of a traditional tiled roof.

2.1.41
1581 x 809 mm 180 Watt photovoltaic panel. Most three-bed ZEDstandard homes can meet their annual electric demand using photovoltaics with 12 to 16 panels

The output of the panels is first taken up by demand in the home. Once this demand has been met, the surplus electricity is exported back to the grid. It is sensible to provide a minimum of 1 kw peak installed PV for a one-bed flat, 1.5 kw peak for a two-bed flat, and 2.0 kw peak for a three-bedroom house or maisonette. This can provide around half of their annual electrical energy demands, providing the ZEDstandards for electrical load reduction are followed. Solar electric installation prices fall every year, making it important to future proof allowing future mounting positions and wireways, even if the present day budget does not allow for initial purchase. Photovoltaic technologies have no moving parts, can pay off their embodied CO_2 within three years, and could last thirty to fifty years in their monocrystalline specification. This is the easiest and most reliable renewable energy technology to incorporate into urban form, and the recent economies of scale achieved in both Germany and China have reduced its financial payback to around twelve years assuming a 5 per cent annual increase in fossil fuel prices.

Micro wind turbines. Micro wind turbines work in a similar way feeding their raw power, be that rectified low voltage DC or wild AC, to an inverter that then feeds back to a fuse board. The advantage of wind turbines is that they work day and night given sufficient wind.

The main problem experienced with wind generators in urban locations is that turbulent wind changes their rotation speed in an unpredictable way. One moment they will be spinning fast, generating considerable raw power, the next they might slow down or stop. A protocol for exporting power to the national grid (the G83 protocol) demands that 3 minutes of smooth power is generated before export can be allowed. With micro turbines in urban areas, this rarely happens. Some of the lower cost turbines are also shipped with inverters that can only achieve grid connection at voltages achieved at wind speeds in excess of 6ms-1, which again is rarely achieved in high turbulence urban areas. Much improved results have been achieved by carefully designing urban form to maximise its aerodynamic performance for both wind turbines and wind driven ventilation. It is not particularly difficult to increase ambient wind velocity by a factor of 1.5 using the wind focusing effect of large building and roof surfaces. Higher factors can be achieved with specially designed buildings, such as the SkyZED model. The future of micro wind turbines lies in carefully designed aerodynamic master plans, and the firm rejection of any ideas that this technology can be easily retro fitted to any situation. We also suspect that the grid connection, vibration isolation and structural support issues that will be experienced mounting any wind turbines to buildings can be easily overcome if a serious research and development initiative was started by a consortium of manufacturers, architects and contractors.

Off grid potential: turning a problem to a solution
To overcome the G83 problem, the raw wild output from urban wind turbines can be fed into an off grid system. The batteries in the system would smooth the wild power peaks while accepting all the power. The smoothed power can then be fed into an inverter to be used in the home and/or exported back to the grid. Such a system would allow a home continue to have electricity during a power cut for a limited time, depending on the number of batteries used and the demand placed upon them. As these systems become more cost competitive, grid connection could reduce in importance. Current proposals allow for about half a days electrical storage – which with sealed recyclable lead acid batteries, can be fitted under the stairs in most family homes. Future developments with pumped electrolyte storage, and possibly the integration of electric vehicles into the home energy system, are likely to further enhance the viability of decentralised energy systems. What is clear, however, is that embedded decentralised electrical storage greatly reduces the peak loads experienced by the national grid – and eliminates the need for investment in costly centralised power stations.

The future – intelligent export
One of the inherent problems with renewable electricity generation is that it relies on the weather. This is one of the key arguments put forward by the nuclear lobby. However, if a small amount of storage was built into every household's generation equipment, the peaks and toughs of power supply could be smoothed out. Legislation is already moving through Parliment that would mean that non-critical devices such as fridges and washing machines would include a device that monitors the grid and shuts them off at times of peak demand. It is not too much of a leap to see how this could be extended to a household's energy systems that not only would switch off non critical demand, but also export some of their stored electricity. This could be incentivised by a energy price market where peak power was expensive while off peak was cheap. The home owner could then set their system to only export once the price went above (say) 20p and kWhr and import when it was below 10p (unless it was a good generating day).

In hotter climates within developing countries - where up to 70 per cent of the peak electrical consumption of major cities is required to run air conditioning systems, the development of solar powered dehumidification and cooling devices could eliminate the need for investment in coal-fired conventional power stations.

Water

Rainwater harvesting
A typical UK household flushes a third of its expensively treated drinking water down the toilet!

In parts of Europe and the USA there is a separate street main for non-potable water that can be used for toilet flushing, car washing and garden irrigation. Sadly the UK is a long way off providing such a utility.

2.1.42
A 4,000 litre rainwater tank

Where rainwater tanks cannot be built into the foundation, an alternative on an individual basis is to install a rainwater harvesting system. This comprises a large fibre glass tank (2,000–5,000 litres) that is buried in the garden. A submergible pump then feeds a separate non potable water circuit for WCs, garden taps and washing machines. The system also includes an automatic main top up facility and level gauge.

Depending on lifestyle patterns, up to 50 per cent of water usage can be saved with such a system.

There are now excellent pre-packaged rainwater harvesting kits ideally suited to low density projects. Most of the pump and control gear can however be easily modified to suit larger projects, with the obvious caveat that the collecting surface area / occupant ratio is lower. Significant water savings can be easily made at almost no additional cost by bulk buying spray taps, showers, water / energy saving white goods and installing flow reducers.

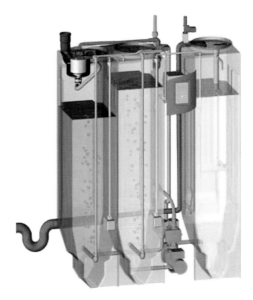

2.1.43
Sophisticated grey water recovery units can work well but can have a high electric consumption

Low water usage fittings

A significant saving in water can be made by fitting water saving taps and shower fittings. High quality fittings save water by aerating the water flow. This makes it appear that there is a large volume of water coming out of the tap as well as making the water feel 'soft', but in actual fact the volume of water is very low. High-quality low water shower heads work on a similar principle.

Grey water recycling

Technologies are now on the market that can treat grey water (water from baths and showers) and make it usable for toilet flushing. These do use energy so should only be used where a rainwater tank is not feasible.

Products in development

Cooling and dehumidification

As summer temperatures increase and climate changes, affordable coolth will become as important as affordable warmth is today. ZEDstandards are also not only designed to be limited to the UK and are relevant to other climates with the addition of some further low energy technologies.

Work has been carried out by ISAW, Nottingham University, ZEDfactory and Arup to design a low energy heating, ventilation, and air conditioning (HVAC) system that can be integrated into the ZED wind cowl based heat recovery ventilation system.

The low energy nature of the system is achieved through the combined use of desiccant dehumidification system, total enthalpy heat exchangers and a solar thermal driven evaporative cooling system.

The system will rely on a combination of different renewable energy sources, assembled in such a way to absolutely minimise the electrical load. In some cases this will involve the use of ground source heat pumps for summer cooling and winter heating, but only when absolutely necessary. Many countries do not have access to biomass energy crop, making it important to develop ways of providing heating, cooling and hot water that rely entirely on the renewable energy available within a typical sites boundaries. This is of course more difficult, and the combination of wider

2.1.44
Spray taps and showers reduce water demand

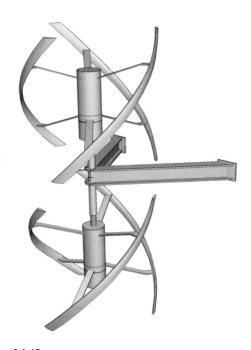

2.1.45
A 1.6 kWp ZEDfabric building integrated wind turbine
suitable for mounting on the sides of aerodynamic
buildings

climatic extremes with no access to a national communal renewable energy resource
results in the need for larger areas of both photovoltaic panels and evacuated tube
solar collectors.

Vertical Axis Wind Turbine

Vertical Axis Wind Turbines (VAWT) have the advantage of being more tolerant for
changing and inconsistent wind directions, making them ideal for utilisation in an
urban context.

This product is currently in design and development stage – basic design, calculations and preliminary design drawings have now been completed. A UK light
engineering firm has already expressed interest in prototyping and manufacturing
this product.

ZEDfabric is developing an integrated system to utilise the combined wind and
solar energy output with one installation. This is suitable for upgrading existing flat
roofs, particularly for schools and offices.

The integrated system consists of a wind cowl (with conventional Heat
Exchanger), 2 x 2.7 m diameter wind turbines, 1 kWp PV panels and a Solar Thermal array (evacuated tubes) – meeting 100% of a ZED building's electrical demand
and hot water in the summer. Each Hybrid assembly services approximately 100
m^2 of floor area. The hybrid system is being designed to be delivered on a flat bed
as one complete unit, minimising on site installation costs and the number of roof
penetrations.

2.1.46
Each turbine meets the annual electric demand for a ZEDstandards two-bed flat.
APA – ZEDfactory architects – PortZED, Shoreham

2.2   The ZEDphysics Model

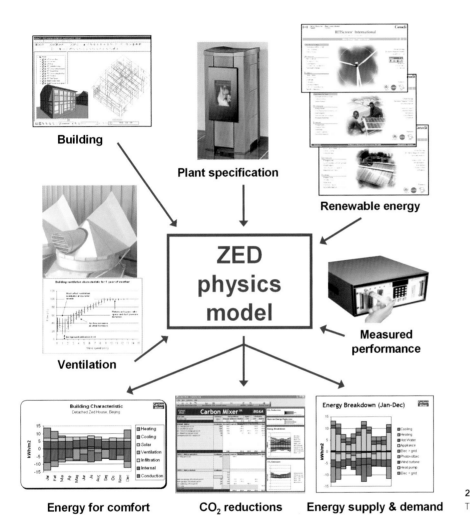

2.2.1
The ZEDphysics model

The ZEDphysics model is an integrated set of sophisticated tools which analyse the performance of the various aspects of the development. These include models of:

- building physics, including energy flows, comfort analysis and ventilation models
- renewable energy collectors and generators – wind turbines, photovoltaics, solar hot water
- models of heating plant for various fuels (biomass, gas, oil, etc.)

- combined heat and power (CHP) plant, again, for various fuels including biomass
- cooling and dehumidification plant
- heat pumps and ground cycled cooling
- carbon emissions accounting using Carbon Mixer™.

The models are based either on detailed simulations of the system's performance or measurements of performance, or a combination of the two.

The Carbon Emissions Accounting Tool integrates all of the above models to show whether a zero energy balance has been achieved, or what level of carbon emissions are present. This tool can also provide summaries of electrical energy, thermal energy, fuel consumption and system and running costs.

Building physics

The building performance can be simulated using a number of software packages. In the studies shown here the IES-Virtual environment software[1] is used to model the energy flows and comfort levels within the building (see Figure 2.2.2). It is important that a tool capable of a full thermal analysis is used in order to show the effect of the thermal mass and other aspects of building physics accurately. For this reason standard assessment tools such as UK SAP/NHER or SBEM are avoided. An example of the thermal heat flows and thermal energy demand for a building is shown below. This type of output is described in more detail in Chapter 2.5.

The heating demand (and cooling and dehumidification loads if present) is taken from this type of analysis and used in the CO_2 emissions model.

Other models are integrated into the base building physics model when required. For example a sophisticated model has been developed for the ZEDfactory wind cowl heat-recovery ventilation system. This is described in detail elsewhere. Its effect on improving the rates of air and heat exchange in the building are fed back into the base building physics model to ensure that it is included in the calculations of building performance.

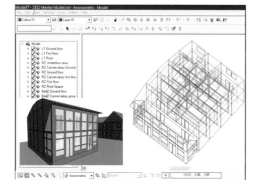

2.2.2
A thermal model of RuralZED forms part of the ZEDphysics model

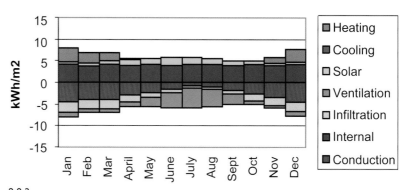

2.2.3
Example of thermal heat balance for a building

Unfuelled energy supply systems – wind, solar hot water, photovoltaic

Unfuelled systems have no CO_2 emissions in use as they burn no fuel (though they will have embodied CO_2 emissions from their manufacture). Therefore any energy they supply will not add to the CO_2 emissions of the site. The wind, solar hot water (SHW) and photovoltaic (PV) potential for the site is modelled using the Retscreen software[2] which is designed for use in assessing the renewable resource on a site based on local weather data and the characteristics of the system considered. Outputs are based on the power curve and system efficiency characteristics for the particular renewable technology. The output is calculated on a monthly basis and is used in the model to offset either the domestic hot water demand or the electrical demand as appropriate. Excess electrical energy is usually assumed to be exported to the grid resulting in a negative CO_2 emission.

Fuelled energy supply systems

Burning fuel, either directly or indirectly at the power station, is what causes CO_2 emissions. Fossil fuels have high CO_2 emissions, renewable fuels such as wood chip have minimal CO_2 emissions associated with their harvest and distribution. This is all accounted for in the emissions conversion factor for the fuel. The thermal demand and boiler efficiencies are taken into account when calculating the amount of fuel burnt. This is then converted into CO_2 emissions using the appropriate conversion factor.

A CHP system is modelled as an electrical generator and has an efficiency rating (typically around 30 per cent) which is used to calculate the quantity of fuel burnt and hence the CO_2 emissions. Having assumed a certain electrical output, the performance data for the system is used to calculate the quantity of 'free' heat produced, typically 1 kWh of electrical output gives 2 kWh of thermal. If excess electrical energy is produced this will be exported to the grid resulting in negative CO_2 emissions.

Where biomass (wood chips, pellets, etc.) is used as the fuel for the boiler or CHP system it is almost carbon neutral since the CO_2 released on burning was relatively recently absorbed from the atmosphere while it grew. It is not quite neutral as energy is expended harvesting and transporting it. A figure of 5 per cent of the equivalent emissions from petroleum is sometimes used though this will depend on the management of the crop and the location of use relative to the crop. Assumed emissions factors for biomass are now given in building regulations though it is not clear what assumptions are made. The resulting CO_2 emissions are relatively trivial.

Ground source heat pumps are characterised by a coefficient of performance (COP) of the system. This is used to scale the electrical demand by the thermal demand for heating and hot water. Note that this must be the COP for the whole system, taking into account any additional electrical load due to pumps and fans additional to normal heating controls, and is typically in the range 2–4 depending on the source of heat. The COP of the heat pump itself may be higher than this. COPs will vary for different climatic conditions and this must be assessed for each site.

Cooling and dehumidification plant can also be characterised by a COP which can be used to scale the electrical demand by the cooling and dehumidification load. Detailed calculations and measured test data have been commissioned from Nottingham University for low-energy cooling systems. These will be characterised by an electrical COP and also a thermal COP for systems which use thermal cooling methods and require a calculation of the number of solar collectors. These systems are described in more detail later in Part 2.

Case studies in Parts 2 and 3 show how all of these effects are integrated to give the calculated reduction in carbon emissions.

2.3 Characterising a Development for Energy Use and Carbon Emissions

The various physics models are used to assess the energy use of the site and the results are integrated to assess whether the development is a Zero fossil fuel Energy Development, or a Zero net Carbon Emissions Development.

The balance of energy demand and supply on the site can be assessed by looking at an energy breakdown graph as shown in Figure 2.3.2. This shows the thermal (heating, cooling, hot water) demands below the zero line being supplied by a heat pump (thermal), photovoltaic and wind generators (electrical) above the line. This type of summary can be carried out for any mixture of energy supply systems.

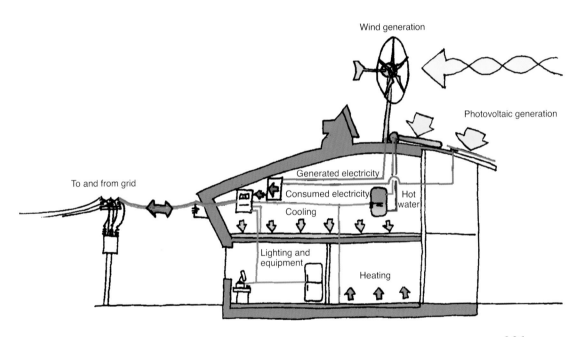

2.3.1
Schematic of some of the energy demand and supply systems in a ZED house

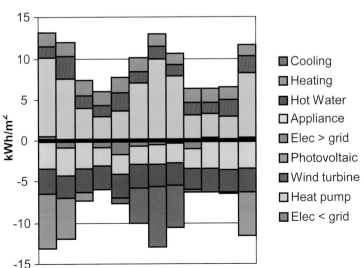

- ■ Cooling
- ■ Heating
- ■ Hot Water
- ☐ Appliance
- ■ Elec > grid
- ■ Photovoltaic
- ■ Wind turbine
- ☐ Heat pump
- ■ Elec < grid

2.3.2
Thermal and electrical energy demand and supply balance for an example house in a hot climate – energy breakdown, January to December

In Figure 2.3.2 it can also be seen that some electricity is being exported to the grid (bright green) when there is an excess. This is shown as an artificial system demand.

Figure 2.3.3 shows the CO_2 emissions resulting from the energy supply strategy shown in Figure 2.3.2. The electrical appliance demand has been cancelled out by electrical supply from the photovoltaics and the wind generator and so no emissions are shown. The thermal supply (heating, cooling, hot water) from the heat pump is fuelled by electricity which nominally generates CO_2 emissions, however these are also cancelled out by the generation of electricity. This is shown on the graph because some of the CO_2 offset comes from exporting electricity to the grid (bright green) but some comes from the on site generation bonus (dark green). This bonus is an aspect of UK building regulations emissions factors. Where electricity is supplied it is assumed to be at the average efficiency for the whole grid. Where electricity is generated on site, it is assumed that this will enable the least efficient, most polluting, power stations to be taken off line for longer and so there is a 'bonus' on the assumption that you are saving more than the average CO_2 emissions. This methodology is up for debate, and is not necessarily appropriate in other countries.

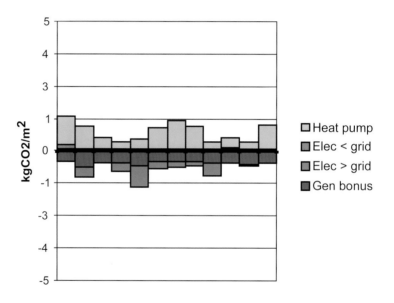

2.3.3
CO_2 emissions are very low and balance to give zero net emissions for the
ZED house – CO_2 emissions, January to December

2.4 Characterising a Development for Comfort

Any building can be made to use zero energy by turning off the gas and electricity and wearing more clothes. However in these circumstances most buildings in most climates would not be very comfortable. Conversely if a limitless supply of energy is available, almost any building can be made comfortable no matter how draughty and uninsulated in winter or overglazed, unventilated and poorly shaded in summer. A well designed building will be comfortable in summer and winter and will require very little energy input to achieve this comfort.

Buildings come in many different shapes and sizes and operate in many different ways. This can make it hard to compare performance. How do you compare the performance of a ZEDfabric building with an Elizabethan manor? One way is to set a comfort requirement for a building and examine the energy flows necessary to maintain them. The buildings can then be compared by looking at the energy required per square metre of occupied space to maintain this level of comfort. Examples of energy flows are shown in Figure 2.4.1.

The comfort requirement will typically be a minimum temperature in winter and a maximum temperature in summer. In addition a required humidity range may also be important particularly in warmer and tropical climates. The comfort requirement will usually be for people, but could be for a machine, for example a computer server room, or for a product, for example a cold room or humidity-controlled storage area.

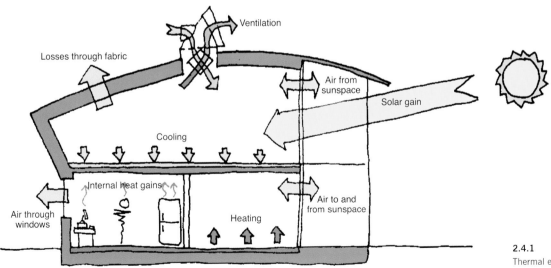

2.4.1
Thermal energy flows into and out of a building must balance on average to maintain comfort levels

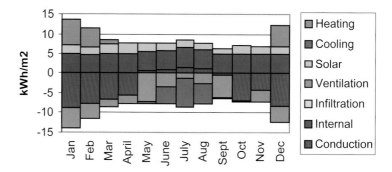

2.4.2

Heat energy balance – detached ZED house, Beijing

Having characterised the building's capacity to be comfortable in terms of energy use, the supply options can be assessed and thus its potential to become a zero fossil fuel energy, zero net carbon emissions development.

Figure 2.4.2 shows an example of the thermal energy characteristic for a building for which temperature comfort levels have been specified.

This graph shows the energy balance required to maintain comfort in the building throughout the year. The blocks above the zero line show how heat is gained each month, blocks below the line show how heat is lost each month, resulting in a balance which maintains the comfort level. The comfort of the building in this case is being controlled by adding energy in winter in the form of a heating load (red), and in summer a cooling load (blue). Thermal energy is also being captured from heat given off by lighting, equipment and the people in the building (purple), and from solar gain (pale yellow). Solar gain is useful in winter but adds to the overheating risk in the summer and so the graph shows how well solar shading is applied by preventing the solar gains from increasing in summer. Thermal energy is being lost through the walls, roof, floor and windows – that is, the building fabric (brown) – and through ventilation (mid blue) and infiltration around windows and doors (light blue). This particular building has a sunspace which can be used to buffer heat loss and even provide extra heat input in the spring and autumn, or as a ventilated buffer for passive night cooling in summer. For example in October in this particular case it can be seen that the ventilation losses are cancelled out by the warm air gains from the sunspace and so the net ventilation losses are zero.

This technique can be applied to any type of building to show the energy requirements for maintaining comfort equilibrium. It can use data from simulations or from the measured performance of a real building. It allows a quick visual assessment of how buildings compare. Big bars on the graph are indicative of energy-hungry constructions. Small bars are indicative of energy efficient constructions.

Case study
Comparison of thermal performance for three UK properties

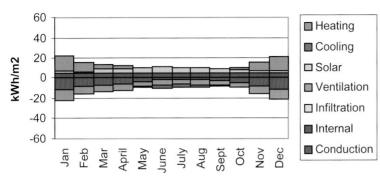

2.4.3

Case 1 – A typical Building Regulations house. Notice heat losses through trickle ventilation (mid blue). Also the solar shading has been poorly thought out, resulting in high solar gains in summer and low gains in winter (yellow). Heating input is moderate (red). The suggestion that cooling is necessary (dark blue) indicates that there would be an overheating risk in the free running building which should be investigated in more detail.

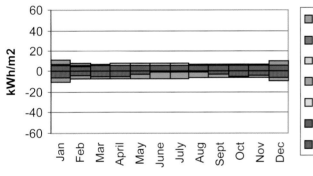

2.4.4

Case 2 – A well operated ZED home with very little additional energy input beyond that used for equipment (cooking, electrical equipment, etc.). The solar gain is spread more evenly through the year. The ventilation is via passive heat recovery systems based on wind cowls, so ventilation losses are minimised (mid blue). The sunspace will be acting as a buffer, reducing the losses through the fabric (brown) in winter. In summer the ventilated sunspace can be used to provide night cooling for the heavyweight material of the building (mid blue) resulting in almost no overheating risk unless the building is left sealed up.

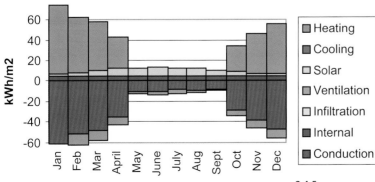

2.4.5

Case 3 – A house typical of existing stock. High heating input required, sending bars off the scale, (red) because of large losses through uninsulated walls and floors and single glazed windows (brown). There are large ventilation losses due to poor draughtproofing and risk of overheating in summer (dark blue) due to poor solar design (yellow).

RuralZED development in a flood plain

2.5 The Effect of Climate

For a given design of building, the energy demand will depend on the site and the local climate, which will influence the heating requirement and also possibly the need for cooling. The local climate will also affect the ability to produce renewable energy from wind and solar energy. The ways in which energy demand can be minimised will be examined shortly, but first consider how much natural energy may be available on the site, to get an idea of the limitations.

If we assume that as a maximum 75 per cent of the footprint of the building could be devoted to PVs mounted on the roof,[1] and that a nominal 1 kW wind turbine could be installed for every 50 m^2 of footprint,[2] then this implies the following amount of available energy for different locations, based on the availability of wind and solar energy (see Figure 2.5.1).

Now compare this with the thermal demand per square metre of example super low energy ZEDstandard buildings whose performance has been simulated in different climates (see Figure 2.5.2).[3]

The thermal loads are for floor area rather than plot area and so can be multiplied up to see how many floors of the building could be supplied from the resources on the roof. It would appear that the available supply of between 100 and 250 kWh/m^2 would be sufficient for 2 to 15 floors of thermal demand depending on the thermal requirement. Changsha in China is particularly challenging, with almost no wind power and a similar solar power to London, making only 100 kWh/m^2 available on

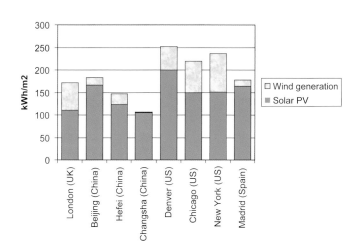

2.5.1
Annual energy yield from building

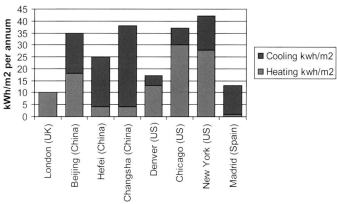

2.5.2
Thermal demands in different climates

the building footprint, but requiring nearly 40 kWh/m² for each floor of the building, a large amount of which is summer cooling.

But this assumes a 1:1 correlation between thermal demand and electrical supply in kWh. If a standard electrical system is used it is likely to be worse than this; if heat pumps are used it could be a factor of four better. Also wood pellet burners (potentially CO_2 neutral) could be used in regions where biomass is readily available, reducing the electrical demand for heating.

While the electrical need to meet thermal demand can be reduced, there are still other demands to account for. The electrical equipment in the building could easily double the electrical demand. An equipment demand of 35 kWh/m² of floor area per annum is not unusual. Another potentially high demand is for dehumidification. This can double the cooling demand in a hot humid climate.

These considerations show that a building must be designed to very low energy standards if it is to have the potential to be powered from on site renewables. Even with off site renewables such as biomass for a community heat main or an off site wind turbine, the building demand must still be minimised so that it does not demand more than a fair share of the national resource of renewable energy. If countries are to succeed in meeting the massive reduction of CO_2 emissions that are required, the demand for energy must be reduced as much as the ability to generate national renewable energy must grow. Even optimistic predictions show that the potential national resource of renewable energy is only likely to meet 30 per cent of the current demand, so it is important that new buildings put as little demand on this national resource as possible.

This assessment shows that if a building is designed to run at very low energy levels it is possible to have a design several floors high that will support itself with on site resources. Higher designs such as apartment blocks designed to ZEDstandards might be able to have zero net energy in some climates and would minimise the need for additional energy to optimise comfort in other climates.

In the event that additional energy were not reliably available to optimise comfort levels (e.g. if local power cuts are a problem), the building should be designed so that it still provided at least an acceptable level of comfort. For example, studies of poorly designed air conditioned buildings in hot climates show that internal temperatures would reach 50°C within half an hour of a power outage.[4] These buildings could become unusable if rising oil prices and the failure to find new reserves make power shortages a regular occurrence.

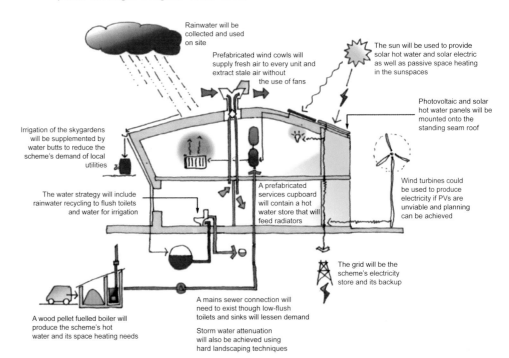

Rainwater will be collected and used on site

Prefabricated wind cowls will supply fresh air to every unit and extract stale air without the use of fans

The sun will be used to provide solar hot water and solar electric as well as passive space heating in the sunspaces

Photovoltaic and solar hot water panels will be mounted onto the standing seam roof

Irrigation of the skygardens will be supplemented by water butts to reduce the scheme's demand of local utilities

The water strategy will include rainwater recycling to flush toilets and water for irrigation

A prefabricated services cupboard will contain a hot water store that will feed radiators

Wind turbines could be used to produce electricity if PVs are unviable and planning can be achieved

The grid will be the scheme's electricity store and its backup

A wood pellet fuelled boiler will produce the scheme's hot water and its space heating needs

A mains sewer connection will need to exist though low-flush toilets and sinks will lessen demand

Storm water attenuation will also be achieved using hard landscaping techniques

2.5.3

The local environment presents challenges on opportunities for the demand and supply of energy

2.6 Building and Upgrading existing Houses and Workspace to Zero Carbon Standards

Five steps to a Zero Carbon Upgrade Home

Time to take personal action – stop exporting your carbon footprint and join the 'microgeneration'.

Almost the same building physics model and supply chain used for new build can be used to reduce the CO_2 footprint of existing homes and workplaces. The same principles of draughtproofing, external insulation, radiant internal massive surfaces and microgeneration using renewable energy systems can be applied to existing buildings – creating a far larger potential market, and the opportunity for faster manufacturing economies of scale, and faster cost reductions to the public. ZEDfactory is currently testing the effectiveness of the following technologies on a number of existing homes, and believes that a simple upgrade process could be made available to the general public.

The most important commodity to save is electricity – with each unit having three to four times the carbon footprint of gas. Gas prices increased 25 per cent last year, and as international stocks deplete will rise steadily for the foreseeable future. With electricity pegged to approximately four times the price of gas and a future shortage of national generating capacity ZEDfactory recommend avoiding home technologies that use large amounts of electricity – particularly heat pumps, ventilation fans and resistance heaters. Payback on solar electric panels is now reduced to around 12 years.

- *Step 1*. If you install 2 W LED or micro compact fluorescents in existing low voltage down lighters you can have every light on in a typical three-bed home, and still only burn less than 100 W. If you are able to turn lights off in unused rooms, this could drop to 20 W, without stumbling around in darkness. Mains electricity has three times the CO_2 footprint of mains gas – so saving electricity becomes a priority.
- *Step 2*. If you run a class A++ dishwasher, fridge and induction hob, use a washing machine once a week and turn off TV and computers rather than leaving them on standby, it is possible to limit annual electrical consumption to 750 kWh/year/person. Don't use a tumble dryer, and put a clothes drying rack above the bath.
- *Step 3*. With three people living in this house, it is easily possible to live on 2,250 kWh/year. If £5,000 worth of solar electric panels are installed, this will produce 1,350 kWh of renewable electricity, dropping the overall consumption to 900 kWh/year. Fitting a convenient electrical consumption display will help you weed CO_2 intensive devices from your home.

- *Step 4.* If a small, 1.7 m diameter micro wind turbine is installed as a further upgrade, powering a small battery bank that provides half a day's worth of storage, running both lights and computers, this will contribute 450 kWh/year within most parts of the South East, mostly on dark, rainy winter nights. This storage system greatly reduces the peak demand on the national grid. If the turbine is not obstructed by surrounding buildings and trees, and the post mounted within the roof space – penetrating the roof tiles at the highest point or ridge – then the wind could be locally accelerated, possibly doubling output to somewhere between 450 and 700 kWh/year. The micro wind turbine is able to generate small amounts of electricity on cold, rainy winter nights or blustery winter days – providing a useful top up when solar energy is scarce. If your home is in an area of high turbulence and low wind speed, please do not insist on a wind turbine, as its output will be minimal. Spend the same budget on increasing the quantity of photovoltaic panels.
- *Step 5.* Replace the gas boiler with a wood pellet boiler, in conjunction with solar thermal collectors (so that it doesn't have to turn on in the summer). Providing that thermostats are turned down, and insulation upgrades are installed, it is possible to just about stay within each UK citizen's fair share of the UK national biomass reserves of around half a dry tonne/person/year without losing productive agricultural land.

It is straightforward to draught strip windows and insulate under floor-boards, and this represents the usual DIY activity carried out by many households over an intensive week – the material cost should be under £1,000. Add another £5,000 for solar thermal collectors and a small wood pellet or condensing gas boiler, and the average three-bed home's carbon footprint should be around 70 per cent lighter. ZEDfactory propose meeting the capital cost of these measures by taking out an energy mortgage. This enables a typical household to more or less meet the annual payments servicing the £11,000 capital cost loan funding the energy efficiency and renewable energy features within the £1,000 per year budget that the same household would have spent annually on fossil fuel – although there would still be a requirement to purchase wood pellets.

This strategy provides ordinary people with the tools to decelerate climate change. Real step change reductions in carbon footprints will have to emerge from the grass roots and be funded by micro credit, not the top-down high investment strategy proposed by the power generation industry. When enough of us small people join the 'microgeneration', then there will be a large enough political mandate to redirect the massive central finance reserves towards funding a social infrastructure no longer reliant on nuclear or fossil fuel.

ZEDfact

Reducing the cost of environmental innovation

Ethical finance options:

- conversion of existing two floor maisonette to first/loft-level maisonette with studio flat at ground floor (to be sold or rented to cover costs of upgrade)

- estate or terrace renovation by landlord or other to claim bulk discounts

- single private dwelling – re-mortgage to finance upgrade and extension as opposed to moving home

- ten-year ZERO CARBON upgrade plan – future proof strategy

- always reduce demand for heat and electricity before installing renewable energy harvesting systems.

Case study
ZEDup – where to spend your money

This section looks at how CO_2 emissions can be reduced compared against both a 2002 Building Regulations house and a Victorian house. The aim is to reach zero carbon status in each case.

The technologies are tested against projected lifecycle costs, additional running costs and income. (Assumptions made can be found below.) The additional cost of the technology is then divided by the percentage reduction in CO_2 realised over the 2002 house. The cost per percentage point improvement can then be seen (the so called 'bangs per buck').

By projecting fuel costs for the next 45 years, payback can be worked out, both in cost per percentage CO_2 reduction and overall expense/income experienced. If you just lived in a 2002 Building Regulations house, your CO_2 reduction would be zero and the cost/income experienced would be zero.

Energy generators of course have a straight income stream that improves as energy prices increase, tempered by the need to replace them. Saving energy is also treated as an income as it puts more pounds in your pocket than you would have had living in the 2002 house.

Technologies that use energy to save CO_2 are costed at the cost of the energy used at the grade it is used, less the cost of the energy saved at the grade it is saved. Hence fan or heat pump heat recovery ventilation powered by electricity saves heat energy powered by gas.

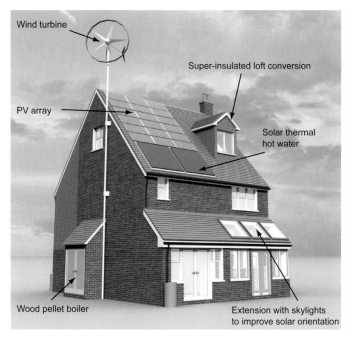

Wind turbine

Super-insulated loft conversion

PV array

Solar thermal
hot water

Wood pellet boiler

Extension with skylights
to improve solar orientation

2.6.1
Micro-generation added to a typical volume house builder's standard product. Up to 70 per cent CO_2 reduction is achievable using the same supply chain as zero carbon new build homes. The economies of scale from the refurbishment programme will reduce installation costs for new construction

Income or cost are then multiplied by the number of years of the projection scenario and added to the original cost of the technology. The total cost of the technology over the building's life can then be seen as well as the total cost per percentage point reduction of CO_2.

Assumptions

- The typical Victorian house is of standard 9-inch solid wall construction with internal plaster and fitted with a 60 per cent efficient gas condensing boiler. All heat demands to calculate gas cost are therefore divided by 0.6.
- It is assumed that a gas condensing boiler would be installed immediately despite the existing 60 per cent boiler still being serviceable. However by the time this gas condensing boiler comes up for its first replacement, the only boiler legal to replace it with would be another gas condensing boiler so the payback income stream would cease. This in fact would be the best case for payback for a gas condensing boiler as the existing 60 per cent boiler may have required replacement well before this time.
- The technologies are added in order with each attempting savings out of the CO_2 production left by the preceding technologies. For this reason the first technology applied looks very good. However if it was applied later in the order, there would be less CO_2 produced so its ability to save would be reduced.
- ZEDstandard construction is assumed to cost £8,260 for external insulation and £6,000 for new windows, doors and roof lights. This includes a new entrance porch and mini rear sunspace.
- Electric heat recovery ventilation is assumed to cost £2,500.
- Wind-assisted passive stack ventilation is assumed to cost £3,250.
- Solar hot water is assumed to cost £2,000.
- The solar hot water is assumed to cost its whole price in replacement in 30 years and cost £200 to maintain every 5 years.
- Biomass hot water and space heat is assumed to cost an additional £4,000 for the biomass boiler and system minus cost of the gas boiler now not needed.
- Biomass fuel is assumed to match and trak the price of gas over the projection.
- The biomass boiler is assumed to cost its additional price in maintenance/ replacement in 15 years.
- The wind turbine is assumed to cost £1,500 installed, generate 1,150 kWh a year and cost its whole price in maintenance/replacement in 10 years.
- The PV panels are assumed to cost £5,400 and then £1,500 for their installation and inverter. A 50 per cent grant is then applied, bringing the total additional cost to £3,450.
- The PV system is assumed to cost its whole price in maintenance/replacement in 25 years.
- The PV system is assumed to generate energy at a rate of 832 kWh per kWp installed.

2.6.2
Low carbon conversion of Victorian villa – ZEDfabric upgrade. 25 Thetford Road, New Malden. Designed by Jim and Lynette Dunster

2.6.3
Internal view of new kitchen/living room at 25 Thetford Road, New Malden

Summary of findings

It was generally found that any technology that used electricity to save heat energy ended up costing more to use than it saved. This was particularly pronounced when looked at against the percentage point reduction in CO_2. From a purely financial standpoint, mechanical heat reclaim ventilation costs more to run than it saves in fuel, even with the existing 60 per cent efficient boiler.

Again, in pure financial terms, the quickest technology to pay back and one of the biggest CO_2 savings to be made is by fitting a gas condensing boiler. Although this is still a fossil technology, the amount of gas used to heat a typical Buildings Regulation house is so large that the reduction in gas used that can be achieved by changing from a 60 per cent efficient boiler to a 92 per cent efficient one is extremely significant. This CO_2 saving and then some could be made by going straight for biomass heating, but this would then consume large amounts of wood. The CO_2 saving for biomass does not appear dramatic in this study as it has been assumed that biomass heating would only be installed after the ZEDstandards construction upgrade.

ZEDstandard construction upgrade scores very highly. Again this is because the typical Building Regulations house uses so much heat that any upgrade in the building fabric can make very large savings.

Once these gross energy use reductions have been made, the next best savings are due to microgeneration of electricity. The high future value of electricity ensures payback. The heat fuel saving technologies of wind assisted heat recovery ventilation and solar thermal panels then follow.

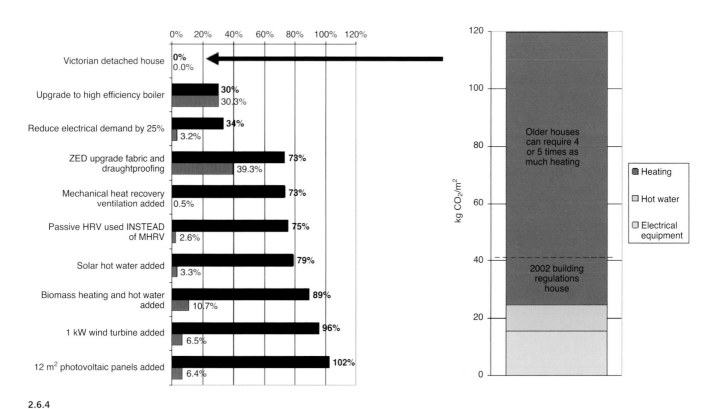

2.6.4
(a) Percentage reduction of CO_2 emissions
(b) CO_2 emissions for Victorian house and 2002 building regulations house

Conclusions

1. If you are only doing one thing, fit a gas condensing boiler.
2. If you are doing two, upgrade the fabric and fit carbon neutral heating (biomass and solar thermal). Solar thermal will reduce/eliminate summer fuel usage, which is particularly important if a manual feed stove is used or storage facilities for biomass is limited. There is little point in installing any further carbon saving technologies unless fabric upgrade and heating fuel usage are first looked at, as these are an order of magnitude greater savings than any other technologies.
3. Fit micro-generation, either PV or wind depending on your location, and preferably both as they are both income generators.
4. Wind-assisted ventilation reduces fuel use even further, though payback is long due to the pure additional cost for the technology as it does not replace an expense that would have normally been experienced (as it does in new build housing).
5. Do not use fan-powered heat reclaim ventilation. It is the most costly way to save CO_2 and will always cost more to run than the cost of the heat it reclaims.

2.6.5
Internal view of new kitchen/living room at 25 Thetford Road, New Malden

The route to a ZEDup – the recommended upgrade

'A', 'A+' and 'A++' rated appliances

Again this is always the first step in any carbon reducing strategy. In an upgrade situation this is likely to be incremental as appliances come to the end of their practical lives, as a comprehensive 'chuck out' would normally be wasteful of the embodied energy in the appliances.

ZEDstandard construction

As stated in the previous section, there is no point in considering upgrading if this is not first tackled as any further savings would be a drop in the ocean of carbon that an un-insulated house produces.

Biomass heating with solar thermal

Once gross heat demand has been reduced as much as possible, the use of biomass for heating becomes practical.

The heat fuel saving due to using solar thermal should be theoretically the same as for a 2002 Building Regulations house as again it is only replacing summer fuel use. Unlike electricity generating devices, solar thermal has limited ability to export or store surplus, so while in the summer it may be generating 150–200 per cent of demand, this surplus cannot be credited in this study. However, unless the Building Regulations house being upgraded in the example is also upgraded with low water use fittings, including bath tubs and so on, hot water usage may well be higher than a 2002 house, so the financial saving could be higher (same percentage saving but of a bigger amount).

2.6.6
Internal view of home office at 25 Thetford Road, New Malden

The main argument for solar thermal is likely to be that the space available to store biomass fuel is limited, so the cost per kWh for the fuel once delivery charges are included makes the payback on solar thermal attractive. Alternatively, ZEDuppers may opt for manual feed stoves. Not having to manually fill and light these would be very welcome as would removing the unnecessary space heating output from such stoves in the summer.

Burning vast amounts of biomass is also not sustainable/feasible due to the limited space in the United Kingdom/Europe available to grow it. Using a solar thermal system in combination with a biomass boiler allows personal consumption of biomass to fall within national resource constraints.

Microgeneration

The next best payback technology is electrical microgeneration due to the high financial value of electricity and the ability to sell back to the grid in times of surplus.

Technologies not chosen

Gas condensing boiler

Although offering an initial fantastic payback due to the saving in gas used over the existing 60 per cent efficient boiler if this was a first step, this payback would be slower if the house was insulated. It also requires the assumption that the existing boiler would not have been replaced anyway. With the new Building Regulations requiring a condensing boiler to be fitted anyway, it could be argued that this step would not have been an upgrade and hence there would be no income stream. Still, if only one step is being considered with no plans for any further upgrades within the next (say) 10 years and the property does not already have a condensing boiler, such a boiler should be fitted.

Heat exchange ventilation

The very small percentage point reduction in carbon achieved by these systems, together with the fact that they cost more to run than the cost of the energy they save, makes them an easy technology to reject.

Wind-assisted passive stack ventilation

Although this technology makes a steady payback, it is by small amounts each year. The main cost of installing the technology can end up being the builder's work for ducting the air pipes. On an existing house this may or may not be a considerable sum so would have to be looked at on a case by case basis. It may well be that an existing chimney flue layout would make the technology sensible, but for the sake of this typical case scenario it is excluded.

How to ZEDup

Load reduction

As we have repeatedly stated, the cheapest way to generate energy is to not need it!

If you are looking to reduce your demand from the national grid by 75 W, you can either buy a 75 W solar panel for £300 or replace a 100 W traditional light bulb with a 25 W energy saving one for £3. Which would you do first?

This principle applies to all uses of energy in a home:

Lighting

- Energy saving (compact fluorescent) light bulbs have been with us for a long time now and are almost a standard item. They give very good colour rendition but have their detractors due to their slow warm up and bulky nature. Being bulky means the choice of light fittings is limited and they can only provide flood lighting. However with clever design, they can be effectively incorporated into a lighting design. New bulbs are becoming available that can give better directionality but they do not compare with traditional tungsten halogen spot lights for focus and brightness.
- LED lighting is currently undergoing something of a revolution. Coloured LEDs have been available for many decades. White LEDs started appearing about 10 years ago but were generally low powered and rather blue in colour. Recently pure and warm white high powered LEDs have become available that actually provide useful light. The small size and focusing nature of LED bulbs have made it natural for them to be used as direct replacements for low voltage tungsten halogen spot light fittings (MR16 or GU10). Although LEDs have an ultra-low power consumption when used singly, the new generation fittings can consume up to 9 W. While this is much better than the 50 W tungsten halogen they replace, indiscriminate use of fittings can still add up to a significant amount. Careful design is required to produce the visual effect required while using the best fittings for any job to provide the lowest overall power consumption.

Cooking

Cooking appliances remain the largest gross power consumers in a home. Electric ovens are generally rated at 3 kW at least while electric hob rings are normally 2–3 kW each.

- An instant reduction in household electrical power consumption can superficially be made by cooking less! However since food is one of the biggest single contributors to an individual's carbon footprint, there are considerable carbon savings to be made elsewhere by home cooking of locally produced unprocessed food. Eating out more is sadly not the answer; eating more raw food may be!
- Gas ovens and hobs are not considered an option for two reasons. First, gas (currently) is a fossil fuel. Second, naked burning of gas, that is as an open flame rather than in a balanced flue system, releases considerable amounts of water vapour into the air inside the house as one of the main products

2.6.7
DIY – 1.1 kWP photovoltaic panel installation on a London roof terrace

Code 5 residential regeneration
for the Accord Housing
Association in Wolverhampton

of combustion. This will require increased levels of ventilation to maintain internal air quality and hence energy loss due to that ventilation.

- Therefore, electric ovens should be used, as highly rated for energy performance as possible (A, A+ and A++). Careful use should also be made of them and when they are on, space heating should be switched off so the waste heat from cooking can heat the home.
- Electric hobs should be magnetic induction. These work by making the metal of the pan heat up rather that a hot plate that then conducts its heat to the pan where the pan touches it. Not only are these 25 per cent more energy efficient since they do not waste energy heating up a hot plate as well as the pan, they also offer a cooking experience akin to gas in its controllability.

Other white goods

- Fridges are one of the biggest consumers of household electricity, not because they are particularly highly powered (100 W is not unusual), but due to the fact that they are always on. Storing something in a fridge or freezer is actually a very expensive method of preservation once the cost of the electricity has been factored in. Fridges and freezers should be the highest energy rating possible but should also be as small as possible. There has been an unhelpful trend recently to use a fridge as a store cupboard for all sorts of food rather than just for food that needs to be kept cold. By reducing the size of the fridge so it just fits what is essential to be keep refrigerated, a significant energy saving can be made.
- Washing machines again should be as highly rated as possible for energy efficiency. However there has recently been a retrogressive step in washing machine design. No doubt in an effort to drive down manufacturing complexity and hence cost, machines are increasingly only available with just a cold fill. An electric element then heats the water up to the temperature required. In a household with zero carbon biomass or solar thermal heated hot water, this does not make sense. An A++ rated machine with hot fill should be sought. This also applies to dishwashers.
- Tumble dryers are not available with high energy efficiency ratings because they are energy inefficient. In a zero carbon household it would be very expensive to use a tumble dryer since the additional electrical generation equipment required to balance the demand of the dryer would be extremely costly. Habitual use of a tumble dryer can at least treble a household's annual electricity consumption and hence at least treble the quantity of the renewable electricity generating equipment required to meet the load. A zero carbon home should be designed to provide a covered drying space where clothes can be conveniently hung to dry naturally. Sunspace conservatories have been found to be very good at performing this function and new build ZED houses come with built in retractable drying racks in these spaces.
- Computers, TVs and audio equipment all consume power when left on standby. While this situation has been improving with high power standby modes being removed, it can still add up to a considerable power consumption once all the appliances in a home have been taken into account. Wiring

such devices via multi-plug adapters with a single switchable supply can make switching all these devices off convenient.

- This can also be a solution for phantom loads from equipment such as mobile phone chargers, camera chargers and low voltage light transformers. These all consume power even when the device they power is not plugged into them. If it is possible to take such devices out of the equation by using dedicated solar or wind up chargers, so much the better.
- And of course you should only ever boil as much water as you need in a kettle rather than habitually filling it up.

Heat

Space heat

The temperature considered to be normal inside a house has increased in recent years. Whereas it used to be common practice to only heat the room being occupied, now the whole house is heated to 20°C. This is partly to do with the increased thermal standards houses are built to – allowing a whole house to be heated for what was previously the cost of heating a single room – and partly to do with the relatively low cost of fuel. Much has been made of this take up of efficiencies by more wasteful use. However human nature is such that acceptable levels of effort/risk/expenditure/ inconvenience are always settled at. (Average traffic speed in London has been 11 mph for the last 150 years. If it decreases, fewer people travel so it increases back to 11 mph. If it increases, more people start travelling so it decreases back to 11 mph).

Taking this principal on board, the zero carbon house should insulate to a point where heating becomes irrelevant. It is just nice and warm without any heating.

Of course if the home is not insulated to these levels, large heating fuel savings can be made by turning the thermostat down a few degrees, heating fewer rooms and wearing more than just shorts and a tee shirt. However many may see this as a retrogressive step in their living standards and may resist.

Hot water

Water saving fittings such as well designed, low volume shower heads and aerated taps can help by restricting the flow while still giving a feeling of plentiful water. Aerated taps produce what appears to be a good fat flow of water but it is in fact mainly bubbles of air. The bubbles in fact enhance the washing experience as they make the water feel 'soft'.

- The principals for not wasting hot water are well known.
- Take a shower, not a bath (well at least not every day).
- Run a basin instead of washing in running hot water.
- Don't have the hot water set to too high a temperature, in fact have it set as low as you can.

Water use reduction

It is generally agreed that as climate change progresses, one of the effects will be to make rainfall less reliable and when it does come, it will be more likely to come in sudden downpours. Exactly what that means is not known but it is thought likely that our current water collection and distribution system will struggle. To mitigate this, two approaches are suggested:

Demand reduction
This can be achieved by the use of low volume (2/4 L) dual-flush toilets, aerated taps, low volume showerheads and the use of the highest available energy rated water consuming white goods (washing machines, etc.).

Water collection
- *Rainwater.* If a suitable roof area is available, rainwater can be collected for non-potable uses such as toilet flushing, plant irrigation, car washing and washing machines. At least 50 per cent of potable mains water can be saved if these uses are supplied by rainwater. Collecting rainwater also has the effect of reducing storm water run off, so mitigating the effects of large downpours that might otherwise cause flooding downstream. Rainwater collection can be as simple as a water butt connected to a rainwater down pipe, but it is much better as a large capacity tank buried in a garden or under the building. Collected rainwater can be pumped into a separate non-potable water circuit that gives the same level of amenity that a entirely mains plumbed system would give.
- *Grey water.* If sufficient roof space is not available, as may be the situation in muilti storey urban locations, domestic grey water treatment machines can be installed that clean grey water from baths and showers to a level suitable for use for toilet flushing. Since toilets count for a third of average domestic water usage, this is a worthwhile mains water saving. However grey water treatment machines require electrical power to run them (about the same amount as a fridge over a year), so should only be installed where rainwater is not available.

Insulation
This involves maintaining the internal environment at a comfortable temperature without using energy.

Loft/roof insulation
It will be no surprise that this is still the most effective place to add insulation. The opportunity to increase the thickness of insulation in the loft or roof to at least 300 mm should be sought.

Avoiding condensation
Care must be taken not to block ventilation of the underside of the waterproof membrane that forms the roof covering. Air slowly moving (breathing) though the house ceiling and insulation will gradually increase its relative humidity as its temperature decreases. By the time it reaches the waterproof membrane on top of the roof it will be desperate to condense its moisture load. In previous decades, this was prevented by reducing insulation so that the dew point (point at which the air

gives up its moisture) was never reached within the roof build up. This was achieved by basically not letting the air cool down sufficiently, or, to put it another way, chucking out loads of heat.

There are two approaches to avoiding moisture build up due to condensation in a well insulated wall or roof:

- Internal vapour barrier. Much loved by the volume house builder in their timber framed systems. A plastic sheet is pinned/stapled to the inside of the timber frame to prevent internal air entering the wall or roof construction. Theoretically, this system works well when looked at on a two dimensional drawing. Unfortunately on site if the sheets of plastic are not properly joined and sealed at their edges or round a penetration such as a ceiling joist, or if they get torn, internal air can enter the construction, so rendering the whole exercise pointless. This was highlighted by the famous Panorama exposé of the volume housing industry in the 1980s. Despite this, the practice continues, although modified by using foil backed plastic insulation products.

- Breathing wall construction. Working on the principal of 'condensation will happen – deal with it', this philosophy looks to allow any moisture that does condense to then evaporate away as temperatures rise again. The most likely place for condensation to form is on an impervious cold surface. For this reason either such surfaces are avoided and replaced with a breathing membrane, or plentiful ventilation is allowed to the underside of the surface. A vapour barrier is not generally used in the wall construction, though sometimes a vapour control layer may be used. As the name implies, this looks to reduce the amount of moist air passing through the wall construction rather than preventing it completely. Allowing walls to breath, that is, absorb moisture, is considered healthy as it helps stabilise the internal environment (never too moist, never too dry) by either absorbing or releasing moisture into the room. For this reason vapour control layers are not generally recommended unless spaces have exceptionally high vapour pressures (sauna or pool room).

ZEDupgrade recommends the breathing wall philosophy.

If insulation is just being added to an existing loft, care must be taken not to block ventilation at the eaves under the felt. Proprietary inserts are available that maintain a 25 mm gap, or a carpentry solution may be simpler. Maintaining this gap allows air to circulate underneath the roofing felt, above the insulation, evaporating any condensation that may form.

If a loft conversion is being undertaken, which often happens at the same time as a ZEDupgrade, there is the opportunity to change the impervious roofing felt for a modern breather membrane roofing felt. Insulation can then be properly and more simply built into the roof structure, as an air gap would not have to be maintained under the membrane. However if the new roof was to be weatherproofed with an impervious membrane such as bituminous felt, rubber or metal, an air gap would be required under this final surface.

Wall insulation

This is one of the trickiest topics to generalise about for an upgrade. To upgrade wall insulation to sensible levels on a house with either a very small or no cavity requires the addition of external insulation. Filling the existing 50 mm cavity with mineral fibre insulation if it hasn't been already done will help significantly, but even current minimum standards of the Building Regulations ask for a filled 100 mm cavity.

Internal insulation. Internal insulation is not normally an option for several reasons:

- It decreases the internal floor area, so decreasing the value of the property, even if the spaces were still to work (beds and baths could still fit in the rooms).
- It could pull the dew point into the middle of a soft brick wall that may become unstable due to the additional moisture.
- And, perhaps most importantly from an energy perspective, it isolates the thermal mass that is normally found in traditional masonry construction from the internal air of the home, so reducing the thermal storage of heat from incidental (occupation) and solar gains. This in turn leads to peak load heating and cooling systems being required and reductions in internal air quality. However this is not always the case. Victorian terraces were often built with a central massive cross wall to allow the floor joists to span from the front wall to the cross wall and then from the cross wall to the rear wall. This wall by itself may be thermally massive enough to help moderate the internal temperature of the home. The external walls may be such a small proportion of the wall area of the home that adding insulation to the inside of them may not make a significant spatial difference. All there is then to worry about is the effect of the dew point on the bricks!

External insulation. From an energy and building fabric perspective, external insulation is always the best solution. The existing thermal mass is kept exposed to the internal environment, the structure is protected and kept warm and dry, and a useful amount of insulation can be added to get towards a zero heating level of heat loss.

On the downside, people tend to like the way their houses look. Conservation officers 'may' (hmm ...) object to brick or stone properties in conservation areas being overclad, and even if not in a conservation area, the local planning department might want to get involved. All of which could add up to delay and expense, so every upgrade should be looked at on a case by case basis. It was not long ago that local authorities were insisting that stone-built houses were cement rendered and pebble dashed! As climate change rises up the agenda anything is possible.

ZEDfactory have undertaken a ZEDupgrade where external insulation was not an option. A high standard conservation area and powerful conservation officer combined with a handsome brick building with fine brick detailing that only the most aesthetically illiterate energy enthusiast would have demanded be overclad, at least today. After 10 more years of peak oil, we may all think differently.

In this case, the maximum amount of insulation possible was added to the roof, the highest thermal performance windows available installed, and the whole façade repointed in lime mortar outside and in. Wet applied clay plaster and decorator's caulk then ensured the envelope was absolutely as airtight as possible. We await the heat energy monitoring figures to see how much of an energy compromise this approach was.

External insulation normally takes the form of a rigid board of insulation that is glued and mechanically fixed to the existing external wall. This is normally then rendered with a modern silicon based render. Lime-based renders may be an option, but there are currently no systems on the market using lime so the home owner would have to take on the risk themselves if specifying lime.

An alternative approach would be to add timber battens, insulate in between, fix a breather membrane with battens and weather board (or some other boarding detail).

Insulation to the ground

There are various competing theories on how much heat is lost to the ground, but evidence from monitoring seems to suggest it is significant. Insulating to the ground in an existing building will depend on its construction. Suspended ground floors can easily be insulated between joists, whereas solid earth, flag stone floors or concrete screeded floors cannot without adding a further build up, which may then compromise headroom and have knock on effects to staircases and door openings.

When insulating a suspended floor, care has to be taken that the floor void remains ventilated. Failure to do so could lead to dampness problems and hence onto rot and insect attack. This is more important once insulation has been added as the void will be colder and the internal air that migrates to it will therefore have a greater desire to unload its moisture on any surfaces. Without insulation, the floor void would be warmer and dryer, but burning fuel to heat a floor void when there is an alternative is not sensible.

In some situations it is possible to insulate to the edge of the property at ground level by excavating externally round the walls to the top of the foundations and adding a layer of waterproof insulation such as EPS (expanded polystyrene). In certain situations this may mitigate the need for under floor insulation as it isolates the ground under the house from heat loss at the edges and it can help provide thermal mass. However a judgement must be made for each particular circumstance and the proof of the success of either approach and its payback will only be obtained by monitoring fuel bills before and after.

Carbon neutral heat

The heat loss of the property should now be as low as it possibly can be (without adding heat exchange ventilation). Providing heat should therefore be a much easier task.

Biomass boilers

The biggest headache with installing a biomass boiler will be finding a space to put it. We have become accustomed to boilers for a whole house being little bigger than a kitchen wall unit. The boiler rooms that used to be built in houses prior to the 1980s have long been converted to other uses.

The best and most likely solution will be the construction of a cellar to take both the boiler and pellet store. This has the advantage of being able to be excavated to exactly fit the space requirements of the boiler and store rather than making a compromise to shoe horn them into an existing space. The pellet store should be fillable

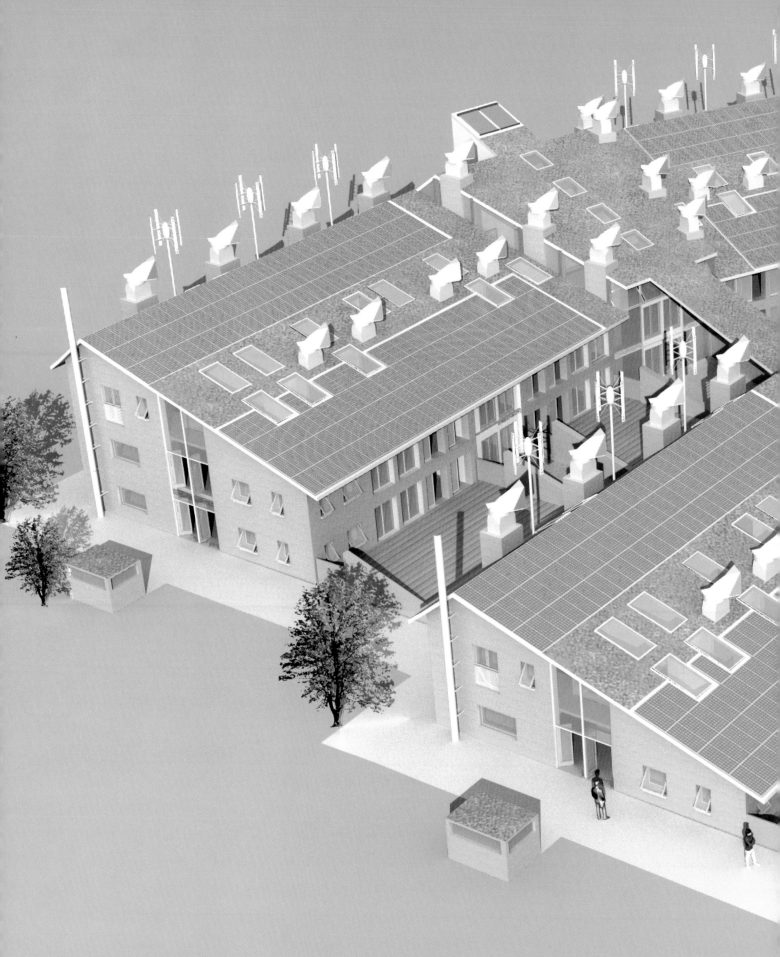

Zero carbon school

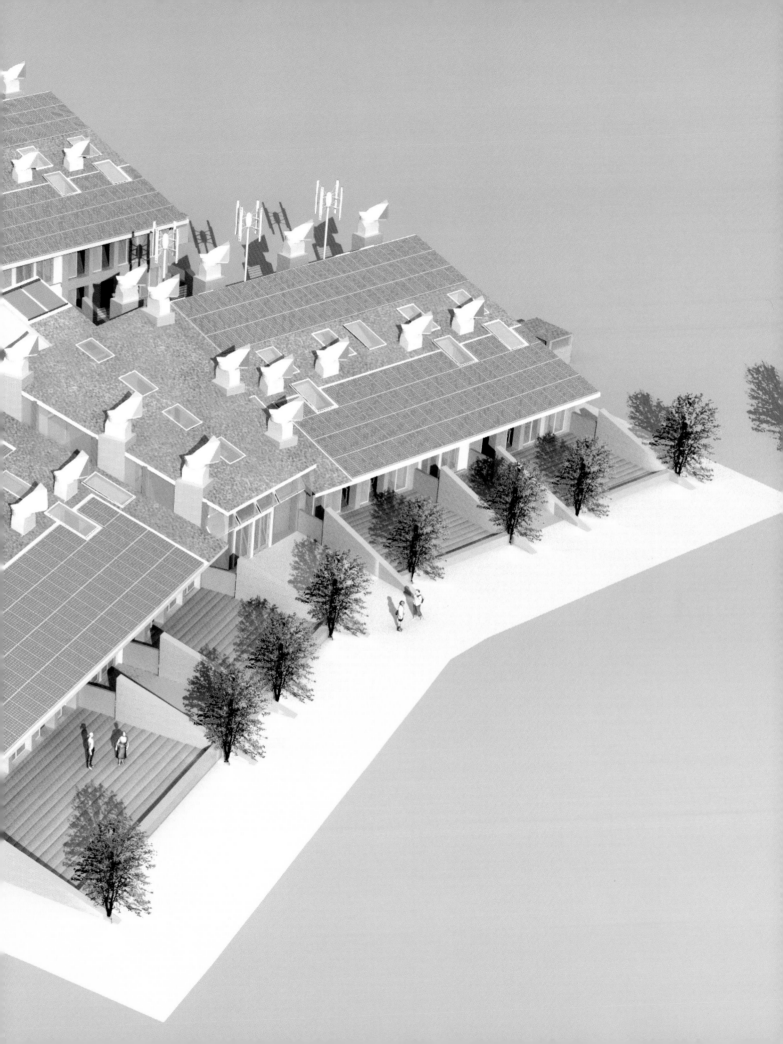

from a part of the property that a delivery tanker can reach. Generally the larger the store the better, as this avoids delivery charges for part loads (same charge whatever the size of load). Tankers start at 10 tonnes so a store should be able to take a full 10 tonnes delivery once the level gauge is indicating a delivery is required. We have found brutally simple level gauges to be best, that is a window in so you can see when it is getting low. This of course would be dependant on where the store is located.

If the property allows it, an outbuilding or garage would also be a suitable place for the boiler and proprietary pellet stores made out of fabric can be used. This is a cost effective, if space hungry solution.

Choice of biomass fuel
There are currently three main varieties of biomass fuel. These are wood pellet, wood chip and wood log. Without going into detail, these are the benefits and drawbacks of each:

- Wood pellet is the most user friendly in that it flows like a liquid, is of reliable quality and can be fed automatically into an automatic boiler that only needs monthly attention to empty an ashpan. The downside is that it is expensive, requires expensive stove technology and relies on a supply chain. All of these are being addressed (more competitive stoves and more suppliers), but like any processed fuel, you will be ransomed to the energy supplier.
- Wood chip is normally from tree surgery waste and rescued from the waste stream. It also undergoes very little processing so is generally a very sustainable fuel. However this same lack of processing can mean it is of variable quality, that is depending on the variety of trees being pruned, and/or variable moisture levels, which may mean in worst case it won't burn at all. Boilers also have to be robust enough to not break when the inevitable brick in the wood chip enters the feeding mechanism. For this reason wood chip boilers tend to be better over the 100 kW size where the machinery is much larger and more robust than is required for domestic uses.
- Wood log is the ultimate in unprocessed fuel. However this will mean the householder will have to spend time processing the fuel themselves. Delivered logs will normally need stacking for seasoning a couple of years to dry them out and bring out their fuel value (burning unseasoned logs wastes a lot of their fuel value on evaporating water). Log boilers are brutally simple and often do not even have a control mechanism more involved than an air flap on a chain connected to a safety value (too hot – less air). Hence they require no electricity for a controller, you just fill them with logs, light them and leave them to it. The load of logs then burns and heats up a very large (2,000 litres plus) water tank. This tank should then last you a number of days till you have to do the next burn.

Other fuels such as rape seed cake pellet and micanthus grass in a domestic fuel version are yet to come to market but are vital energy crops.

Solar thermal

Solar thermal panels can be mounted on most roofs providing they do not slope north. Success has been reported from mounting them on pitched roof where the ridge runs north–south with one panel on the east slope and one on the west. In the summer they are running at well under their capacity so this compromise of orientation will not effect their output. However winter may be a different matter. Only fuel bills will tell.

'J' brackets that fit under the lap of tiles or slates can be used to mount solar thermal panels on most roofs. There are then proprietary tile soakers that allow the water pipes to pass into the property.

Solar thermal panels should provide all the domestic hot water for between 50 per cent and 60 per cent of the year. Outside this time they can be plumbed to provide a useful preheat for water that is then brought up to full domestic hot water temperature by a biomass boiler.

Plumbing for biomass and solar thermal

Biomass boilers like to work at full power and then switch off. Burning at low power has the tendency to make them coke up as well as being inefficient in the use of fuel. For this reason all biomass boilers benefit from working against a large hot water cylinder (known as a thermal store or buffer vessel).

There are then various strategies for taking the heat from the thermal store. All have efficiency/cost/simplicity compromises. Our current thinking on the subject is as follows. However, this may change as more systems are installed and we receive feedback from installers and clients on the installation cost and on fuel bills. We also recognise that other, more control heavy systems may give far higher apparent efficiencies, but from experience, we are always wary of control heavy solutions as they are seldom operated correctly.

Current ZEDupgrade hot water plumbing thinking

This concept is based on the following observations:

- Unvented systems require expensive expansion vessels and come under the jurisdiction of building control.
- Unvented systems require safety blow off valves and large bore tundish pipes to the outside.
- Unvented hot water cylinders are expensive.
- To discourage the fitting of power showers, showers should be at mains pressure.

Our strategy is therefore to use two hot water tanks as thermal stores only, that is vented to a storage tank above the upper cylinder. The upper 'airing cupboard' tank would be a standard sized plumber's merchant vented copper tank. The second 'boiler room' tank would be as large as possible depending on the choice of biomass fuel taken. The water in the tanks would be dosed with an anti-corrosive additive. The tanks would share the same water (be linked). The water in the tanks would be directly heated by the solar thermal panels in one circuit from the small tank, and the boiler in another circuit, from the large tank. Since this water is dosed, it could also be used for the central heating circuit via a suitable mixer.

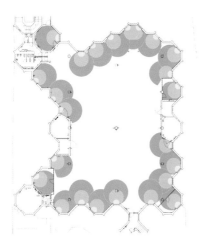

2.6.8
Existing daylight levels of an existing office building

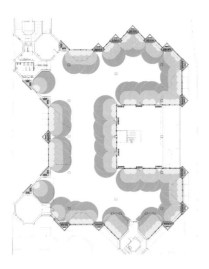

2.6.9
Proposed daylight levels with the addition of new atrium with no loss of area of commercial space

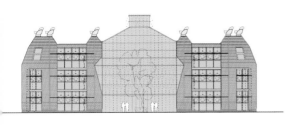

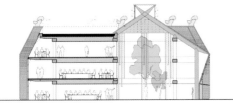

2.6.10
Proposed section and elevation of the building

Where space is at a premium, the functionality of these two tanks can be combined into one large tank at the expense of being able to make maximum use of a solar thermal system without providing a top up from the boiler. (The same energy harvest would be made but this would only preheat the water in the single large tank rather than producing water hot enough for domestic use by itself as it might be able to if it was only heating a small tank.)

To supply domestic hot water (DHW) at mains pressure, cold water would enter a hi-flow heat exchanger in/on the small water tank. If the solar thermal panels had heated up this tank sufficiently, this water would be thermostatically mixed to a safe temperature and supplied directly to the household's taps. If the water is too cool on leaving the first heat exchanger, it would continue to a similar heat exchanger in the big tank before going to the taps, again via a mixer valve.

The advantages of this system include the ability of the system to get full benefit of any preheating the solar thermal panels have managed even in winter. They may only raise the temperature of the incoming water from 5 to 20°C, but this is still 15°C of useful work and so reduces the heat that would otherwise be stripped from the biomass thermal store, hence displacing fuel use.

Thermostatically mixing the water allows the tanks to reach very high temperatures without risking scalding from the hot water they produce. After a 'burn', the water in the biomass tank may reach 95°C. The mains water passing through this may be heated up to 90°C by passing through the heat exchanger, but this is then mixed first with water from the small solar tank and then, if need be, with cold water to bring the hot water down to a safe 45°C.

By connecting the store water of the two tanks, boiling the small tank during sunny spells while the property is unoccupied can be avoided. A thermostat on the tank would detect when the tank was approaching boiling point and energise a small pump to circulate water to the large thermal store. This may also increase the usefulness of the solar thermal array into the autumn and spring due to its ability to store heat from a whole sunny spring or autumn day, rather than shutting down once the small tank had been filled. Again this would reduce the frequency of a boiler burn and reduce biomass fuel use.

Microgeneration

To become a truly Carbon Neutral Home, the ability to generate electricity must be considered. It is assumed that by this stage a ZEDupper will have already installed every energy saving fitting and white good they can and be being conscientious about phantom energy use (standby energy, phone chargers etc. being left energised).

Domestically there are currently two methods available to generate your own power. These are solar electric (known as photovoltaic (PV)) and micro wind turbines.

Domestic CHP is not seen as viable as first, it uses fossil gas as its primary fuel, and second, it is only generating electricity when it is producing heat. As heat loads have already been minimised, the opportunity to generate electricity will be limited, especially if solar thermal panels are installed.

Electricity from the sun

Solar electric is probably the easiest method of generating electricity if you have a south-facing roof. Mounting panels is relatively straightforward using the ZEDfabric 'J' brackets and uni-strut kit. The panels plug together so their voltage adds up to that required by the inverter. The inverter then converts their DC current to mains synchronised AC current. This current then pushes back into your household mains where it is first used by your household appliances. Anything left is then exported to the national grid. If you have an old electricity meter with a spinning disk it will even run backwards when you are exporting.

2.6.11
Proposed street scene

Electricity from the wind
Micro wind turbines are similar in that when spinning sufficiently, they send wild AC current to an inverter that converts it into mains synchronised AC before pushing it into the household mains.

Wind turbines tend to be much fussier about their location than PV. Generally the higher they can be, the smoother the air flow and hence the more time the will spend steadily generating. The problems first generation of wind turbines had were mainly to do with the fact that they have to generate 3 minutes of consistent power before the inverter would push into the grid. Badly positioned turbines could never achieve this.

To get a turbine in a good position requires a pole mounted to a solid part of the house structure. Ideally the post should go all the way to the ground so forces can be resolved right down to the ground floor. Chimney breasts can work well if properly pointed. Bed reinforcement using a helifix bar can be used to spread the load of the fixings. The turbine mounts to the top of the pole with its wires passing down the middle of the pole. They can then either leave the pole via a hole at a point that is not structurally critical, or leave at the bottom of the pole. From here they go to the inverter.

Micro wind turbines have had some bad press, but we firmly believe that even if their potential yield is only a quarter of what was originally claimed, and once the export protocol problems are resolved, they will be a very cost effective way of generating power for the home.

2.6.12
Existing view of office building

Wind-assisted stack effect heat exchange ventilation (WASAHEV)
Although not included in the general recommended menu, WASAHEV should be mentioned as in some circumstances it will be easy to install and have working effectively. A house with an existing large multiple flue chimney breast could have a wind cowl added without too much difficulty. The rules for coal fireplace flues are very similar to those for passive ventilation ducts, so each room that was originally provided with a fire place could be provided with heat exchange ventilation.

If such a house was to be upgraded and the full range of upgrades already discussed could also be applied, it is possible that full carbon neutrality might be achieved within a UK wood fuel footprint. True environmental sustainability.

Upgrading existing workplaces
Most existing workplaces can use the same zero heating/zero cooling specification building physics model and supply chain to achieve a step change reduction in their carbon footprint. Exposing concrete ceilings, installing high density screed raised

2.6.13
Proposed refit to existing building fabric

floor tiles and external insulation, improving daylighting, adding efficient glazing and passive heat recovery ventilation will transform the most inefficient building into a low carbon exemplar. The following steps have been proposed for Northleigh House – an existing electrically heated and air conditioned deep plan office housing the Chichester planning department. Plant failures were becoming increasingly common as the existing mechanical and electrical equipment came to the end of its working life, leaving the council with a large bill to replace and upgrade services to modern comfort expectations. ZEDfactory proposed removing a central portion of the floorplate to create an internal atrium – greatly improving the daylight levels and internal working conditions for staff. A new superinsulated weather boarded rainscreen skin with natural heat recovery ventilation, opening windows and faced air distribution made the perimeter warmer in winter and careful shade/maintenance walkways prevented summer overheating. The fully engineered and costed study showed how the environmental upgrades could transform the experience of working in the building, improve productivity, and achieve an 80 per cent reduction in the carbon footprint – for the same cost as replacing the existing air conditioning plant and a conventional refurbishment.

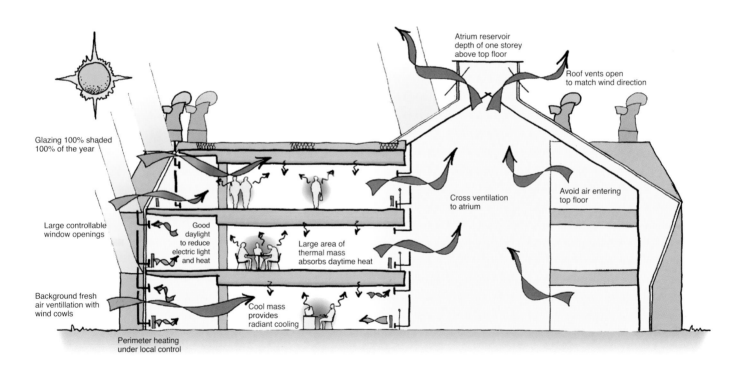

Atrium reservoir
depth of one storey
above top floor

Roof vents open
to match wind direction

Glazing 100% shaded
100% of the year

Cross ventilation
to atrium

Avoid air entering
top floor

Large controllable
window openings

Good
daylight
to reduce
electric light
and heat

Large area of
thermal mass
absorbs daytime heat

Background fresh
air ventillation with
wind cowls

Cool mass
provides
radiant cooling

Perimeter heating
under local control

2.6.14
Building physics principles in a workplace

2.7 Achieving Zero Carbon Emissions on a Large Development

Achieving Zero Carbon on a large development can give the opportunity for sharing efficient plant through community heating schemes such as a large biomass heating system. Combined heat and power (CHP) systems can be a very efficient way of producing site heating and 'free' electricity. Biomass CHP systems are coming to market which do this for (almost) zero carbon emissions.

The development also gives the opportunity for sharing carbon offset technologies. Photovoltaic panels can be put on south-facing roofs and facades regardless of whether they benefit that particular building or the site as a whole. In some cases it is also appropriate to put larger wind turbines on the site.

The site will also have additional infrastructure such as street lighting to be considered. On a large development wider issues can be considered such as ways in which public or shared transport can be incorporated, home working encouraged and schemes to reduce food miles.

Bobby Gilbert & Associates and Best Foot Forward have developed the concept of a carbon emissions accounting sheet where every source of carbon emissions and every means of offsetting carbon emissions are added to the account with the aim of getting a result of zero emissions. The ZEDphysics model is integrated into an example of such a tool, Carbon Mixer™ developed by Bobby Gilbert & Associates, by providing templates of building performance and plant performance. These form a database from which the developer can mix and match building types, plant and renewables quickly and easily to get an estimate of the carbon emissions of a particular site.

Carbon Mixer™ can be configured for a particular location/climate and for use by a particular audience. The following case study shows a configuration available from the North East Assembly for planners and developers in the north east of England. Carbon Mixer™ is used to get a ballpark figure for likely reductions of carbon emissions within five minutes.

Development of tools such as this is essential to enable local government to implement carbon emission reductions.

Case study
Carbon Mixer NE – a micro-renewables toolkit for the north east of England

Carbon Mixer NE was developed by Bobby Gilbert & Associates for the North East Assembly. It is used by planners and developers to help determine how a development can incorporate 10 per cent embedded renewable energy generation. The following is an overview of the process.

The Carbon Mixer interface

The Carbon Mixer NE user interface allows specification of the building and other energy demands on a site, the unfuelled energy supply systems (wind, PV, solar hot water), and the fuelled energy supply systems (boilers, heat pumps, CHP, tri-generation, etc). The graphs on the right give instant feedback on the effect of any changes in terms of reduction in CO_2 emissions (compared with a user defined baseline), reduction in the use of non-renewable energy, a monthly breakdown of energy demand (below zero) and supply (above zero) by type and system, and a monthly breakdown of CO_2 emissions.

2.7.1
Energy demands and supplies are entered into the
Carbon Mixer™ interface to find CO_2 emissions

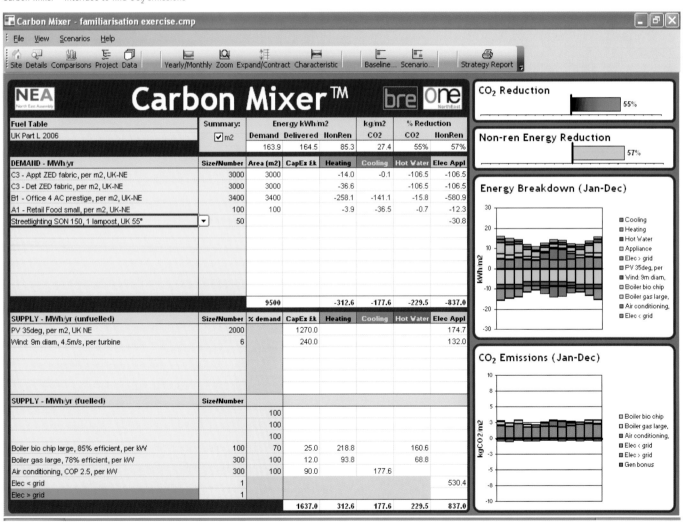

Overview of the process

Buildings have energy demands for heating, cooling, hot water, and power for electrical appliances. Carbon Mixer™ allows you to specify a site from a single building up to a large multi-use development by choosing from a drop down list of building types for the site, each of which will have a demand profile.

Heating, cooling and power supply systems are then chosen to meet these demands by burning fuel either directly or indirectly at a power station. Systems available include boilers of various fuel types, heat pumps, combined heat and power, tri-generation, etc. Pure renewable systems requiring no fuel (e.g. photo-voltaic, wind, solar hot water) can also be specified. Carbon Mixer calculates the amount of fuel and power required by these systems.

Carbon dioxide emissions for the site are then calculated by Carbon Mixer based on this fuel/power requirement.

Having calculated an initial baseline for CO_2 emissions, Carbon Mixer can be used to change the mix of building types, heat and power systems, renewables, etc and a new emissions scenario can then be calculated and compared with the baseline. The baseline may also be moved if the 'goalposts' for the comparison need to be altered. For example it is usually a requirement to show how much CO_2 can be reduced by improving a building, and then how much it can be further improved by using sourced of renewable heat and power. Figure 2.7.2 summarises this process.

Each of the systems specified can have a capital cost associated with it as well as an annual service and maintenance cost. Each of the fuel types also have a cost associated. These costs are used by Carbon Mixer to calculate capital costs, annual

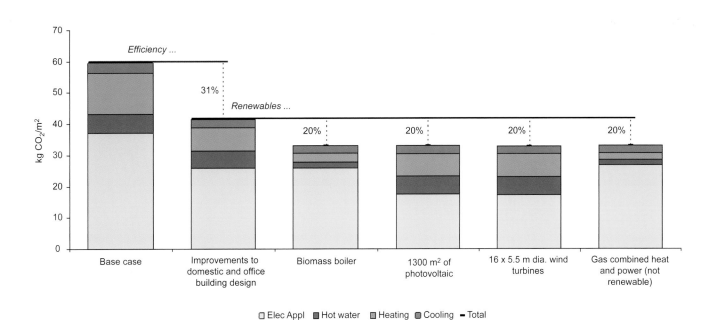

2.7.2
Different mixes of building types and energy supply systems can be compared for CO_2 emissions

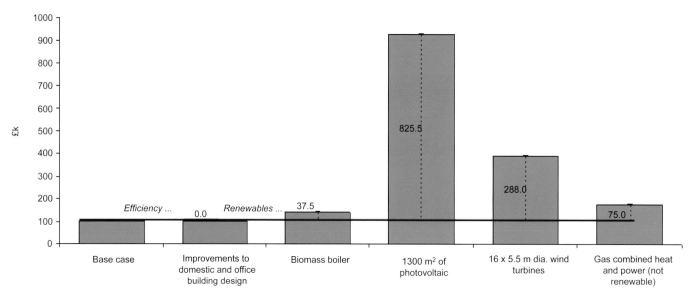

2.7.3
Different options can be compared for up front costs

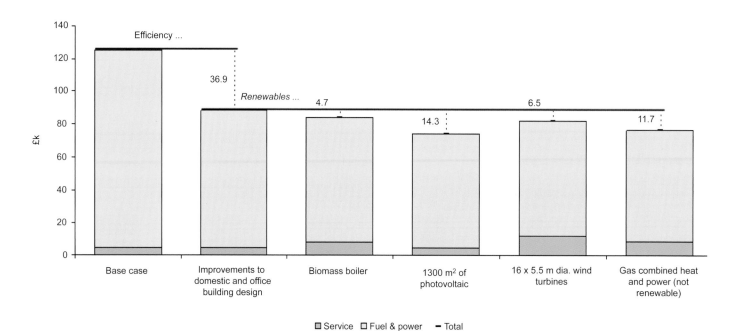

2.7.4
Annual costs for fuel and service may reveal savings
compared with the baseline

costs, and payback periods which can also be compared between different scenarios. Figure 2.7.3 and 2.7.4 show examples of this.

Carbon Mixer NE comes with a locked database of benchmark data taken from publicly available sources and adapted for North East England climate conditions. This can be used to get initial 'ballpark' estimates. Users can then justify changes from this estimate with hand calculations or with Carbon Mixer *Professional* they may add their own data to the databases to refine these calculations and so the results given can then be as accurate as required depending on the accuracy of the data input by the user. Typical sources of more accurate data are detailed simulations of building and systems performance or measurements of buildings and supply systems in use.

Finally a report can be printed off to support a planning application. This will show the reduction in non-renewable energy and CO_2 emissions for the energy and renewables strategy for the site giving details of this and the baseline case it is compared with.

Carbon Mixer Professional

With Carbon Mixer *Professional* a user can build up a valuable database which may contain a portfolio of actual performance of buildings on their estate. Alternatively it may be used as a storage area for performance characteristics of various buildings that have been simulated for consultancy work. It may also be used to store the performance characteristics of renewable and other heat and power systems. The easy access to this data, and the ability to mix and match combinations will form a valuable tool in designing low carbon developments and managing the improvements to existing developments.

The latest information on Carbon Mixer is available at www.bobbygilbert.co.uk or at www.zedstandards.com.

Mixed-use regeneration in Changsha – creating a new urban landscape

2.8 Building Fabric and Insulation

Walls, floors and ceilings

The structure of ZED houses is characterised by high thermal mass, tight sealing from air infiltration, and high levels of insulation. Figures 2.8.1 and 2.8.2 show a section through the walls and floor/ceilings of two types of ZED house – the BedZED blockwork style design and the RuralZED timber frame with heavyweight panel design – which are compared with a typical lightweight Building Regulations house.

Figure 2.8.1 shows sections through the *exterior* walls of the three buildings with U-values marked. The Building Regulations house will lose almost three times as much heat through the walls as the ZED house.

The inside face of the walls is most important to the thermal performance. BedZED clearly has the most thermal mass exposed to the inside of the room with 100 mm of dense concrete block. RuralZED has 45 mm of dense concrete panel. The lightweight house is shown for comparison – it has no dense thermal mass exposed to the room and the moderately dense brick outer skin is effectively shielded from the room by the 90 mm of insulation.

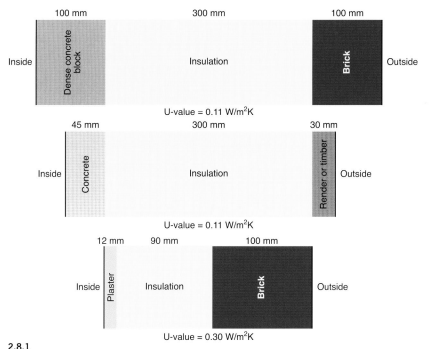

2.8.1

Sections through (top to bottom) BedZED, RuralZED and lightweight exterior walls

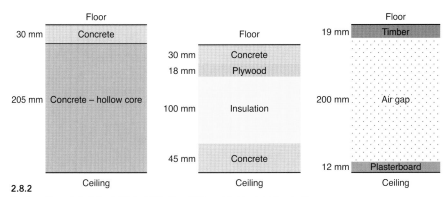

2.8.2

Sections through (left to right) BedZED, RuralZED and lightweight floor/ceilings

The *internal* walls are assumed to be of lightweight stud construction in all three cases.

Figure 2.8.2 shows sections through the floor/ceiling constructions for the three buildings. Again BedZED has the most thermal mass exposed to the rooms with over 200 mm of concrete separating the two floors. The hollow core concrete was represented in the physics model as 150 mm in thickness to take account of the absence of mass in the cores. RuralZED has 30 mm of dense concrete paving exposed at the floor and 45 mm of dense concrete slab exposed at the ceiling. The lightweight house is shown for comparison and has a standard floor construction with no dense thermal mass exposed at the floor or ceiling. No carpeting is assumed in all cases.

The lower storey floor and the upper storey ceiling are of similar construction to those shown above, with just the floor layer or ceiling layer used as appropriate.

The roof of the ZED houses has 300 mm of insulation. The roof of the lightweight house has 150 mm of insulation.

Windows

The windows are low-e double glazed in all cases with a U-value of 1.9, though windows have been used in ZED buildings with U-values as low as 1.0–1.5.

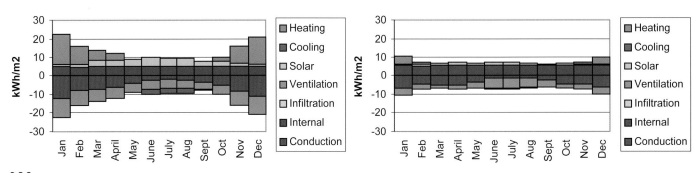

2.8.3

Building regulations house (left) compared with RuralZED house (right)

The heat energy balance charts (Figure 2.8.3) show how the heating energy is reduced in the ZEDfabric building.

Winter

Much less heating (red) is needed for the ZED house, which is heated sufficiently for most of the year from the solar gain (yellow) and from heat given off by people, lighting and equipment (purple).

This is because less heat is lost through the fabric of the building (brown) due to the superinsulation, and also because of the buffering effect of the sunspace. The ventilation system (mid blue) is also more efficient as it has a passive heat recovery system. In sunny months (March) the heat in the sunspace is sufficient that air from the sunspace can be used to warm the house by opening the French windows, it can be seen that the net ventilation losses that month are low due to gains from the sunspace. In less sunny months, the air temperature in the sunspace will still provide an effective buffer to heat loss through this wall.

Summer

The heating system has been turned off, but heat is still being gained by the house from the people, lighting, and equipment (purple). The amount of solar gain (pale yellow) is lower and better controlled than the Building Regulations house due to the design ensuring shading from much of the summer sun.

The building doesn't cool much through the fabric (brown) due to the superinsulation. Instead night cooling from cool air in the ventilated sunspace (mid blue) removes heat soaked up by the thermal mass of the building during the day. This is supplemented by air through open windows and the ventilation system. The use of cooling (dark blue) is negligible, suggesting that this design would not overheat if cooling were not included. See overheating assessment later.

Case study
European Union Performance of Buildings requirements and UK Building Regulations: RuralZED design part L1, SAP 2006

A detached version of the north/south RuralZED design was used as a test case for the proposed new UK Building Regulations designed to meet the requirements of the EU Performance of Buildings requirement (these have since come into force). The assessment showed it to achieve a top (A) rating. See Part 3 for a detailed discussion of RuralZED.

The SAP rating was close to a maximum efficiency component of 100, with the probability of this increasing to a maximum of 120 as an energy producer when the photovoltaic panels on the roof are taken into account in the final version of the regulations.

Background

Changes to Part L of the Building Regulations Conservation of Fuel and Power come into effect on 1 April 2006. Under the EU Performance of Buildings Directive it is now mandatory to look at the performance of the dwelling in terms of its energy consumption and hence its effect on the environment through its carbon emissions.

To effect this Part L1 lays down a procedure for estimating the Target Emission Rate for a dwelling constructed from a set of criteria defined in the approved documents, and then comparing this to a Design Emission Rate calculated for the dwelling based on its actual design parameters.

Method of calculation and scope

The whole calculation process is known as the Standard Assessment Procedure or SAP. The calculation is based on the energy balance, taking into account a range of factors that contribute to its energy efficiency:

- materials used for the construction of the dwelling
- thermal insulation of the building fabric which must meet set minimum standards
- ventilation characteristics of the dwelling and the ventilation equipment
- efficiency and control of the heating systems
- solar gains through openings to the dwelling
- the fuel used to provide space and water heating, ventilation and lighting
- renewable energy technologies.

The calculation is independent of factors related to the individual characteristics of the household occupying the dwelling when the rating is calculated, for example:

- household size and composition
- ownership and efficiency of particular domestic appliances
- individual heating patterns and temperatures.

The Rating is also independent of location so the calculated Rating is valid in all parts of the United Kingdom.

For apartments the rating calculated applies only to the individual apartment and does not apply to the common or access areas.

Other aspects of the SAP calculation include:

- a sliding scale of 1–100 with 100 representing a zero energy cost. This scale has scope to go beyond 100 should the dwelling be a net exporter of energy
- energy for lighting is taken into account
- solar water heating can be taken into account
- renewable energy sources can be included.

Design standards

To obtain an Energy Performance Certificate the Standard Assessment Procedure must be undertaken. This involves calculating a Target Emission Rate (TER) and a Design Emission Rate (DER). Part of this calculation involves the inclusion of an Improvement Factor. This has been decreed within all Part L documentation to be a minimum of 20 per cent. This means that the design building must perform at least 20 per cent better than an equivalent notional building. So even if the dwelling was built to the same standards as the notional building it would still have to be improved by 20 per cent in order to gain a pass and be awarded a certificate.

One of the major influencing factors in the assessment is the choice of fuel for the primary heating system. All fuels have a Fuel Factor, which varies from 1 for gas and biofuels up to 1.47 for electricity. The high factor for electricity represents the inefficiencies incurred in its production and distribution – to produce one unit of electricity requires the input of about three units of a primary fuel.

A Design Emission Rate is calculated for the actual design dwelling. If the DER is less than the TER, the dwelling will be awarded a pass and an Energy Performance Certificate can be issued. This certificate will reflect the SAP rating for the building on the 1–100 scale. This scale relates to a grade for the dwelling of A–G, with A being the highest performing building and G being the lowest; this is the same scale that is applied to the energy efficiency of domestic appliances with the EU Energy label.

SAP rating for RuralZED development

A typical RuralZED as shown in Figure 2.8.5 is designed to perform to significantly higher standards than those prescribed by the Building Regulations.

The building fabric is very highly insulated to minimise heat loss to the external environment and a double height south facing sunspace, thermally separated from the dwelling, acts as a thermal barrier and assists in reducing heating requirements during mid seasons.

The building uses a wood chip boiler to provide spaceheating. This type of fuel is a renewable resource and hence has a very low environmental impact. The boiler also

2.8.4
RuralZED model for SAP calculation

heats hot water in conjunction with a solar hot water generation system. The solar system will have enough capacity to supply all of the dwelling's hot water requirements during the summer months when the main heating is switched off; it will also provide a proportion of the hot water during the winter period. All the pipework and water storage will be highly insulated (150 mm on tank) to keep heat losses to a minimum.

The calculations for a RuralZED clearly demonstrate its performance much beyond a Building Regulations compliant building.

A dwelling with the same form as a RuralZED, if built to the specification as detailed in the building regulations, will have a Carbon Emission Rate of 27.9 Kg CO_2/m^2. A ZED will have an emission rate of just 4.59 Kg CO_2/m^2. This gives a graphic illustration of how much better the ZED performs than a typical regulations compliant building, and how far much more than the mandated 20 per cent energy saving can be achieved.

This emission rate gives the ZED a SAP rating of 90+ and an A band Energy Label.

There is potential for the ZED to get an even higher rating through the use of photovoltaic cells to produce the dwelling's electrical requirements and export surplus back into the grid. It is conceivable that with enough Photovoltaic arrays, the dwelling could gain the maximum SAP rating of 120, though the exact process for accounting for this is still being determined in the new SAP process.

Conclusion

It can be seen that the fundamental principles on which the ZED is based far exceed the requirements of Part L, which has been deemed the minimum standard for good practice in UK domestic development in the twenty-first century. ZED dwellings have very low environmental impact and through the extended use of sustainable technologies have the potential to produce more energy than they consume.

The ZED dwelling is in the very highest band available under the Energy Label and reflects its low energy, low impact credentials. ZEDs have very low environmental impact due to their method of construction and the materials from which they are constructed, and their aggregation into communities further increases their value and impact on the world about us.

Case study
Thermographic imaging of ZED buildings – achieving good quality building fabric in practice

Thermographic imaging is a vivid way of showing whether the actual thermal performance of a building lives up to the intentions of the design.[1] It provides a way of assessing the quality of the build, spotting missing insulation, windows with poor seals and so on, which can then be rectified.

The following examples are taken from a thermal imaging assessment carried out by Living Space Sciences (www.ls-sciences.com). This service is available for all ZED homes. Showing an example report to the builder in advance of the build goes a long way towards ensuring top quality workmanship and a trouble free sign-off of the construction!

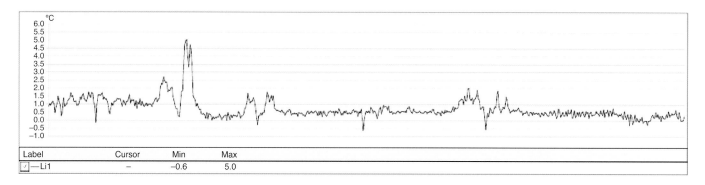

2.8.5
1980s house (left, background) gives a blue glow in thermal image to show greater heat loss than ZED buildings (right, foreground)

Label	Cursor	Min	Max
☑ —Li1	–	–0.6	5.0

2.8.6
Graph taken from line 1 across thermal image shows considerably more heat loss from 1980s building (left 1/4 of trace) than from BedZED (right 3/4 of trace)

Figure 2.8.5 shows the external temperature of a ZED building (foreground right), and a traditional (late 1980s) building (left). The air temperature was -0.5°C. Pink areas show where there is negligible heat loss, that is, most of the ZED building. The image shows that the insulated walls of the traditional building are nonetheless losing as much heat as the ZED windows and considerably more where cold bridging is apparent at the junction of the floor with the wall.

Figure 2.8.6 shows the temperature along line 1 on the image. The traditional building is mostly about 1°C warmer than the ZED building, implying significantly increased heat loss of over 12 W for each square metre of wall area, or 1.2 kW for a 10 m x 10 m wall (based on CIBSE values for external surface thermal resistance).

The histograms in Figure 2.8.7 show the temperature distribution of the two windows shown as Ar1 and Ar2 on the image. Much of the window on the traditional

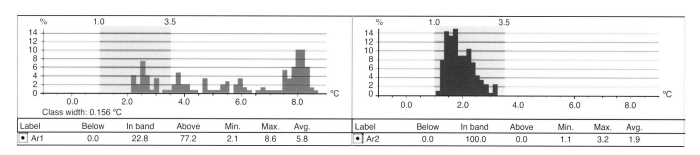

Label	Below	In band	Above	Min.	Max.	Avg.
◉ Ar1	0.0	22.8	77.2	2.1	8.6	5.8

Label	Below	In band	Above	Min.	Max.	Avg.
◉ Ar2	0.0	100.0	0.0	1.1	3.2	1.9

2.8.7
Temperature distribution of 1980s building window (left) shows considerably more heat loss than from BedZED window (right)

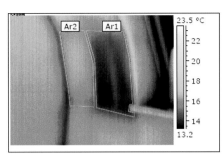

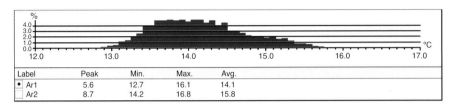

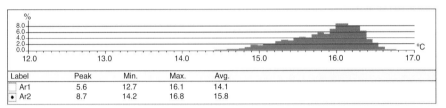

2.8.8

Thermal imaging shows missing insulation, invisible to a normal camera

building is 6°C warmer than the ZED window. This will be partly due to poor glazing, but may also be due to poor sealing compared with the ZED window.

The images in Figure 2.8.8 show an area (Ar1) of missing insulation on a wall. This is of course invisible when looking at the wall without thermal imaging technology (right). The histograms show that the wall is 2°C cooler at this point.

Figure 2.8.9 highlights a window that needs attention due to a poor seal allowing cold air to enter. The image also shows the small area of cold bridging around the edges of the triple glazing caused by the aluminium spacers. This is why the effective thermal resistance of a window is always lower on average than the theoretical value at the centre of the window pane.

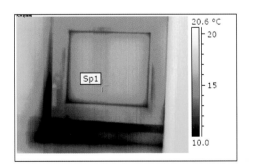

2.8.9

A poor window seal shows up with thermal imaging as does cold bridging around the edge of the glazing panel.

2.9 ZEDfactory Wind Cowl Passive Heat Recovery Ventilation System

The ZEDfactory Wind Cowl passive heat recovery ventilation system supplies and extracts air to and from a building to maintain good air quality while minimising heat loss.

Passive ventilation systems typically rely on trickle ventilators in windows for air inlet and stack effect ducting systems which work like chimneys, relying on the buoyancy of the warm air in the building to rise up a vertical duct to be exhausted through an outlet in the roof. These outlets can be designed so that airflow across them from the wind results in negative pressure and helps draw out the exhaust air.

Active ventilation systems typically are driven by electrical fans and have dedicated inlet ducts as well as outlet ducts. These ducts can be brought together to pass through a heat exchanger where the incoming air gains heat from the outgoing air, reducing the amount of heat loss. They can often be over 70 per cent effective, but the energy recovered through the heat exchanger is offset by the energy required to drive the electrical fans.

The ZEDfactory Wind Cowl works like an active ventilation system, having dedicated inlet and outlet ducts and a heat recovery system, but instead of using electrical fans to drive the air flow it uses the wind to create both positive pressure at the inlet and negative pressure at the outlet, ensuring a throughput of air with no electrical input. In low wind conditions it will continue to produce reasonable ventilation levels through stack effect.

The heat recovery system used is 70 per cent efficient. The effect of the heat recovery system can be seen in Figure 2.9.4 which shows how the loss of energy through ventilation is much reduced with the heat recovery system (blue bars).

Removing the heat recovery unit (right) increases the heating load.

2.9.1
The original wind cowls provide efficient ventilation at BedZED

2.9.2
Design iterations reduce the size of the wind cowl and bulk manufacture brings down price

2.9.3
The wind cowl heat exchanger is 70% efficient at pre-warming incoming air with heat from exhaust air.

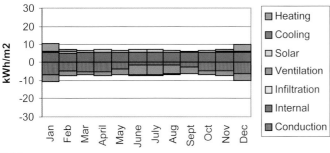
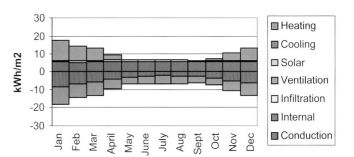

2.9.4
Without the passive heat recovery ventilation system (right) the ventilation losses increase resulting in increased heating load

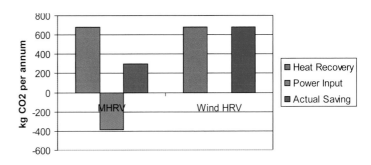

2.9.5
Much of the heating CO$_2$ savings are lost running the electric fans in a mechanical heat recovery ventilation system

Heat recovery ventilation and CO$_2$ emissions

A ventilation system that includes heat recovery will reduce the heating requirement of a building and hence the associated CO$_2$ emissions. Consider the example of a house containing a volume of air of 380 m^3 with a ventilation rate of 60 l/s (just over half an air change per hour). This is typical of the capacity of a single Wind Cowl system. If we assume the heating season is 9 months of the year and during that time the outdoor temperature is on average 10°C and the indoor temperature 20°C, the rate of energy extract in this scenario is 780 W. With a heat recovery unit operating at 70 per cent efficiency, this will drop by 546 W, which adds up to a saving of almost 3,600 kWh of heat energy over the 9-month period. If the heat is provided by a gas powered system this would result in a reduction of 684 kg of CO$_2$.[1]

However if the heat recovery ventilation system is not passive and requires an electric fan to power it then this will result in some CO$_2$ emissions, so will reduce the overall effectiveness. If we assume that a pair of 50 W fans are required (supply and extract) to force 60 l/s through the ductwork for 9 months of the year (windows can be opened in the summer) then this will require 657 kWh of electrical energy. If mains electricity is used this will result in an emission of 388 kg of CO$_2$, which more than halves the effectiveness of the heat recovery ventilation system, as shown in Figure 2.9.5.

This often results in a system with a negative payback, as electrical energy usually costs considerably more than the thermal energy (typically gas) that it is saving.

The Wind Cowl systems have no electrical energy requirement and instead are powered by the very air that is used to ventilate the building. The ZEDphysics model is used to quantify the ability of the Wind Cowl system to supply ventilation so that it can be designed into new buildings to provide the maximum reduction of CO$_2$ emissions.

The performance of a Wind Cowl system

The performance of the Wind Cowl system is based on a number of effects which are included in the ZEDphysics model. These are:

- Wind Cowl performance characteristic which has been assessed during wind tunnel testing
- ducting resistance characteristics calculated from standard design tables (test results could also be used if available)
- stack effect pressure changes based on mean stack height of the system and temperature difference
- background infiltration levels assessed from pressure tests and air change tests
- weather (wind speed and temperature) based on a year of representative hourly measurements from a local weather station.

The overall system is largely self-regulating so that good ventilation rates are nearly always achieved. When wind speeds are low, stack effect will perform a base level of ventilation until the wind picks up again. As wind speeds get high, the air flow is limited both by a bypass valve in the cowl opening, and by the increase in resistive pressure in the duct work. The physics behind each of the effects is described below. Each of these has a characteristic property and once calculated, these can be combined to give the overall building ventilation characteristic.

Wind Cowl characteristic

The characteristic of the Wind Cowl, that is, its ability to supply air flow at different wind speeds for different resistive pressures, has undergone a number of wind tunnel tests at the National Physics Laboratory.[2] Figure 2.9.6 shows an example of a Wind Cowl being tested in a wind tunnel. The results are used to calibrate the cowl and produce characteristics (Figure 2.9.7).

Once the cowl has been characterised, a two dimensional formula can be used to predict the flow rate as a function of resistive pressure and wind speed within the tested range of the cowl. The same process is carried out for both the cowl *supply* and *extract* characteristics. The cowl can now be treated as if it were two (wind speed dependent) fans, one supplying air and one extracting air.

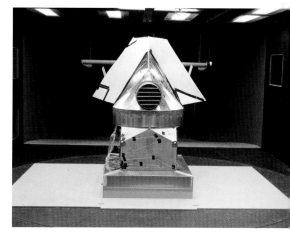

2.9.6
A cowl being wind tunnel tested

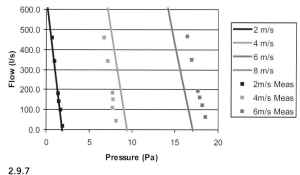 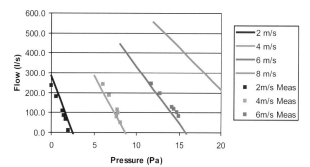

2.9.7
Wind Cowl characteristic showing wind tunnel measured values where available

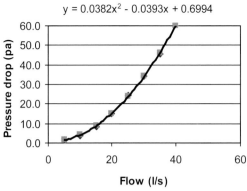

$$y = 0.0382x^2 - 0.0393x + 0.6994$$

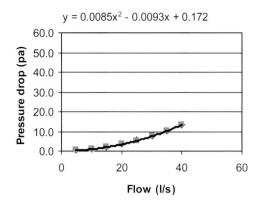

$$y = 0.0085x^2 - 0.0093x + 0.172$$

2.9.8
Calculated characteristic for a single length of duct work
(left) and for a system of eight supply ducts (right)

Ducting characteristic

The ductwork in the building also needs to be characterised. This is usually done by using standard design formulae to calculate the pressure drop across the duct work for a given flow rate.[3] Very low pressure drops are achieved by using large diameter pipes and having a maximum of two 45° bends.

Characteristics for ductwork and the mathematical formula for a trend line used in the physics model are shown in Figure 2.9.8. The standard Wind Cowl can have up to eight supply ducts and eight extract ducts. The characteristics for these are combined as a resistance network. This results in a lower overall resistance and so, not surprisingly, more ducts results in a larger flow of air into the house (though slightly less per duct). A similar characteristic would be calculated for the extract ducts.

Stack effect

The average height difference between the duct outlets and the Wind Cowl, and the temperature difference between indoor and outdoor temperature, will drive the stack effect passive ventilation. This is a particularly important effect when there is low wind. The stack effect is assessed by calculating the pressure difference caused by

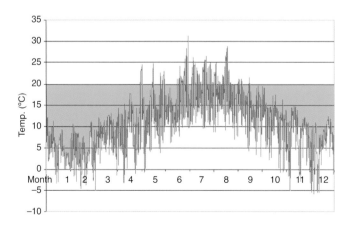

2.9.9
Outdoor temperature variation for a year showing stack
effect potential (shaded)

the temperature and height differences,[4] and then applying this as an offset to the ducting resistance pressure.

Figure 2.9.9 shows a trace of the hourly temperature for a year in south-east England. The difference between the outdoor temperature and the indoor temperature will drive the stack effect ventilation due to the relative buoyancy of the hot indoor air. This is shown as the shaded area (assuming the indoor temperature to be 20°C). It will be greatest in winter and during the night in summer.

Infiltration

Air can also enter the building by infiltration. The rate of infiltration can be estimated by pressure testing the building to 50 pascals, as required by UK Building Regulations, and dividing the pressurised air change rate by twenty,[5] or by taking direct air change measurements using tracer gas decay testing which involves releasing a tiny quantity of a trace gas into a building and measuring its dispersal over time. See the case study on measurement of infiltration and ventilation of ZED houses for more details on this method of testing.

The whole building ventilation characteristic

The effects described above can be combined for a given building in the form of a building characteristic plot. The Wind Cowl will try to produce a certain air flow for a given duct pressure, however the duct pressure will vary depending on the flow of air through it. This balancing process forms a natural control mechanism for the system because if high winds result in increased air speeds, the pressure in the duct will increase and control the air flow.

In the physics model the effects are equated against each other and solved to find the air flow and balancing pressure. This is carried out for a range of wind speeds and air temperatures in order to produce the whole building ventilation characteristic. This can also be carried out for each hour of an example year of weather conditions to simulate the behaviour for any given climate.

The example shown in Figure 2.9.10 is for the extract system of a three storey building with an internal temperature of 21°C.

Where measurements of real weather are combined with the building ventilation characteristic the relative importance of the different parts of the characteristic can

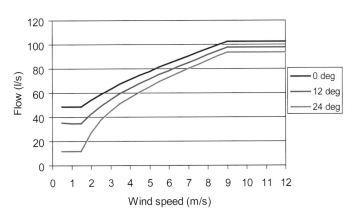

2.9.10

Example of building ventilation extract characteristic
including effects of wind cowl, ducting and infiltration

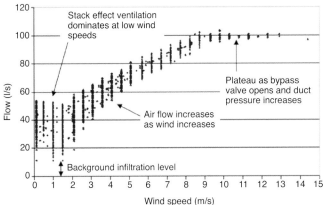

2.9.11

Building ventilation characteristic for
south-east England

Table 2.9.1: Three-storey building with two vents on top floor, three on mid floor, and two on bottom floor for extract and the same for supply. Internal temperature assumed to be 21°C. Infiltration rate 0.11ac/h or 11 l/s

	Extract				Supply		
Flow (l/s)	Outdoor Temperature C			Flow (l/s)	Outdoor Temperature C		
Wind speed (m/s)	0 deg	12 deg	24 deg	Wind speed (m/s)	0 deg	12 deg	24 deg
0.5	48	35	11	0.5	48	34	11
1.0	48	35	11	1.0	48	34	11
1.5	48	35	11	1.5	50	38	15
2.0	54	43	27	2.0	55	44	30
2.5	59	49	38	2.5	58	49	38
3.0	63	55	45	3.0	62	53	43
3.5	67	59	51	3.5	65	57	48
4.0	71	64	56	4.0	68	61	53
4.5	74	68	61	4.5	71	64	57
5.0	78	71	65	5.0	74	68	61
5.5	81	75	69	5.5	78	71	65
6.0	84	78	73	6.0	81	75	69
6.5	87	82	76	6.5	84	78	73
7.0	90	85	80	7.0	87	82	76
7.5	93	88	83	7.5	90	85	80
8.0	96	91	87	8.0	94	89	84
8.5	99	95	90	8.5	97	93	88
9.0	102	98	93	9.0	101	97	93
9.5	102	98	93	9.5	101	97	93
10.0	102	98	93	10.0	101	97	93
10.5	102	98	93	10.5	101	97	93
11.0	102	98	93	11.0	101	97	93
11.5	102	98	93	11.5	101	97	93
12.0	102	98	93	12.0	101	97	93

be seen. Figure 2.9.11 shows the airflow performance for an example building in southern England. At low wind speeds stack effect and infiltration are the dominant effects. As the wind speed increases, the forcing effect of the Wind Cowl dominates. The rate of increase drops off as the back pressure from the ducts increases. Eventually the characteristic hits a plateau as the bypass valve opens in the Wind Cowl.

Table 2.9.1 is a pre-calculated air flow characteristic for a three-storey house with ZEDstandard ducting arrangements.

Case study
Sensitivity analysis of the Wind Cowl system in different conditions

The whole building ventilation characteristic was used to compare the sensitivity of the system to different weather conditions and different climates. The following shows an assessment of the levels of ventilation of a three-storey building through eight ducts, two on the top floor, three on the mid floor and two on the ground floor. The assessment was carried out for two sites in London, one with a low average wind speed of 3.2 m/s and one with a higher average windspeed of 4.4 m/s. It was also carried out using weather data from Beijing in China to see how it would cope in a climate with high summer temperatures and very low wind speeds.

Gatwick
Annual average wind speed – 3.2 m/s

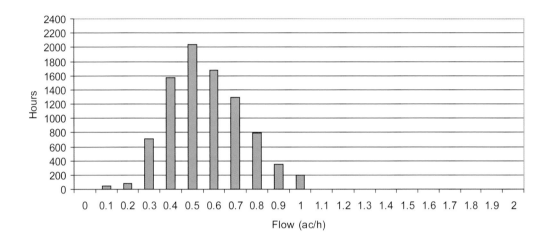

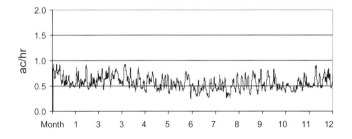
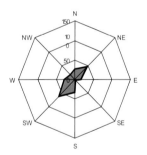

2.9.12 (clockwise from top)
Hours of air flow at each level (air changes per hour)
Available wind energy (kWh/m²)
24 hour averaged flow (ac/hr)

This first example uses weather data from Gatwick for a below average (for London) year of wind. The top graph in Figure 2.9.12 shows the distribution of the air change rates over the course of the year. The majority of the time the ventilation rate is between 0.5 and 1 air changes per hour. The graph below shows that it falls below this rate generally in summer, when there can be reduced stack effect as well as low wind. Night cooling for the house will ensure that it receives purge ventilation through open windows at these times.

The wind rose graph shows the amount and direction of wind energy which gives a visual assessment of the site. The direction is not important as the cowls will rotate to face the wind.

Heathrow
Annual average wind speed – 4.4 m/s

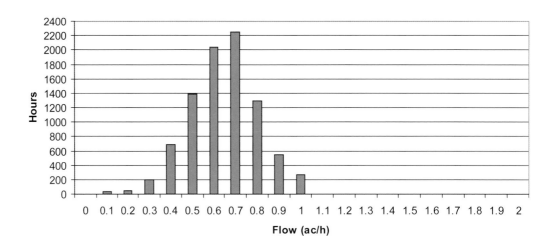

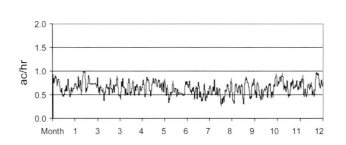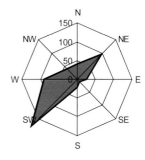

2.9.13 (clockwise from top)
Hours of air flow at each level (air changes per hour)
Available wind energy (kWh/m^2)
24 hour averaged flow (ac/hr)

The Heathrow example (Figure 2.9.13) is for a higher wind speed more typical of London. It can be seen that the air change rate is still between 0.5 and 1 air changes per hour for the majority of the time with fewer occasions in summer where it drops below this. The maximum rate is much the same as the previous, less windy, site showing that the bypass valve in the wind cowl, and the increased back pressure in the ducting, effectively stabilise the air change rates.

Beijing

Annual average wind speed – 2.5 m/s

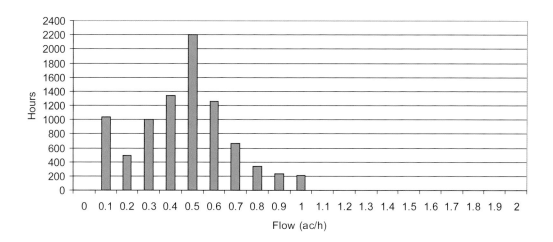

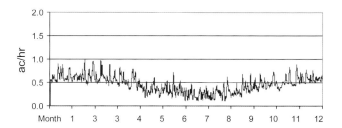

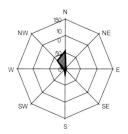

2.9.14 (clockwise from top)
Hours of air flow at each level (air changes per hour)
Available wind energy (kWh/m²)
24 hour averaged flow (ac/hr)

In Beijing (see Figure 2.9.14) the wind speed is very low in summer and the outdoor temperature high, and there is a noticeable reduction in ventilation rates during this period. In a hot, low wind environment such as this additional fan power may be required. In particularly hot and humid environments air cooling and dehumidification will be needed as well as fan power. The description of ZED low energy cooling/dehumidification technology in this book shows how this is tackled in conjunction with the Wind Cowl system which still provides good ventilation in winter, and assists the fans in summer.

Case study
Infiltration and ventilation rates achieved in practice in ZED buildings – tracer gas decay measurement

In order to understand fully the energy performance of a building, knowledge of the air change rates is necessary. This will help one understand both air infiltration rates and the performance of the ventilation systems. The technique used to measure these directly is the tracer gas concentration decay method, carried out in accordance with ISO 12569: 2000 (E), *Determination of air change in buildings – Tracer gas dilution method*.

A calculated, small amount of tracer gas is introduced into the internal air space and thoroughly mixed to ensure a uniform concentration. The tracer gas is then sampled at intervals (as detailed in Figure 2.9.15) and analysed to determine the exponential decay in the gas concentration with time.

In order to produce accurate measurements, five samples are usually taken (minimum required in ISO 12569 is two samples). These five samples are usually taken with the passive ventilation inlets and outlets sealed over in order to determine the air infiltration air change rate (h^{-1}). To establish the ventilation rate (h^{-1}) during the same test, a further five samples are taken with the ventilation inlets and outlets unsealed, that is, normal conditions.

The ten samples can then be analysed using a gas chromatograph. The results from the analysis provide the concentration levels of the tracer gas in parts per billion (ppb), which can then be used to calculate the air exchange rates as follows:

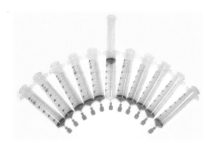

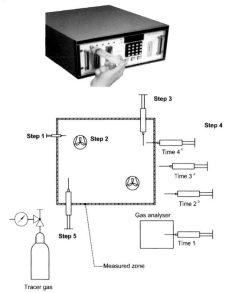

1   Introduce tracer gas
2   Mix tracer gas with space
3   First sample
4   Second to fourth samples at pre-determined intervals
5   Final sample
6   GC Analysis for ppb concentration

2.9.15
Typical tracer gas decay measurement procedure in accordance with ISO 12569:2000

$$n_{av} = \frac{\ln C(t_1) - \ln C(t_2)}{t_2 - t_1}$$

Where

n_{av} is the mean air change rate (h^{-1})

ln is the normal (Napierian) log

C is the tracer gas concentration

t_1 is the time of the first sampling

t_2 is the time of the second sampling, and so on …

Figure 2.9.16 is an example of measurements of a ZED house carried out by Living Space Sciences showing it to have an infiltration rate of 0.11 air changes per hour (ach^{-1}) from the first five samples.[6] The second five samples illustrate the ventilation rate (by unsealing the ventilation inlets and outlets) of 0.45 ach^{-1} on that particular day.

The graph visually illustrates the 'decay' of the gas with time at each of the ten sampling points according to the ventilation regime, that is, no ventilation (infiltration only) and normal ventilation conditions. The time for the ventilation regime change is indicated for reference, in this case three hours into the test. It is worth noting that this method is a 'snap-shot' test under normal conditions, that is, the properties are not subjected to any controlled conditions such as pressure testing. This has advantages and disadvantages as listed at the end of this case study section.

It is particularly important in the case of installations employing passive heat recovery ventilation systems that the infiltration rates are kept to an absolute minimum. If infiltration rates are high, this means that the cold air from outside will bypass the heat exchanger, reducing the efficiency of the system. The infiltration rate in this instance is 0.11 ach^{-1}, which roughly equates to 2.2 ach^{-1} @ 50 pa. The 2006 revision to Building Regulations Approved Document AD L1a requires that dwellings have a maximum 10 ach^{-1} @ 50 pa. It is good practice to have an air permeability rate of less that 5 ach^{-1} @ 50 pa in installations that employ passive heat recovery

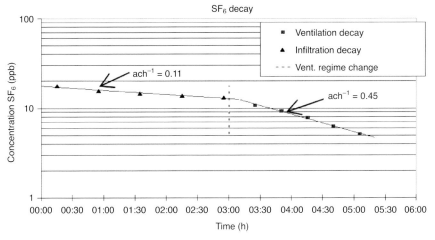

2.9.16
The tracer gas decay test shows ZED building to be well sealed against infiltration but to have good heat recovery ventilation

ventilation systems. A value of 2.2 ach^{-1} @ 50 pa illustrates very good infiltration control and will not compromise the efficiency of the heat recovery system.

The ventilation rate achieved in this case study was 0.45 ach^{-1}, equating to a flow rate of 10.2 l/s for the measured volume, or 0.32 l/s/m^2. Ventilation is required primarily to provide breathing air for the occupants, but also to ensure suitable air exchange to prevent the build up of condensation and mould growth which will damage the building fabric and may have health implications for the occupants. Both of these conditions can generally be satisfied if the ventilation rates are between 0.4 and 1.0 ach^{-1} (CIBSE Guide A – Table 1.1).

The wind conditions during the day of this test were very low. Higher wind speeds would induce greater pressure differences, resulting in greater air change rates. Therefore, the results from this particular test could be viewed as 'worst case', that is, the air change rate is unlikely to be below 0.45 ach^{-1}. The 2006 revision to Building Regulations Approved Document F requires the minimum ventilation rate should not be less than 0.3 l/s/m^2 and therefore the measured value of 0.32 l/s/m^2 falls within this range. The new AD F also requires that the minimum whole building ventilation rate is 13 l/s (based on a one bed dwelling with two occupants). This particular test property, now approximately six years old, would not need to comply with this requirement. However increasing the airflow by this small amount would simply require an additional (or larger) inlet and extract valve – an improvement that can be easily incorporated in the ZED concept.

Tracer gas tests – advantages and disadvantages
Advantages:

- extremely accurate results
- not much equipment required on site.

Disadvantages:

- 'snap-shot' nature means different results according to weather (in particular wind) conditions – this is why pressure testing is often the test of choice although it is less accurate
- time consuming
- requires laboratory analysis (expensive).

2.10 Passive Solar Design

Passive solar design features for minimising heating load in winter include:

- large amounts of south-facing (in northern hemisphere) glazing to capture low winter sun
- a sunspace to trap heat to minimise that lost through conduction through the south wall (northern hemisphere)
- allowing air exchanges between the building and the sunspace if it heats up to a higher temperature than the building
- high thermal mass to allow solar gain to be soaked up by the building without raising the temperature above comfort levels. This heat will then be released on cloudy days, keeping the building warm without additional heating.

Passive solar design features to minimise the need for cooling in summer include:

- minimal east/west glazing. West glazing in particular can result in severe building overheating as the low afternoon sun shines through the window deep into the building
- shading overhangs over the south-facing windows which prevent the high sun from penetrating into the building
- well ventilated sunspace in summer to exhaust any solar gain (and also to allow night cooling)
- high thermal mass to soak up solar gain. This heat can then be exhausted from the building at night via night cooling ventilation.

A row of houses designed to be orientated with the main windows facing south and smaller windows to the north (for northern hemisphere) is ideal for passive solar design, as the amount of solar gain received by the house can be controlled by having overhangs over the south-facing windows. These block out the high summer sun, helping to prevent overheating, but allow in the low winter sun for passive solar heating.

However it is not always possible to have a north/south orientation and so an east/west ZED house has also been developed. East/west orientations make it harder to control the solar gain into the building. In particular in the summer, the low afternoon sun will penetrate any western windows, increasing the risk of overheating. For this reason, and also because there is no sunspace to buffer heat loss through windows, the glazing is reduced on the east/west house compared with the north/south in order to minimise the drop in thermal performance. This comes at the cost of a drop in the availability of natural lighting, and hence a need for more artificial lighting.

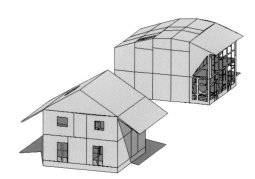

2.10.1
Examples of solar shading models of east/west detached house (top, foreground) and north/south detached house (top, background). These would ideally be built within terraces as shown in the site scheme (bottom)

Case study
Designing for orientation – the effect of climate

This case study looks at simulations of a number of building types. First of all a north/south ZED house designed to optimise passive solar effects is compared with a standard Building Regulations house in a high solar climate (Denver, Colorado). Then the performance of the north/south ZED house is compared with an east/west ZED house, both in a mild solar climate (London) and in a high solar climate (Denver). Finally the overheating risk of each of the designs is assessed and compared with the standard house for a hot summer in London.

Comparison with a Building Regulations house

Figure 2.10.2 compares the heat energy performance of a ZED house (left) with a conventional UK Building Regulations lightweight house in a sunny climate (Denver).

The sunspace of the solar house not only reduces the heat conducted through the wall fabric (brown), but also allows hot air to be circulated from the sunspace into the main house (mid blue) even in midwinter, when temperatures can drop to -23°C, resulting in a much reduced heating load (red). In summer the solar gain is greatly reduced (light yellow) and the ventilation through the sunspace (mid blue) means that cooling (dark blue) is significantly reduced.

Energy assessment

The amount of winter sun will significantly affect the level of difference between the two building types, so an energy assessment was carried out for two examples of climate. The London climate was chosen to represent cloudy winters with little solar gain but mild conditions. The Denver climate was chosen to represent sunny winters with much colder temperatures.

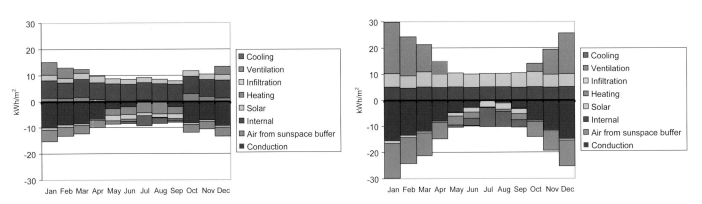

2.10.2
In a sunny climate (Denver, Colorado – heat energy balance) the passive solar design (left) performs much better than a conventional house

Mild cloudy climate – London

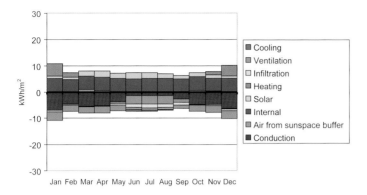

2.10.3: north/south design

The north/south design uses 11.8 kWh/m2/annum for heating.

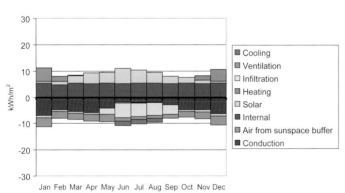

2.10.4: east/west design

The east/west design uses 13.3 kWh/m2/annum for heating, an increase of 13 per cent over the north/south model despite the smaller amount of glazing. It also shows a need for cooling in summer if the temperature is to be kept below 24°C. The overheating could probably be prevented with heavy external shutters, but this would reduce light levels in the building.

Cold sunny climate – Denver

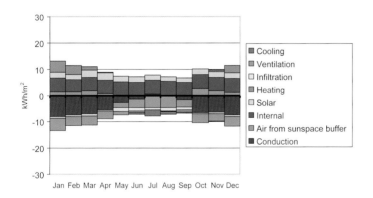

2.10.5: north/south design

The north/south design uses 12.8 kWh/m2/annum for heating. Notice the increased effect of the air from the sunspace heating the house in winter, and being used for night cooling during the cool summer nights. The north/south passive solar design means that the heating required is very similar to London despite much lower winter temperatures in Denver.

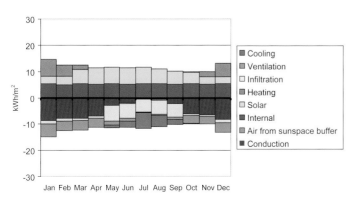

2.10.6: east/west design

The east/west design uses 19.7 kWh/m2/annum for heating, which is 54 per cent more than the north/south model. The additional heating is required because this design cannot use passive solar heating to the same extent. Again, external shutters would be needed in summer to cut out the sun and prevent the need for cooling.

In summary, the north/south design is more adaptable and requires a similar amount of heating for very different climates, due to its ability to use passive solar heating to compensate for colder, but sunnier, conditions. The east/west design's performance will be more dependent on the climate. The examples show that the difference in performance could be equivalent to a greater than 50 per cent increase in heating requirement for the east/west design, depending on climate.

The differences would be even greater if the glazing on the east/west design had not been reduced compared with the north/south design. A further assessment in the London climate showed that even in the United Kingdom, if the ability of the sunspace to trap heat were removed (by leaving sunspace windows open), this would result in a 26 per cent increase in heating requirement.

Overheating assessment

For the overheating assessment the cooling systems were turned off and the summer free running temperature was monitored for a realistic level of ventilation control (windows being opened if the room is occupied and it is overheating). The assessment was carried out for a hot month in London when outdoor temperatures rose to 30°C. Peak temperatures would be reduced if more attention were paid to ventilation by the occupants.

Figure 2.10.8 shows that the three ZED designs all perform similarly for typically warm conditions (first 2 weeks) and better than the lightweight building regulations house which is included for comparison. The hot spell during the third week resulted in the east/west house heating up to almost 4°C higher than the north/south house, though this was still 6°C lower than the peak temperature of the lightweight house. This could be improved by adding external shutters to the east/west house for use in very hot periods, and also by increasing the amount of ventilation. The ventilation is greater in the north/south designs as it is easier to maintain security by ventilating via the sunspace. Ease of ventilation and the possible addition of blinds should be considered for the east/west house as once it has overheated the effect of the high thermal mass will be to make it likely to stay at high temperatures through the night.

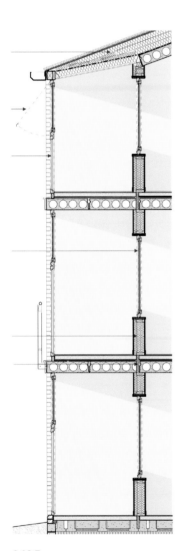

2.10.7
50% of the outer glaze screen opens in summer changing the conservatory into an open air verandha with the floor shading the internal galze screen

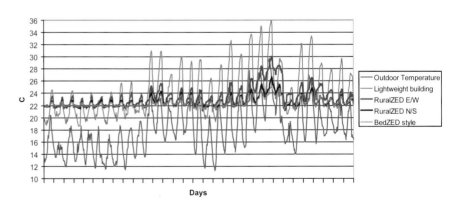

2.10.8
The east/west house is more at risk from overheating than the north/south house, but the thermal mass means that it still outperforms the lightweight building

Case study
Sunspace performance in the United Kingdom

A sunspace should be built optimised for orientation, and with high thermal mass available to soak up any available solar gains.

Figure 2.10.9 shows the results of simulations of a ZED sunspace during the months January to May for a location in the south-east of England. It shows the percentage of the time during the day (10am–8pm) that the temperature in the sunspace is above a given value (blue line). It also shows the same analysis for the external temperature for the same period, and for a period 3 months later.

The sunspace has a floor area of 15 m² on the ground floor with a further 10 m² on a first floor balcony. There is no heating in the sunspace other than that provided by solar gains.

It can be seen that for 50 per cent of the time the temperature is above 16°C in the sunspace and for 25 per cent of the time it is above 20°C. The temperature is typically 6°C warmer than outside.

Another way of considering this is that the climate in the sunspace is 3 months ahead (i.e. warmer) than the climate outside. So winter feels like spring, spring feels like summer. Sunspaces should not be heated as the glass does not give good insulation compared with a ZED wall and so a lot of heat would be lost to the environment. Instead they should be used as an outdoor terrace which can continue to be used for most of the winter.

The sunspace will also act as a buffer, reducing losses from the building on that side because the outside appears to be a whole season warmer. For 25 per cent of the time the temperature in the sunspace is above 20°C and the doors into the main building can be opened to allow heating of the main building.

The United Kingdom tends to be cloudy in winter. Sunspace performance will be improved in sunnier climates.

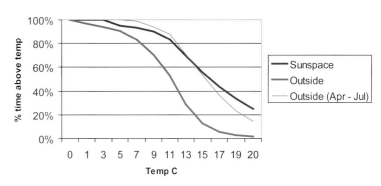

2.10.9
Sunspace daytime temperature range, January to May

High-density solar urbanism with linear parks housing retail and workspace

2.11 Thermal Mass

The addition of thermal mass to a building will affect its comfort and its thermal efficiency through the ability to stabilise temperatures by soaking up heat when there is an excess and releasing it later when it is cold. The following shows an example of this.

Figures 2.11.1 and 2.11.2 show results of simulations with a lightweight wall and a heavyweight wall with equal levels of insulation.[1] A row of output shows the temperature and heatflow through a section of the wall. Temperature is shown by colour: red is hot, pink is warm, white is cold. Heat flow is shown by the black arrows and is mostly from the inside of the room (left surface) through the wall to the outside (right surface).

Each successive row of output is for the same section of wall but shows the condition an hour later.

In this case the walls are being heated up in winter by solar gain coming through windows. On the sunny days the room and lightweight wall get very hot but get cold at night and on sunless days. The heavyweight wall however stays constantly warm, soaking up the excess heat from the room without letting it overheat and then releasing it back into the room at night and on sunless days.

The heat arrows show where heat is being absorbed from the room and when it is being released back into the room.

A heavyweight building is at its most energy efficient when there are sources of excess heat. In summer it will moderate the building temperature and can exhaust excess heat through night cooling, reducing the need for high energy air conditioning systems. In winter it will absorb spare heat energy, which might be from solar energy, from cooking, from computers, televisions, lighting and so on, and re-emit this heat at cooler times.

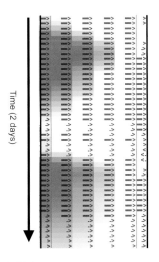

2.11.1
Heat flow in a simulated core through a lightweight wall shows high temperature changes through the day

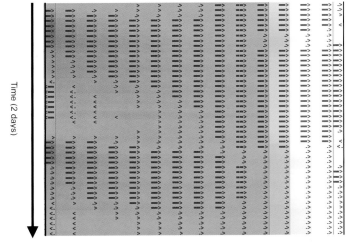

2.11.2
Heat flow in a simulated core through a heavyweight wall shows almost constant temperature through the day

Another benefit is that heating equipment can be sized low to meet only the average needs of the building and then run flat out at high efficiency as the 'storage heater effect' of the thermal mass will mean that temperatures are maintained at comfortable levels through hot and cold days. Conversely lightweight buildings have to have equipment sized for peak loads as they have little ability to maintain temperatures; this equipment then runs inefficiently for most of the time. They also need responsive heating systems and may not perform well with underfloor heating, which although very efficient (assuming it is not electrical) is not particularly responsive.

Lightweight buildings can be more energy efficient in situations where use is very intermittent, or there is a requirement to heat the building up quickly, and there is no risk of overheating. Examples of this might be holiday homes and seldom used community rooms with little glazing.

Lightweight buildings are also traditionally favoured in hot humid climates as they will cool down quickly at night if well ventilated. However, at best they will have no lower temperature inside than the ambient temperature outside (if well ventilated and shaded). This is fine when it is acceptable to the occupant (as of course it was for thousands of years before they had the option of an air-conditioning system), but where a lower temperature is required, thermal mass allows night cooling to be used, or in situations where this is not possible due to the low diurnal range typical of the tropics it can be used to ensure that cooling plant does not have to be oversized and can be run efficiently.

Overheating risk and low energy cooling systems are discussed elsewhere in this book.

2.12 Overheating Risk Assessment

As well as designing houses that require minimal energy for heating it is also important that they have a low overheating risk. For many climates it is possible to design a house with appropriate use of high thermal mass, night cooling, shading and orientation, which will require no cooling even in hot summers. Where houses are too lightweight the overheating risk increases to the point where occupants may install air conditioning which will generally result in high carbon emissions and so should be avoided.

In some climates cooling becomes inevitable if the occupants require moderate internal temperatures. In these cases the well designed house will limit the cooling load and allow a low energy cooling system to be fitted, as described elsewhere in this book.

The following case studies show how ZEDstandard houses compare with typical lightweight houses.

Case study
Overheating risk assessment – comparison of RuralZED, BedZED and lightweight house

RuralZED and BedZED both have highly massive building fabric. BedZED is built using high thermal mass materials. RuralZED is built as a timber frame structure, with thinner high thermal mass panelling resulting in the same area of thermal mass but to a lesser depth. The fabric is described in more detail in Chapter 2.8. This case study looks at how well the RuralZED design compares with the BedZED design in hot weather. A typical UK lightweight Building Regulations house is used for comparison.

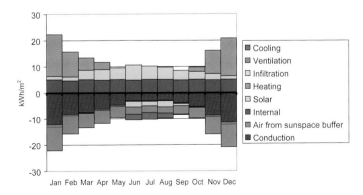

2.12.1
Where a significant cooling energy requirement is identified (dark blue) an overheating risk assessment should be carried out if cooling is not part of the design

Usage assumptions

Usage is probably the most important factor in how a building behaves and will significantly affect the likelihood of overheating. For the overheating assessment, two extreme levels of usage were initially defined: one that would maximise the ways in which the building could be kept cool in summer, and one which would minimise them to see the level of overheating in a worst case scenario. A number of intermediate scenarios were then set up to represent more realistic levels of effort on the part of the occupants to control the temperature in the house. This was to show that while it is possible to keep most buildings reasonably cool if every effort is made, some buildings tend to stay naturally cool for little effort, whereas others tend to overheat if care is not taken. The following are overviews of the usage patterns considered in this assessment.

Cool

This is the best case scenario for keeping the houses cool, though probably unrealistic due to the excessive use of blinds.

- Conservatories in the ZED houses have full ventilation and the French windows are opened as necessary for night cooling until the indoor temperature is below 22°C.
- All of the windows in both buildings have internal blinds in place permanently. This would make the building very dark.
- All opening external windows have temperature controlled opening whenever the inside temperature is above 22°C and the outdoor temperature is cooler.

Good control

This case assumes a high level of control of the building without being unrealistic.

- It was assumed that most people would not operate blinds regularly. It is particularly unlikely that they will close them in the morning before leaving the house in anticipation of a hot day that may not happen. Therefore blinds were removed from all windows in the houses except for where they were designed to be permanently in place for the summer, that is, the opening windows in the ZED conservatories and also on the ZED roof lights.
- The ZED opening sunspace windows are designed to be kept open all summer and have appropriate security arrangements. It was therefore assumed that they would be opened at the beginning of the summer and left open until the heating season starts in autumn.
- The French windows from the house into the conservatory were only opened for night cooling if the external temperature was below the internal temperature.
- Non-fixed external windows in all buildings were opened whenever someone was at home (4pm–8am) if the indoor temperature was above 22°C and it was cooler outside. This assumed that the occupants were effective at opening all windows as and when necessary, and not just the ones for the room they were in.

Realistic control

This scenario was more relaxed and was intended to reflect the amount of effort most people would put into controlling the temperature in their house. The ZED buildings are designed to have summer settings that do not have to be adjusted day by day (the sunspace windows being open and having permanent summer blinds); these were left unchanged from the previous scenario, as they require no day to day effort.

In the rest of the house:

- French windows were now opened whenever it was hot, rather than strictly for night cooling. This is counter productive when it is hotter outside than inside, but it was thought that most people would tend to open them regardless of the outside temperature.
- The roof light in the ZED houses was still assumed to have blinds and to open automatically whenever it was above 22°C. This implies some form of automatic opening device in the design similar to those used to open greenhouse windows.
- For all three houses, other opening external windows were now only opened when someone was actually in the room. This was taken to be 4–7pm in kitchen/dining areas, 7–11pm in the living area and 11pm–8am in bedrooms.

Poor control

In this scenario there were elements of poor control in the building usage. In summary, it was assumed that the occupants do not do anything to pre-empt overheating on a daily basis and only react when they are too hot. The scenario was the same as the 'realistic' scenario with the following changes:

- The roof light was kept permanently closed with no blinds in place in the ZED house.
- The lightweight house has been rotated to an example which is east/west orientated instead of north/south, making pre-emptive shading or window operation more important. This was justified because it is unusual for orientation to be taken into account on the layout of typical housing estates. This orientation caused problems particularly in the afternoon as the sun is lower in the sky and large amounts of solar gain come in through the west windows. The ZED house was not rotated because it was designed to be built only in a north/south orientation (east/west designs are also available and are considered elsewhere).

Hot

This was a worst case scenario. All windows were closed including in the conservatories, there were no blinds and all buildings get afternoon sun through west windows (the lightweight house is east/west orientated; the conservatories of the ZED houses have some west windows).

Other conditions

Of the other conditions, casual gains from people, lighting and equipment were the most important as they are a source of heat in the buildings. All rooms in all houses (not including the conservatories) had casual gains of 2 W/m² of floor area when occupied during the day and 1 W/m² at night. The casual gains were zero during the day. This was a fairly low level of casual gain and assumes high efficiency low energy appliances. Conditions were kept the same for each day with no account taken of weekends or holidays.

Results and analysis

The buildings' performance was simulated over the course of a hot summer month for the different usage scenarios. Figure 2.12.2 shows the main weather inputs for the month. The green line shows outdoor temperature, which peaks at 30°C and has a diurnal range of 5–12°C. The red line shows the level of solar radiation each day, giving an input of almost 1000 W/m² on some days, of which up to half could penetrate the windows depending on time of day and orientation. The black line shows the wind speed, typically 5 m/s (11 mph) or less. This affects the levels of ventilation in the houses when the windows are open. Hot, sunny, windless days are the worst combination for overheating. This would suggest that the third week of the month would be particularly problematic.

Figure 2.12.3 shows an example of the output data from the simulations. Temperatures were logged on the ground floor and on the first floor of all buildings. In each plot the RuralZED house response is shown in blue, BedZED in pink, and the lightweight house in red.

It is clear that the lightweight house is much more responsive to changes in temperature, with brief peaks to high temperatures during the day, and drops to lower temperatures when the outside air is cool and the heat is exhausted through the windows.

The temperature stratification is evident in the ZED houses where the first floors peak 2°C hotter than the ground floor. Both ZED houses respond very similarly, suggesting that there is adequate thermal mass in the RuralZED house. The additional mass in the BedZED house is demonstrated in its greater inertia. On the ground floor

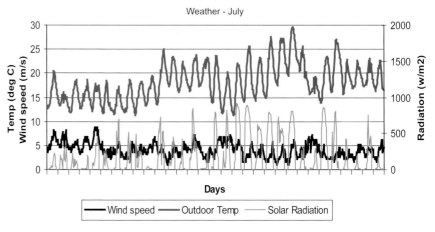

2.12.2
Weather data used for simulations

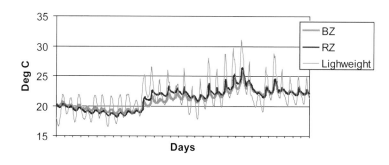

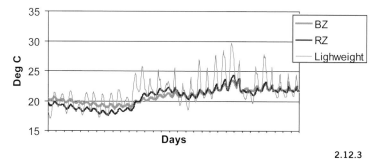

2.12.3
Example of output data for the 'good' usage scenario: (top) first
floor hourly results; (bottom) ground floor hourly results

it can be seen that the temperature does not drop so low during the first quarter of the month, and does not rise so high in the second quarter. The hottest peak is also slightly lower. The difference is small, however, suggesting that the fact that the surface area of exposed thermal mass is the same in both houses may be more important than the differences in quantity of thermal mass for this climate. The usefulness of additional thermal mass would become apparent in hotter arid climates.

To simplify comparisons for the various scenarios, a set of overheating indicators was chosen to represent the behaviour of the buildings over the month for each usage scenario. These were:

- Maximum temperature measured at 4.30pm downstairs. This time was chosen because it was half an hour after the occupants had returned and opened windows and so on. It would give a measurement of how hot the building was after allowing time for the worst of any overheating to dissipate.
- Maximum temperature at 12.30am upstairs. This was a measure of how hot the bedrooms were when people were trying to sleep. It is at least one and a half hours after the bedroom windows have been opened. Note that in some cases the lightweight house could be cooler at this time than the heavyweight buildings because its low thermal mass allowed it to cool down faster from the daytime temperatures.
- Percentage of time when the temperature was above 28°C downstairs. This was an indicator of how long a building overheats (which may not be indicated by the peak temperature). It included the time when the buildings were unoccupied.

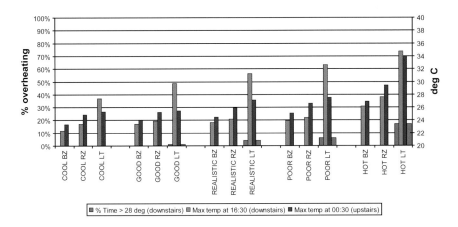

2.12.4
Summary overheating indicators for the three different
buildings and five different usage scenarios

The summary (Figure 2.12.4) shows the overheating indicators for the buildings in the different usage scenarios. It can be seen that all of the buildings can be kept reasonably cool in the best case scenario, with the lightweight house performing worse during the day but almost as well as the RuralZED house at night. In the worst case, the lightweight house has severe overheating with temperatures of 34°C at night and above 28°C for almost 20 per cent of the time. It is also interesting that the heavyweight houses have higher temperatures upstairs at night than downstairs during the day, whereas the lightweight house is the other way around. This is because the temperature stability in the heavyweight houses means that the temperature stratification between upstairs and downstairs is the dominant effect. For the lightweight house, whose temperatures follow the exterior temperature more closely, the time of day is the dominant effect.

Now consider the ability of the buildings to cope with poor levels of occupant control. Are they naturally cool buildings or are they only cool if the occupants are particularly vigilant with cooling strategies?

It can be seen that as the usage scenarios become more relaxed, from the 'cool' base line through the 'good' level of control to the 'poor' level of control, the lightweight house shows a marked increase in its tendency to overheat, with the 4.30pm temperature going from 27°C up to 33°C. The ZED houses, however, appear to be much more stable and the performance only deteriorates a little as the level of control decreases, with the 4.30pm temperature varying from 23°C up to 24°C for RuralZED and from 22°C to 24°C for BedZED.

The heavyweight performance starts to deteriorate in the 'hot' extreme, with no windows being opened, but still regulates the temperature to below the 28°C overheating level on the ground floor, as the hottest period does not last many days and the temperatures are slow to rise due to the thermal mass.

A real dilemma in a lightweight house in a city is the decision whether to have a cooler but noisy night with the windows fully open, or a hot quieter night with them closed. The heavyweight house gives you more flexibility in this regard, particularly if the hot spell is short and casual gains are not particularly high (as is the case here), so heat can be exhausted through open windows during the next cool day rather than relying on night ventilation.

Case study
Overheating risk assessment – comparison of RuralZED and lightweight house upgraded with heavyweight material

In order to see the effect of retro fitting thermal mass to a lightweight house the following assessment was carried out to compare it with the RuralZED house.

The lightweight house was modified to have 29 mm cement particle board fitted on the inside of the external walls in place of the 12 mm of gypsum plasterboard, to see to what extent this additional thermal mass would bring the performance closer to that of the ZED houses.

Cement particle board is a dense board with high specific heat capacity and relatively high thermal conductivity, making it good at absorbing and storing heat. The properties are shown in the following table together with those of the gypsum plasterboard, and also those of the concrete panels used in the RuralZED house.

Figure 2.12.5 shows the temperatures on the first floor for the original 12 mm gypsum case, the result when the cement board was added to the inner face of the external walls and the result when the extra cement board was also used on each face of the internal partitions. The combined effect is a reduction in peak temperature on the hottest day of 3.5°C.

Table 2.12.1: Thermal properties of material options for wall internal surfaces

	Cement board	Gypsum plasterboard	RuralZED panels
Density (kg/m³)	1250	950	2400
Thermal conductivity (W/mK)	0.23	0.16	1.4
Specific heat capacity (j/kgK)	1800	840	840

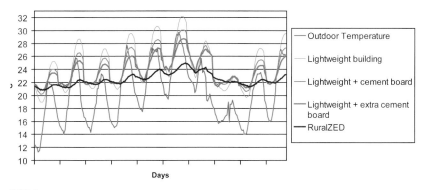

2.12.5
Summary overheating indicators for the three different buildings and five different usage scenarios

It can be seen that, although the addition of cement board to the lightweight house has brought the peak temperatures down, they are still considerably higher than the ZED house for which the peak temperatures are a further 4°C lower. This is due to the extra thickness of thermal mass in the ZED house and the additional area (as thermal mass is also present in all ceilings and floors).

2.13 Low and Zero Carbon Heating and Hot Water

Solar hot water

A solar hot water system can be used to pre-heat domestic hot water supplies. Figure 2.13.1 shows results of calculations of the percentage of heating supplied throughout the year by the solar hot water system (orange). The balance (purple) must be supplied by another system – typically a heat pump, immersion heater or wood pellet boiler. Clearly, the climate will affect the amount of heat that can be obtained from solar hot water.

The system was assumed to be based on high efficiency evacuated tube solar collectors with an average of one collector (footprint 1.1 m²) per person. This assumed that 40 litres of water per day at 60°C were required on average by each person.

In the two examples in Figure 2.13.1, both systems supply 100 per cent of the heating in mid summer but the Beijing example (right) continues to supply 50 per cent of the heating in winter whereas the London example (left) provides less than 20 per cent. This will be mostly due to the amount of sunshine but will also be affected by the air temperature and source water temperature, which varies through the year. Over the course of the year an average of 65 per cent of the hot water is supplied at the London location and 80 per cent for Beijing.

Note that heating controls and plumbing must be well designed to take full advantage of solar hot water systems. If a tank of hot water is heated every morning by a boiler before the sun has risen, there will be little input from the SHW system. ZEDfactory thinking on optimal plumbing of hot water systems is discussed elsewhere.

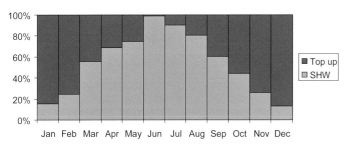
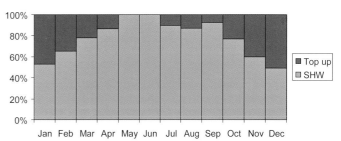

2.13.1
Ability of same solar system to supply hot water in (left) London and (right) Beijing

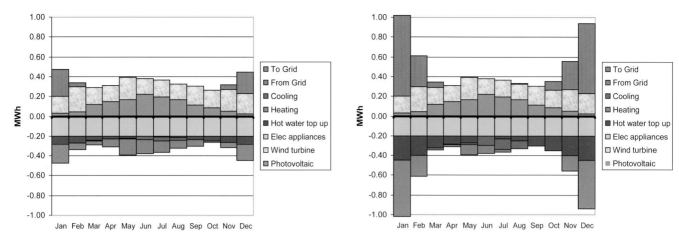

2.13.2
Electrical energy supply-demand graphs show that energy can be provided by renewables for heat pump (left),
but the same building would require a large additional input from the grid with conventional heating (right)

Heat pumps

Heat pumps are another way of reducing energy demand and are useful for developments that have no ready access to biomass for wood pellet burners or where cooling is required in summer. They can produce up to four units of thermal energy for each unit of electrical energy used. They can also be run in reverse for cooling applications in which case they absorb typically three units of thermal energy for each unit of electrical energy. Figure 2.13.2 compares electrical energy demands for heat pumps and conventional electrical heating.

Heat pumps will work particularly well as underfloor heating/cooling in buildings of high thermal mass because they can be sized to meet the average requirement and run at full load and maximum efficiency to keep the mass of the building at the desired temperature. Any peaks and troughs in the average air temperature will be balanced by the heat source/sink of the thermal mass. By contrast, in a lightweight building, a heat pump must be sized to meet the peak load if the temperature is to be effectively controlled, even though it will be mostly run on part load.

Another advantage of using heat pumps in a building of high thermal mass is that if power has to be drawn from the grid to meet peak summer cooling or peak winter heating demands it can be done at night using off-peak power because the thermal mass will retain its temperature during the following day. Cooling can continue during the day using power from the solar PVs.

Heat pumps will only be zero carbon if the electricity they use is supplied by a renewable source such as PVs on the roof of the building.

Groundwater heating and cooling

The ground under a building can be used as a large heat source/sink. Ground cycle water cooling involves circulating water through pipes buried in coils in the ground or in bore holes. The ground stays at a constant temperature of about 12°C throughout the year and so the water emerging at this temperature can be used to cool a building through underfloor cooling. It is important to assess the humidity if this is done as condensation may form on the floor, making it slippery if dehumidification is insufficient.

This is a very efficient form of cooling as it only requires the electrical input of a water pump. This can be supplied by a renewable source.

Ground cycle water can also be used in combination with a heat pump to supply a relatively warm supply of heat in winter which will increase the heating efficiency of the heat pump.

Biomass heating

An alternative to using heat pumps is to provide space and water heating with a biomass system such as a wood pellet burner. This will be approximately carbon neutral if the wood fuel is grown in a renewable manner. It will remove the load from the electrical systems and reduce reliance on grid electricity to meet peak demand and so is generally to be preferred in situations where biomass is readily available and particularly if there is no demand for summer cooling.

If combined with a solar hot water system, the pellet burner need not be used during the hot months of summer. Figure 2.13.3 shows that using a wood pellet boiler (right) instead of a heat pump (left) results in spare electricity that can be exported to the grid. Alternatively the quantity of photovoltaic panels could be reduced for this building. Figure 2.13.4 shows how the demand for heat from the pellet burner drops off in summer as the solar hot water system starts to provide the bulk of the hot water.

Larger scale biomass heating systems can be used to provide a community heating main for a group of houses or apartments. This could also be a combined heat and power (CHP) system which would also provide electricity for the community.

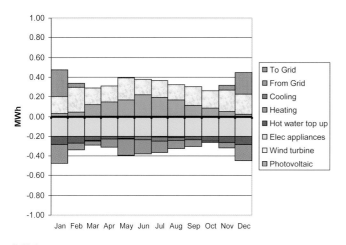
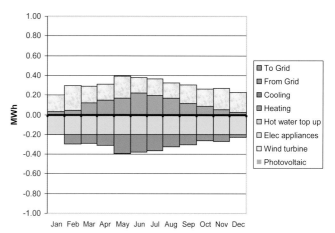

2.13.3
Electrical energy supply-demand graphs show that providing heating and hot water with a wood pellet boiler (right) will remove the winter requirement for grid electricity compared with the heat pump system (left)

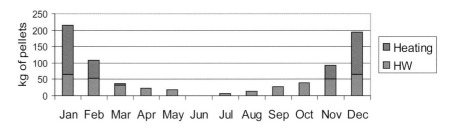

2.13.4
Example of calculation of quantity of wood pellets required for space and
hot water heating assuming solar hot water system is also present

Table 2.13.1: Renewable wood fuel resources in Great Britain

Oven Dry Tonnes (ODT)	Forest and Woodland	Arboricultural Arisings	Short Rotation Coppice	Primary Processing Co-Products
England	2,394,147	616,060	15,899	289,580
Scotland	2,942,513	34,717	572	413,538
Wales	971,689	19,706	218	165,783
	6,308,349	670,483	16,689	868,901

Notes: figures are given in oven-dry tonnes. Woodfuel will never be delivered at this moisture content. Typical moisture contents will vary from 50–60% (measured on a fresh weight basis) for harvesting brash to 25–30% for conditioned woodchips.

Figures are estimates of the annual sustainable production that can be made available taking account of technical and environmental constraints. They do not take account of economic or market constraints

This is discussed in more detail in the section on electricity production.

Burning of biomass should always be used in conjunction with making a building efficient. Ultimately, if everyone relied on biomass as a carbon neutral way of heating their home, there would not be enough to go around.

Table 2.13.1 shows an estimate of the wood fuel resource in the United Kingdom.[1]

This is a total of just under 8 million tonnes per annum to be shared between 60 million people, giving 130 kg of fuel per person oven dry weight, or 160 kg per person at a typical fuel moisture content. Note our own estimates are more conservative but, when straw is included, give a similar per capita resource.

To put this in perspective, a ZED house in the United Kingdom designed for four people is estimated to require three-quarters of a tonne (750 kg) of fuel for heating alone, that is, slightly more than four people's share, and a similar amount for hot water depending on whether solar hot water heating is installed. A ZED upgraded Victorian house is estimated to require over 2 tonnes, or 12 people's share for heating alone. This gets more complicated still when you consider that public buildings must be heated, as well as people's homes.

This quick ballpark calculation shows that even though biomass is a good source of carbon neutral fuel for heating, houses should still be designed to be as thermally efficient as possible. While biomass is probably one of the easiest ways to start creating zero carbon homes, other technologies will also be needed, such as heat pumps driven from renewable sources.

2.14 Low Energy Air-conditioning, Dehumidification and Cooling

Designing with high thermal mass and good passive solar design and shading allows buildings to maintain comfortable temperatures in summer through night cooling and other natural ventilation strategies in many parts of the world. However in more extreme climates, particularly where night-time temperatures are high, additional cooling will be needed if modern expectations of comfort are to be met.

A standard air-conditioning plant works like a fridge, using a heat pump compressor to cool a refrigerant which is then passed through a heat exchanger to cool the incoming air. However in many parts of the world this incoming air will be humid and as it is cooled the level of water vapour in the air will result in unpleasantly high levels of humidity and even condensation and mould growth (which occurs when humidity levels are above 75 per cent). To prevent this, the air is typically cooled to below the comfort level so that the water condenses out of the air at the heat exchanger, where it can be ducted away. The air then has to be reheated to comfort levels (this is not always done, which is why some air conditioned buildings seem to be excessively cold). The dehumidification process can typically use 40–50 per cent as much energy again as the cooling process.

This process is entirely driven by electricity and so results in high carbon emissions. In many parts of the world cooling loads in summer are starting to exceed heating loads in winter. This is due to poor building design, high comfort expectations and energy intensive air-conditioning systems.

Good building design will minimise the cooling load requirement, and can be combined with innovative low energy cooling systems to make it possible to achieve high levels of comfort while meeting the load with on site renewable energy sources.

Technologies that should be included when designing a low energy system include:

- *Evaporative cooling*. This works by passing an airstream over a wet surface (or vapourising water into the airstream). The latent heat of vapourisation of the water reduces the temperature of the air stream, but the humidity level increases. Useful in hot arid regions with low humidity. This system can produce significant cooling with the input of water alone, with a small amount of electricity to drive a low energy fan. The cooled air does not have to have high levels of humidity if the evaporative cooling is carried out via a heat exchanger.
- *Solid desiccant dehumidification*. Air is passed over a surface coated with a solid desiccant such as silica gel. The desiccant removes moisture from the air, reducing the dehumidification load, but raises the temperature slightly,

increasing the cooling load. The desiccant has to be heated to drive off the water absorbed. This is typically done by coating a wheel with the desiccant. As the wheel slowly rotates, it alternates between adsorbing moisture for half of the rotation and being heated to drive off the moisture for the other half of the rotation. The heating cycle could be done with heat from solar collectors.

- *Liquid desiccant dehumidification.* This is similar to solid desiccant dehumidification but because it uses a liquid such as lithium bromide solution there is potential for more flexibility. A reserve of strong desiccant solution can be built up on sunny dry days using solar collectors to drive off excessive moisture. This can be used to absorb water on hazy humid days when there is reduced solar energy but increased humidity. Instead of coating a surface with the desiccant, it can trickle down a surface. Another advantage of this liquid system is that it cleans the air by removing dust, pollen and so on, improving the air quality.

- *Whole enthalpy (temperature and humidity) heat exchange.* In summer a heat exchanger can be used to minimise the amount of heat introduced into a room through ventilation – in effect this is a 'coolth' recovery ventilation system. A whole enthalpy heat exchanger will also reduce the amount of additional humidity introduced through the ventilation by exchanging some of it with the exhausted air.

- *Ground cycle water cooling.* The ground can act as a large heat sink. If pipes are buried in the ground in horizontal coils or in vertical bore holes, then water can be circulated through these, and then through underfloor pipework in the building to remove heat. The water coming from the ground will typically emerge at about 12–15°C, quite cool for summer. This could also be used as a relative source of heat for heat pump heating in winter. This system would have to be used in conjunction with a dehumidification system in most climates or there would be a high risk of condensation on the floors.

The system being developed for ZEDfactory combines these technologies to give control of temperature and humidity appropriate for the climate. It is shown in outline in Figure 2.14.1. A key feature is the whole enthalpy heat exchanger embedded in the wind cowl, which can provide cooling, dehumidification and humidification by successful integration of evaporative cooling and liquid desiccant dehumidification. The system is currently being patented.

All of these technologies have the advantage that the energy inputs can be in the form of low energy pumps and fans (to move air, water or desiccant), or solar thermal where desiccant regeneration is required. This gives the potential for a very good coefficient of performance (COP) of the system where COP is a measure of electrical energy input divided by cooling energy output.

Where additional fabric cooling is required (to offset the heat from casual gains to the building) this can be provided by ground cycle cooling.

The following case study shows how different climates would benefit from a different mix of the technologies.

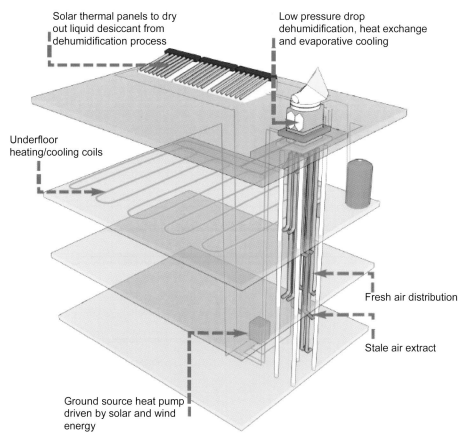

Solar thermal panels to dry
out liquid desiccant from
dehumidification process

Low pressure drop
dehumidification, heat exchange
and evaporative cooling

Underfloor
heating/cooling coils

Fresh air distribution

Stale air extract

Ground source heat pump
driven by solar and wind
energy

2.14.1
Schematic of the layout of a low-energy cooling/
dehumidification system

Case study
Cooling requirements for different climatic conditions

Conventional cooling and air conditioning systems tend to be inefficient and use
large amounts of energy, particularly if dehumidification is required – something that
conventional compressor based air-conditioning does badly. This study looks at three
different climates: a temperate climate represented by London, a hot humid climate
represented by Beijing (particularly in August) and a very hot but arid climate
represented by Riyadh. Consideration of climate allows the most appropriate cooling
systems to be considered, giving opportunities for highly efficient systems that could
be run off building-embedded renewable energy sources.

2.14.2

In London the climate is mild and buildings should be designed to require no active cooling, even in the hottest weeks in summer.

Temp °C

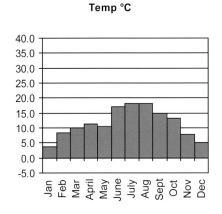

Humidity %

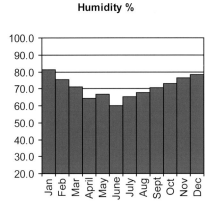

2.14.3

In Beijing, the hot summers correspond with the highest humidity levels. Night temperatures are too high for effective night cooling and dehumidification will be an issue.

Temp °C

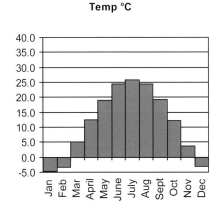

Humidity %

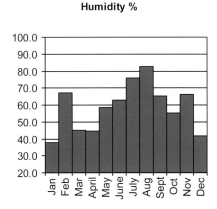

2.14.4

In Riyadh the weather is extremely hot in summer, and no heating is required at any time of year. The humidity levels are very low, below 20% for a lot of the year, so dehumidification is not likely to be an issue.

Temp °C

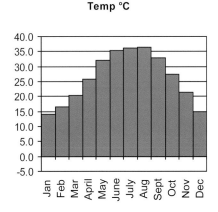

Humidity %

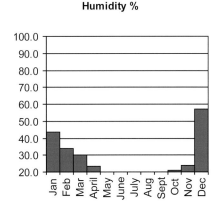

The following analyses show an initial assessment of ZED houses in each of the three climates. As well as the standard heat energy balance charts, latent heat energy graphs show to what degree the humidity levels will need to be controlled. The humidity conditions are controlled to between 30 and 60 per cent. The temperature is controlled to between 20 and 24°C.

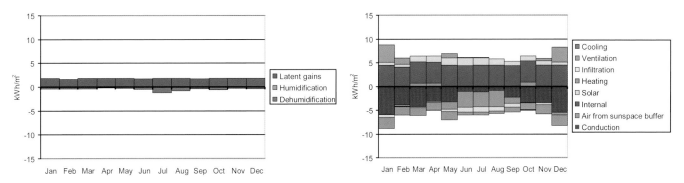

2.14.5
London – naturally ventilated: (left) latent heat energy balance; (right) heat energy balance

Analysis of a ZED building in London shows that it would require no cooling in summer as there is sufficient night cooling through the ventilated sunspace (mid blue) to control temperatures. The latent balance shows some occasions where the humidity produced within the building (from people, cooking, bathrooms – purple – left graph) could exceed 60 per cent and would need to be controlled (blue blocks – left graph) in summer. These are small and could be controlled with purge ventilation when necessary by opening windows. In summary, no cooling system is required.

In Beijing, two scenarios were considered. First, full air-conditioning where all the air entering and exiting the building passes through the cooling/dehumidification heat exchanger in the wind cowl. This shows a large cooling demand (blue – right graph), but a smaller dehumidification demand due to the quantities of outside air being well controlled.

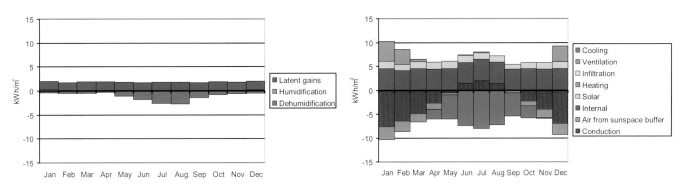

2.14.6
Beijing – fully air conditioned: (left) latent heat energy balance; (right) heat energy balance

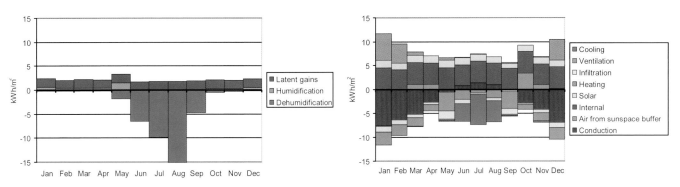

2.14.7
Beijing – Naturally ventilated when possible: (left) latent heat energy balance; (right) heat energy balance

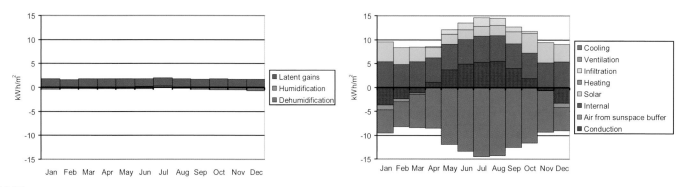

2.14.8
Riyadh – fully air conditioned (left) latent heat energy balance; (right) heat energy balance

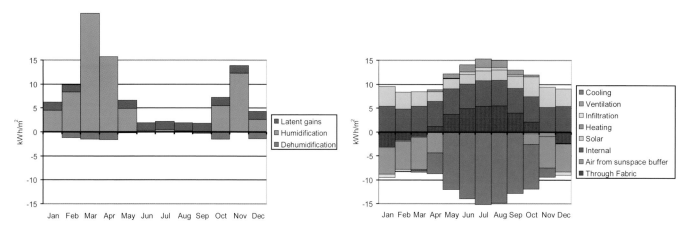

2.14.9
Riyadh – natural ventilation when possible: (left) latent heat energy balance; (right) heat energy balance

Alternatively natural ventilation can be used whenever it is colder outside. The mid-blue bars show the effect of cool air entering from the ventilated sunspace. However this results in a much higher demand for dehumidification (blue bars – left graph) due to much larger quantities of outside air.

The best solution is likely to be the well sealed air-conditioned house, at least for the height of summer, but this will depend to some extent on the relative efficiencies of the cooling system and the dehumidification system. In any case, a reasonably efficient dehumidification system, probably based on liquid desiccant dehumidification with solar desiccant regeneration, will need to be in place to control humidity levels as purge ventilation by opening windows will tend to make the humidity levels higher.

If good dehumidification is in place, then ground cycle water cooling could be considered as a low energy way of cooling the underfloor slab. This should not be considered if high humidity levels inside the building are likely, because it can lead to condensation and slippery floors.

The outline design building for Riyadh does not have a sunspace and has shaded glazing as there is no need to capture solar gains for heating at any time of year.

The fully air-conditioned and naturally ventilated scenarios are considered again. Cooling is required all year round in the well sealed fully air-conditioned example. This can be reduced considerably by using night ventilation to cool the thermal mass of the building during the winter months (mid-blue bars). However this ventilation will be very effective at removing all of the moisture from the building, meaning that large amounts of humidification may be necessary otherwise the environment can become uncomfortably dry with large amounts of static electricity.

The best solution is likely to include evaporative cooling systems which can be run at high efficiencies with very low energy inputs, and can provide humidification as well as cooling. Ground water cycle cooling of the building floors would also be worth considering if the ground water is sufficiently cool. This can be very efficient, as the only energy required is for an electric pump. Condensation on the floor is not likely to be a problem in this case due to the low humidity levels.

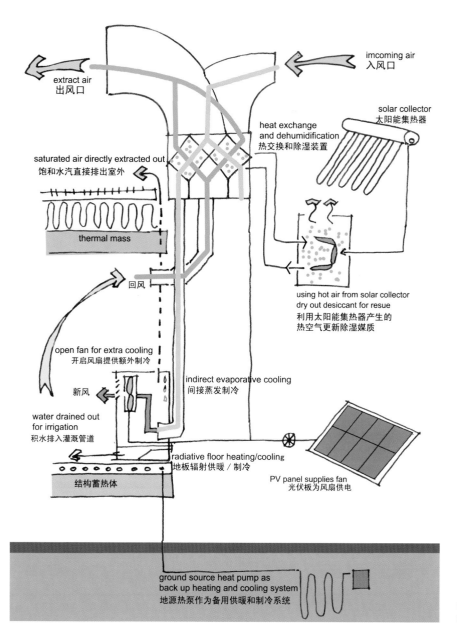

2.14.10
Solar cooling concept for high humidity climatic zones

New country house in Sussex

2.15 Providing a Renewable Electricity Supply

As a house becomes more thermally efficient the focus will move to meeting the demand for electricity in order to achieve zero carbon emissions. This can be done by reducing the demand for electricity by using efficient appliances throughout, and meeting this reduced demand with on-site renewable sources of energy.

A typical house with two to four occupants in the United Kingdom uses 4,000–5,000 kWh of electricity each year. Figure 2.15.1 shows measured annual electricity use at BedZED in London. It shows that electrical demand can be reduced to well under this average with efficient appliances and conscientious users. The average electricity consumption at BedZED is 750 kWh per person per year.

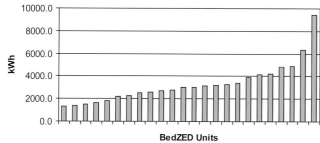

2.15.1
Range of annual electricity usage at different units at BedZED

Photovoltaic panels

Photovoltaic panels (PVs) are an effective and predictable way of producing renewable electricity. They have traditionally been expensive but cheaper panels are now coming onto the market from China and India.

Efficiency of PVs is anything up to 15 per cent (i.e., 15 per cent of the solar energy hitting the panel can be converted into electricity) and depending on the climate, hours of sunshine and so on, over 1,000 kWh of energy can be produced for each nominal kW (peak) of installed panel (typically 7 m^2 of panel area depending on efficiency). This will drop in less sunny climates, and also if the panel has a poor view of the sky.

Up to 50 per cent of the energy produced can come from diffuse radiation, that is, energy coming indirectly from the sun via clouds. A panel mounted horizontally will be optimal for diffuse radiation as it will receive energy from horizon to horizon, but a panel mounted pointing directly at the sun will be optimal for direct

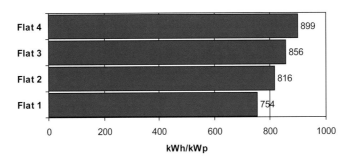

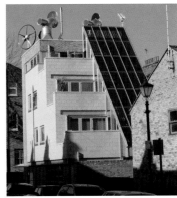

2.15.2
Measured performance results of PV arrays from BowZED show the advantage of
having an unobstructed view of the sky

radiation, so a compromise must be found depending on the climate and practicalities of the building. Figure 2.15.2 shows the measured performance of panels
at BowZED in London. Notice how the panels for the lower flats do not perform as
well. This is because they receive less diffuse radiation because the view of the
sky is blocked out by adjacent buildings, even though the direct radiation is not
blocked.

Micro wind

Wind is another way of producing electrical energy for a building. It is less
predictable than solar energy because nearby buildings and other obstructions
can seriously reduce the available wind to below the average for the location. This
is important because half the wind speed will result in one-eighth of the power
output. Where an exposed area is available on a site it might be possible to install
a relatively large wind turbine, otherwise building-mounted micro wind turbines
should be considered. These should be designed to maximise the amount of
energy that can be produced at low wind speeds even if this lowers the theoretical
performance at higher speeds, which are unlikely to be available in a built
environment.

   Another consideration in a built up area is the likely amount of turbulence
in the wind. This can result in the turbine constantly changing direction and so
missing 80–90 per cent of the available wind. Vertical axis wind turbines are less
susceptible to turbulence. The position in which the turbine is mounted on the roof
can affect the amount of turbulence and should be considered carefully. Ideally a
building can be designed to enhance the available wind by focusing it for the wind
turbine.

Biomass combined heat and power

Combined heat and power systems (CHP) are electricity generators whose waste heat is used to produce hot water. They can run on a number of fuels but biomass is considered here as it is a carbon neutral fuel (almost – there is a small amount of fossil fuel input required for harvesting and distribution of the biomass). CHP systems are highly efficient because almost all of the energy from the fuel is used either as high grade electricity, or as low grade heat. They can also be considered as a lower efficiency heating plant which produces 'free' electricity. Typically twice as much heat is produced as electricity.

A typical biomass CHP system might produce 180 kW thermal and 90 kW electrical output and so would normally be used as part of a community scheme. The amount of biomass consumed can be calculated from the efficiency of the system as a heating plant (44 per cent in one example) with the electrical output then being taken as a 'free' by-product. Biomass CHP systems run at their best on almost continuous load but this can result in a large excess of hot water in summer and so the site should be designed to make good use of this.

Sizing of the CHP system is important. There is a large amount of unused heat in the summer when only domestic hot water is required. However it may still be worth running the plant because the electricity generated will reduce the carbon load on the grid. A CHP system could work well with an application that can soak up excess hot water, for example a community swimming pool. Note that it would be easier to keep it heated in summer when there was more spare capacity than in the winter. Perhaps an indoor and an outdoor (summer only) pool would be worth considering. Probably a better scenario is to use one CHP system to provide all of the domestic hot water and a little heating, and a community biomass heating plant to provide the rest of the heating. The CO_2 implications of this and other scenarios would be assessed in each development.

Lightweight houses with little thermal mass would require oversized systems designed to meet high peak loads for a few hours each day, reducing the efficiency of the system. Heavyweight ZED houses with high thermal mass would require a system sized for only slightly more than the average winter load running continuously. Underfloor heating works well as the whole floor can then act as a storage heater, soaking up heat from the CHP system continuously, without needing high peak loads.

Any form of community heating system needs to have a heat meter for each house, otherwise people will tend to regulate the temperature by opening windows rather than by turning down the heat. This should be included in the system's design.

While biomass is (almost) carbon neutral, this should not be used as an excuse to use large quantities instead of making a building efficient. Ultimately the environmental impact must be considered. Put simply, if we all want to use large quantities of biomass fuels, there will not be enough to go around.

Case study
Energy supply for different climatic conditions

The following are examples of how energy demand and supply can be balanced for a number of different locations using an appropriate mixture of technologies. In each case a 100 m^2 family home is considered and demands for heating, cooling, hot water and electrical equipment are calculated along with how these will be met with renewable technologies.

The ZEDphysics model is used to carry out these assessments, with results taken from an embedded version of the RETScreen software used to simulate the performance of PVs, solar hot water and wind turbines.[1] In all cases good availability of the local solar and wind resource was assumed for the location. The site wind micro-climate and likely turbulence, shading issues, view of the sky, etc., should always be assessed to ensure that this is reasonable.

Denver – USA

An abundance of sun means that the building can be powered by photovoltaic cells alone and achieve a zero energy balance over the year. The large diurnal temperature ranges make this an ideal location for a ZED building. Little heating is required in winter even though temperatures drop to a low of -23°C.

Denver weather data also reports reasonable quantities of wind, so the final site should be assessed in detail for wind micro-climate before deciding to go for PV power only.

In this example the heating is by electrical heat pump but subject to local availability of fuel, a wood pellet burner should also be considered. This would make the demand curve match the supply curve from the PVs more closely.

Thermal demand:
- heating – 1,281 kWh/annum (13 kWh/m²)
- cooling – 443 kWh/annum (4 kWh/m²).

Electrical demand:
- heating – 430 kWh/annum (4 kWh/m²) (Heat pump)
- cooling – 15 kWh/annum (2 kWh/m²) (Heat pump)
- hot water – 190 kWh/annum (2 kWh/m²) (Heat pump)
- electrical equipment – 3,500 kWh/annum (35 kWh/m²).

Supply achieved by:
- RuralZED style passive solar construction
- 18 m² of photovoltaic panels
- 3.4 m² of solar hot water collector
- no wind generator
- heating and cooling by heat pump.

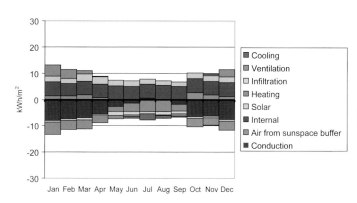

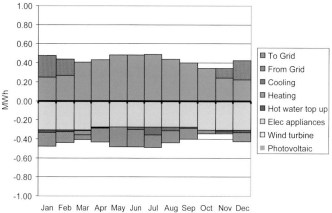

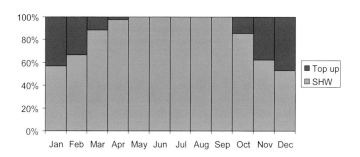

2.15.3
Denver:
(clockwise from top left)
Heat energy balance
Electrical energy balance
Solar hot water

Madrid – Spain

Almost no heating is required in winter but cooling is required in summer.
This results in a demand curve that matches the availability of power from the photovoltaic cells fairly closely. There is little wind reported in the meteorological data from Madrid and subject to a detailed assessment of the site, the wind turbine might be better replaced with some more PV panels in this case.

Thermal demand:
- heating – 122 kWh/annum (1 kWh/m^2)
- cooling – 1,185 kWh/annum (12 kWh/m^2).

Electrical demand:
- heating – 40 kWh/annum (0.4 kWh/m^2) (Heat pump)
- cooling – 400 kWh/annum (4 kWh/m^2) (Heat pump)
- hot water – 230 kWh/annum (2 kWh/m^2) (Heat pump)
- electrical equipment – 3,500 kWh/annum (35 kWh/m^2).

Supply achieved by:
- BedZED style passive solar construction
- 19 m^2 of photovoltaic panels
- 3.4 m^2 of solar hot water collector
- 1,000 W wind generator
- heating and cooling by heat pump.

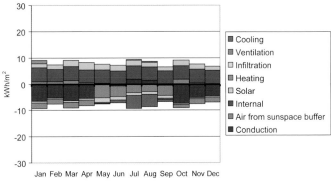

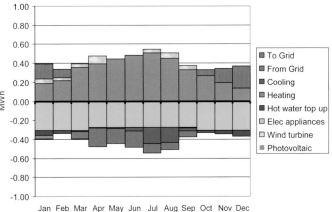

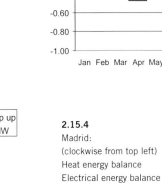

2.15.4
Madrid:
(clockwise from top left)
Heat energy balance
Electrical energy balance
Solar hot water

New York – USA

A good resource of wind provides power to the wind turbine and minimises the area of photovoltaic required. A site survey of the wind micro-climate should always be carried out however.

Heating by wood pellet burner is favoured due to the availability of local wood.

Thermal demand:

- heating – 2,788 kWh/annum (28 kWh/m^2)
- cooling – 1,403 kWh/annum (14 kWh/m^2)

Electrical demand:

- cooling – 470 kWh/annum (5 kWh/m^2) (Heat pump)
- electrical equipment – 3,500 kWh/annum (35 kWh/m^2)

Supply achieved by:

- RuralZED style passive solar construction
- 11 m^2 of photovoltaic panels
- 3.4 m^2 of solar hot water collector
- 1,000 W wind generator
- heating by wood pellet burner
- cooling by heat pump.

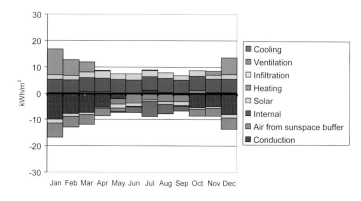

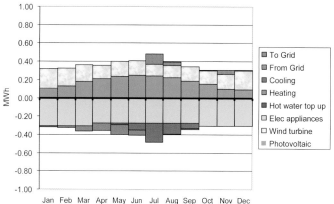

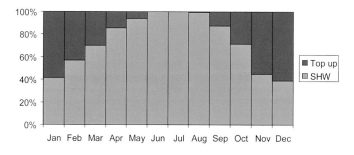

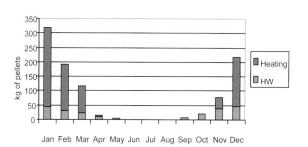

2.15.5

New York:
(clockwise from top left)
Heat energy balance
Electrical energy balance
Biomass – wood pellet requirements
Solar hot water

Chicago – USA

The windy city favours the use of two wind turbines, which minimise the need for photovoltaic cells when combined with using a wood pellet burner for heating.

Thermal demand:
- heating – 3,022 kWh/annum (30 kWh/m²)
- cooling – 781 kWh/annum (7 kWh/m²).

Electrical demand:
- cooling – 260 kWh/annum (3 kWh/m²) (Heat pump)
- electrical equipment – 3,500 kWh/annum (35 kWh/m²).

Supply achieved by:
- RuralZED style passive solar construction
- 3 m² of photovoltaic panels
- 3.4 m² of solar hot water collector
- 2 x 1,000 W wind generator
- heating by wood pellet burner
- cooling by heat pump.

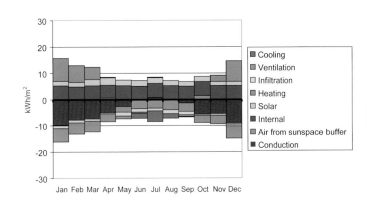

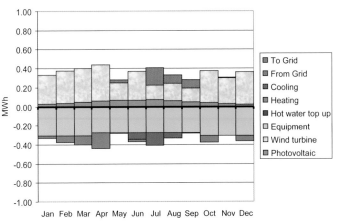

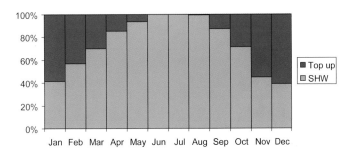

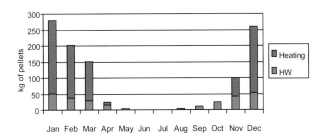

2.15.6
Chicago:
(clockwise from top left)
Heat energy balance
Electrical energy balance
Biomass – wood pellet requirements
Solar hot water

Beijing – China

China is challenging. Local supplies of wood pellets are often not available so heat pumps must be used for heating and cooling. Beijing weather data does not show a large wind resource and the summer diurnal temperature range is not always high enough for night cooling. However where grid electricity is required for cooling it can be used off-peak at night to pre-cool the massive fabric of the building for the following day. This cooling will be topped up by power from the PVs during the day. It is also assumed that low energy cooling and dehumidification plant is fitted.

The following shows two ways of achieving a zero net energy balance. It is always important to assess the local wind micro-climate to see if more output could be achieved.

Thermal demand:
- heating – 1,767 kWh/annum (18 kWh/m²)
- cooling – 1,749 kWh/annum (17 kWh/m²).

Electrical demand:
- heating – 600 kWh/annum (6 kWh/m²) (Heat pump)
- cooling – 600 kWh/annum (6 kWh/m²) (Heat pump)
- hot water – 250 kWh/annum (3 kWh/m²) (Heat pump)
- electrical equipment – 3,500 kWh/annum (35 kWh/m²).

2.15.7
Beijing:
(clockwise from top left)
Heat energy balance
Solar hot water
Electrical energy balance (Option 2)
Electrical energy balance (Option 1)

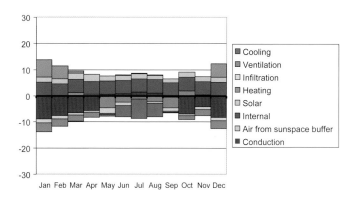

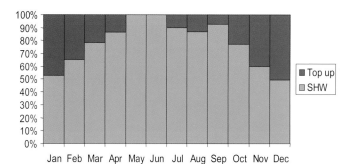

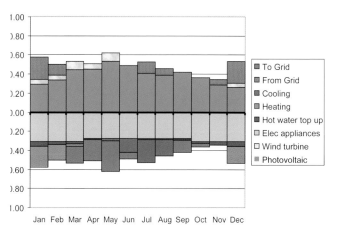

Option 1
- BedZED style construction
- 23 m² of photovoltaic panels
- 3.4 m² of solar hot water collector
- 1,000 W wind generator – 1.5 x wind focusing
- heating and cooling by heat pump.

Option 2
- BedZED style construction
- 18 m² of photovoltaic panels
- 3.4 m² of solar hot water collector
- 1,000 W wind generator – 1.5 x wind focusing
- Equipment demand reduced by 33%
- heating and cooling by heat pump.

Jubilee Wharf across the creek

Part three

Case studies

Code 6 suburban home with sufficient electric
micro-generation to power both house and car

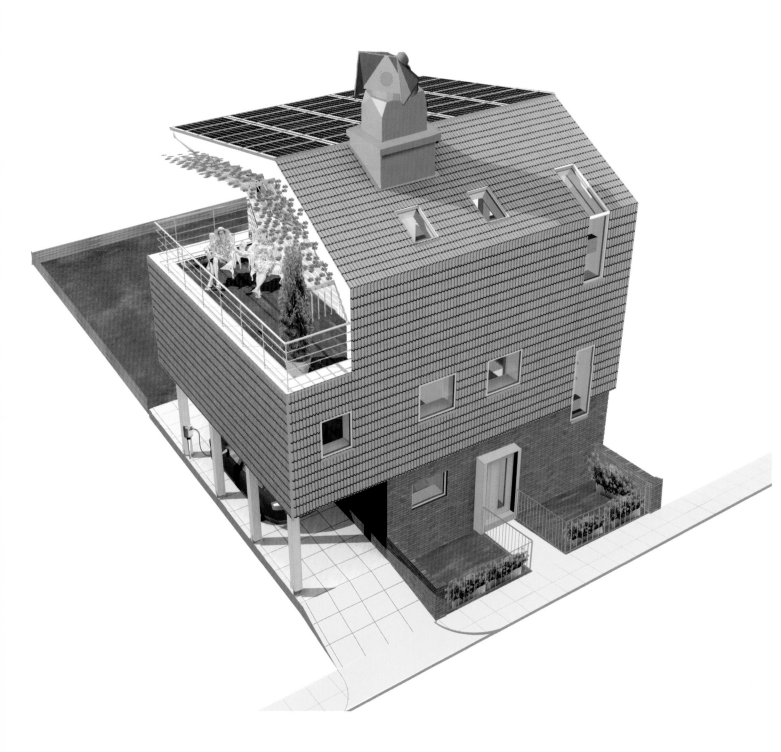

RuralZED

Residential Density 1 to 15 Homes/ha

Typical applications

- detached homes suitable for rural locations
- in terraced form suited to existing village extensions
- suburban infill sites

Prototype

Hope House in Molesey, Surrey was the first model for this typology, now superceded by the RuralZED range of standard house kits. Hope House was designed to sit in a flood plain, with a thermally massive and flood resistant ground floor supporting a two-storey timber frame. A two-and-a-half-storey south-facing conservatory with balcony terrace connects all floors, with the upper surfaces clad in solar electric panels and solar thermal collectors. The house began life 15 years ago with a small gas boiler, but has accommodated a planned set of environmental upgrades as they can be afforded by the household, culminating in a zero carbon specification by summer 2007. Current technologies fitted include a small wood stove for space heating, an automated pellet boiler for domestic hot water in winter, evacuated tube solar thermal collectors providing all hot water from late spring to early autumn, a 1.1 kW peak photovoltaic array, and a 600 W wind turbine. The house was designed

Hope house interior

Hope house

From top
Semi-detached ruralZED
RuralZED village
South facing end terrace ruralZED
Interior view

to facilitate homeworking, with the ground floor being designed with separate entrances, with the future potential for conversion into a granny flat. The house was built using locally-sourced materials and labour, and provides an alternative aesthetic to the surrounding neo Georgian or neo Tudor architecture. The house was designed to both provide privacy from neighbours and harvest sunlight through the obscure glass sunspace for both people and plants, at the same time as providing easterly views to the garden and surrounding landscape.

Production run

RuralZED is a prefabricated kit house. If you can assemble an IKEA sofabed, then you can probably (with the help of a short training course) build your own zero carbon home. The idea here was to reconcile the quick and dry assembly benefits of a gluelam post and beam frame with the passive cooling performance of thermally massive masonry structures. By cataloguing almost every component, and pre-negotiating economies of scale with many small manufacturers, it also became possible to precisely cost the new homes, leaving site labour the only variable. This process minimises the risk of out turn construction costs, at the same time as providing large, small and self builders a simple way of delivering zero carbon homes. All the ZEDstandards microgeneration features are built into the frame kit, leaving site layout and elevational treatment to respond to local context. Two laminated timber frame kits are offered – one lower cost using eastern European FSC softwood, the other using Sussex sourced chestnut from overgrown coppices. The thermally massive lining planks and floor finishes are from a mixture of ground granulated blast slag concrete, reclaimed aggregate and white Cornish china clay stent, and do not need plastering if carefully rubbed down and finished with a natural wax sealer. The basic frame kit provides good levels of airtightness, superinsulation and thermal mass, and can easily be assembled into terraces or flats up to four floors. A number of detachable features such as roof trusses, double glazed sunspaces, balconies, garages and communal boiler rooms enable the system to be used within most masterplans without sacrificing its individual microgeneration performance or high standards of energy efficiency.

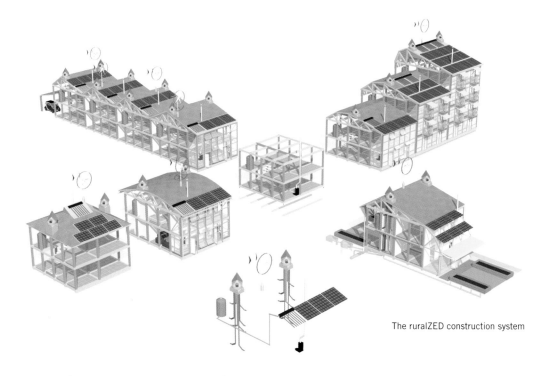

The ruralZED construction system

Merton Rise

ZED House 1
ZED House 2
ZED House 3
ZED Mews 5   Parking
1B Flats   In left plot 40 spaces
2B Flats   right plot 78 spaces.
Sun Space   Total car spaces 118

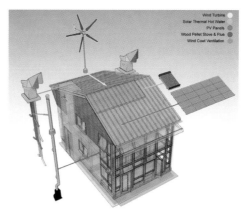

Wind Turbine
Solar Thermal Hot Water
PV Panels
Wood Pellet Stove & Flue
Wind Cowl Ventilation

Energy – microgeneration appliances provide carbon neutral energy, with the use of rainwater storage and composting toilets RuralZED can be an off grid stand alone unit.

Amenity – RuralZED kits with gardens provide private outdoor space which is at a premium in todays new developments.

Energy
PV / (kwp/br)	0.4
Installed CHP / (kwe/br)	0.7
Ground source heat pump / person	no
Micro wind / (kwh/br/yr)	112
Onsite generation ex biomass	60%
Onsite generation inc biomass	100%

Amenity
Sunspace / (m²/br)	3.4
Public open space / (m²/br)	3.5
Private garden / (m²/br)	8.4
Children's play space / (m²/br)	no
Sports facilities / (m²/br)	no

Workspace
Home office space / (m²/unit)	bedroom sockets
Area rentable workspace / (m²/br)	no
No. workspaces/ha (m²/br)	no

Transport
Private parking (sp/unit)	1.5
Car pool / (sp/unit)	0.02
Veg oil filling station / (sp/unit)	personal
Charge points / (sp/unit)	no
Bike storage/ (bikes/unit)	2.9
Public transport	no

Food
Communal growing space	no
Private growing space	0.5 with garden
Farmers market / person	no
Cafes	no
Shops	no

Biodiversity
Undisturbed wildlife habitat / ha	none
CO_2 saved per unit over lifetime	617 t

SuburbanZED

Residential Density 15 to 75 Homes/ha

Typical applications

- creates medium density perimeter block layouts
- suitable for expanding new towns
- creates new suburban districts
- suitable for urban estate regeneration

Prototypes

Francis Court in Halesowen for Accord Housing Association, Birmingham was the first model for this typology, now accompanied by new terraces being completed for Presentation Housing Association at St Mathews, Brixton and Testway Housing Association in Artists Way, Andover. All of these projects carefully respond to their context in different ways. At St Mathews the street frontage was south facing – so a joint venture between PRP Architects and ZEDfactory developed an alternating composition of sunspaces and balconies that provided both defensible space, sunlight and reasonable privacy. In Andover and Halesowen, the terraces are approached from sheltered arcades to the north, allowing more private patio decks and terraces opening out from south-facing sunspaces. All projects share communal wood-fuelled pellet boiler heating systems, with solar thermal collectors on Andover and Brixton used to minimise wood pellet consumption in the summer period.

Above – Francis Court

Upton development phase 1. Code for sustainable homes, level 6 units

The ZEDstandards allow for future photovoltaics upgrades by allowing simple mounting rails to clip onto the standing seam aluminium roof without costly disruption or modification to the building fabric. In Andover, durable mounting brackets and electrical conduits have been installed for micro wind turbines, enabling this promising future technology to be added on a plug and play basis. Simple plan layouts, with disabled flats on the ground floor, south-facing living rooms and north-facing bedrooms for cool summer nights, maximise the benefit of the passive solar building fabric.

Production run

The suburban typology can be built in both the RuralZED prefabricated system and using a thermally massive traditional masonry construction system. Choosing which method almost entirely depends on the masterplan dimensions, street layouts and whether the more standardised plan dimensions of the prefabricated system can work within the plot layout. Buildings that turn corners, have radiused frontages or support full roofgardens should probably adopt masonry construction. A typical masterplan – as illustrated at Merton Rise, an urban extension to Basingstoke, with highly irregular triangular street layouts – shows how a mixture of one-off special corner blocks and regular terraces can create a varied streetscape, rising and falling with the steep site contours, and managing to create a village atmosphere with shared green spaces overcoming the tyranny of an excessive parking allocation. By relaxing the placement of sunspaces – only using them in locations receiving good annual solar exposure, and taking care to provide every home with a clear street frontage with its own front door, it is possible to reconcile the concerns of traditional urban design with the microgeneration agenda. An important addition to the simple repertoire of south-facing terraces with glazed sunspaces was the development of new plan types allowing front doors and entrances from both the north and south – depending on the urban layout. This introduced a new idea, alien to most traditional streetscapes: the north elevation of the street will always be completely different to

RuralZED MMC glue laminate frame

Artists Way, Andover

Upton, corner of Millpond Drive

the south. Far from this being a problem, we believe that this should be celebrated by the architectural form. Similar concerns encountered trying to maintain the same levels of building integrated renewable energy microgeneration on new homes facing east or west (inevitable within most perimeter block layouts) led to the development of a serrated south-facing roof system. This appears on the streetscape as a series of dutch gables, with the south-facing surfaces of each pitched roof providing opportunities for photovoltaics and solar thermal collectors. Juggling the requirement for unobstructed sunlight to photovoltaics with the unobstructed airflows maximising the performance of the passive heat recovery ventilation cowls has produced a carefully honed roofscape – hopefully expressing the natural forces informing the architectural language.

This new streetscape can be seen in its purest form in the theoretical RuralZED urban block studies where the grim internal parking court beloved by traditional urban designers has been replaced by a communal orchard and children's playspace. The new development at Upton for the Metropolitan Housing Trust, working within a strict Princes Foundation masterplan, manages to create mews type spaces by imposing 45° street corners and a varied streetscape by juxtaposing two- and three-storey blocks. All of this is achieved at the expense of added construction detailing complexity and compromised microgeneration performance – which may be beneficial, depending on personal hierarchies of the importance of these complex and often paradoxical form generators. However, what is important is that the debate between preconceived streetscape concepts and environmental performance actually takes place, and when budgets are tight, difficult choices are made as the result of informed debate.

Upton

I Floor Layout Area 6

Energy – Terraces in this development can benefit from a single wood pellet boiler for top up heating requirements.

Amenity – On a development of this size the units have smaller private gardens but benefit from improved communal space and parking.

Mews terraces at Upton

Energy

PV / (kwp/br)	0.4
Installed CHP / (kwe/br)	no
Ground source heat pump / person	no
Micro wind / (kwh/br/yr)	112
Onsite generation ex biomass	100%
Onsite generation inc biomass	100%

Amenity

Sunspace / (m²/br)	2.8
Public open space / (m²/br)	5
Private garden / (m²/br)	14
Children's play space / (m²/br)	1
Sports facilities / (m²/br)	no

Workspace

Home office space / (m²/unit)	bedroom sockets
Area rentable workspace / (m²/br)	no
No. workspaces/ha (m²/br)	no

Transport

Private parking (sp/unit)	1.4
Car pool / (sp/unit)	0.04
Veg oil filling station / (sp/unit)	personal
Charge points / (sp/unit)	no
Bike storage/ (bikes/unit)	0.9
Public transport	yes

Food

Communal growing space	no
Private growing space	inc in garden
Farmers market / person	no
Cafes	no
Shops	no

Biodiversity

Undisturbed wildlife habitat / ha	0.28
CO_2 saved per unit over lifetime	646 t

Live/workZED

Residential Density 75 to 120 Homes/ha

Typical applications

- integrated workspace for true live/work communities
- suitable for densification of existing residential areas
- potentially minimises need to travel, reduces congestion
- helps achieve 24-hour communities
- significantly promotes social cohesion
- enhances take up of shared facilities such as food deliveries and car pool
- provides useful alternative to the monofunctional housing estate
- provides useful alternative to the monofunctional office park
- creates both employment and housing on the same plan footprint

Above – BedZED aerial and sky gardens

Prototypes

BedZED was the first prototype. The idea was to show how it was possible to combine workspace with housing while matching the residential densities of the surrounding dormitory suburb, and actually increasing overall standards of amenity – particularly gardens and public open space. This was achieved by matching south-facing rows of single aspect residential terraces with north-facing live/work units or workspace. By placing gardens on the workspace roof, it was possible to give almost every home a garden or terrace, while achieving high levels of cool northlight within the office space. Five years after full occupation, there has not been one complaint from residents about workers on the site, indicating that the combination of different uses has been complementary on the whole. The design team tried hard to do

BedZED village square

the right thing in the right place. A complex mixed-income residential brief from Londons' oldest housing association – the Peabody Trust – asked for one-third of the homes to be social rent, one-third shared ownership and one-third private for sale. A requirement for a mixture of both large and small family homes as well as one- and two-bed flats led to a wide variety of different plan unit types, each changing to suit the position within the masterplan and cross section. North-facing workspace can be divided up into small units, each with its own front door to the street, or knocked through to create one large workspace the length of an entire terrace, with enough deskpace for a 30 to 40 person office. This enables a mixture of fairly sizable and micro start up companies to integrate themselves in this community. Lintels and blocked up doorways were provided linking ground floor homes to the adjacent workspace, should residents wish to either expand their homes or seamlessly connect home and business. This flexibility greatly increases the ability of self-employed parents with families to juggle with a better work–life balance, and came directly from our experiences of running the ZEDfactory office from Hope House. BioRegional reclaimed were very successful at reclaiming structural steelwork and softwood walling studs from local demolition sites for remanufacturing into useful new structural components. Most bulk materials and labour were sourced within a 50-mile radius of the site, enabling the completed embodied carbon to compare favourably with that of a volume housebuilder's industry standard product – despite having thicker walls and considerably higher thermal mass.

BedZED is just about large enough to merit its own on site water treatment plant and woodchip fuelled combined heat and power plant (CHP). Although the plant can be accurately sized to meet demand, staff maintenance costs on an isolated island site of this size can become prohibitive, although this problem will be overcome as both these community-scale technologies become more commonplace in south London. Biomass CHP works very well on mixed use zero heating specification developments, as the thermal demand is for hot water only, and remains consistent all year, with oversize hot water storage tanks that can meet peak demands while still allowing trickle recharging throughout the day. This allows the power plant to more or less match average electrical demand, exporting to grid when surplus power is generated on site – and importing to meet peak demand. On balance over a year, if the plant performs reliably, with only its planned maintenance downtime, slightly more power is generated than is actually required on site. If this surplus power is between 5 and 15 per cent of annual demand, it should be possible to pay off both the embodied initial construction carbon and the planned maintenance / replacement carbon footprint. The advantage of the biomass CHP system is that very similar amounts of biomass are burnt compared to a conventional heat only boiler, as the electricity is generated from flue gases that would be unlikely to have been harnessed to the same efficiency in a more conventional combustion process. This makes it much easier to stay within the national biomass quota, while still inhabiting higher density urban infrastructure.

Four-bed townhouse terrace

Production run

After completing BedZED, the ZEDfactory team understood that reducing construction complexity and component cost had to be tackled to convince potential

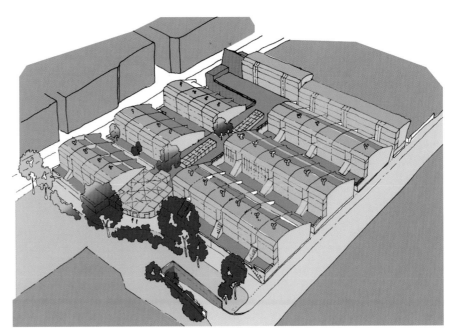

EdZED ZEDinaBox school

developers to roll out this typology. The ZEDinaBox concept rationalises the terrace concept to ensure maximum repetition for continental in situ concrete tunnel forming techniques, or repetition of simple precast concrete elements if more traditional low cost construction techniques were preferred for smaller projects. The bridges have gone, front gardens have been extended, space standards increased for better private sector take up, live/work units have been given their own gardens, and the maisonettes' sky gardens have improved privacy with no overlooking. The gaps between the blocks have been slightly increased to improve solar access, and achieve on street parking and deliveries in front of every home. Each home and workspace has both its own front door, accessed directly off the street, and its own private garden. The area of solar electric panels per home has been increased, and a wide range of standard housetypes – from one-, two- and three-bedroom flats to maisonettes, townhouses and live/work units – can be accommodated within its simple crosswall construction logic. A variation of this theme is the MedZED and EdZED concept – where the live/work northern volume provides either hospital wards or classrooms which can be joined up by a linear north–south axis street to both create larger institutions and provide key worker housing for the staff who work in them.

Cross section through MedZED

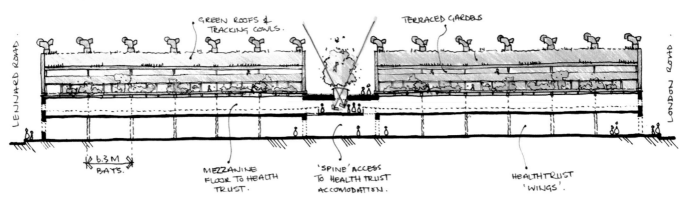

Forests Forever – the same concept of living and working within small self-contained communities – is currently proposed for an urban extension about 30 km outside Beijing for developer the Modern Group. Instead of following a Western suburban model and creating a dormitory suburb reliant on high levels of private car use, each home was provided with a home office accessed directly from the street, with the masterplan focusing on a central commercial hub / telecommuting centre containing farmers market, restaurant, tea house and convenience store / newsagent. A reedbed placed on the centre's roof cleans the water for a centrally placed traditional Chinese fishing lake, allowing some of the more expensive executive homes to catch their supper from their own veranda. The larger homes are inter-generational, allowing younger couples a measure of independence in a self-contained basement flat, grandparents with restricted mobility bedrooms on the ground floor, and the normal suite of bedrooms at first floor level. A wide range of different housetypes, from stacked maisonettes to townhouses and villas, are used to suit a variety of different incomes and space requirements, with a wide variety of different housetypes designed – depending on whether the home is accessed from the northern face of the street or the southern. A central pedestrian park with mountain bike training track and skateboard ramp provides useful public open space and secure play areas for children. All the homes have enough south-facing roof area to harvest enough solar electricity to meet their annual electricity demands, including heat pump winter heating and summer cooling, with additional areas of solar thermal evacuated tube collectors to power the dessicant dehumidification and domestic hot water requirements. A communal larger turbine placed at the centre of the site provides power for the community building and site-wide external lighting and lake water purification.

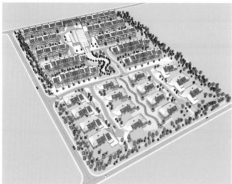

Solar urbanisation on the outskirts of Beijing

Each three-generation home has its own private lawn and fishing island

ZEDinaBox

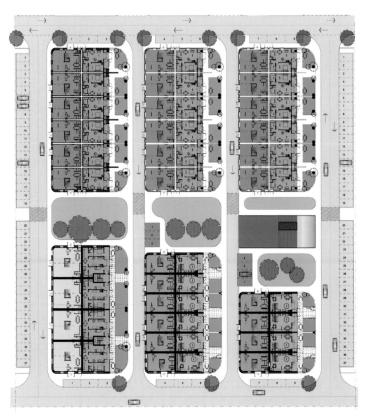

Energy

PV / (kwp/br)	1.7
Installed CHP / (kwe/br)	no
Ground source heat pump / person	no
Micro wind / (kwh/br/yr)	yes
Onsite generation ex biomass	15%
Onsite generation inc biomass	100%

Amenity

Sunspace / (m²/br)	6.4
Public open space / (m²/br)	5
Private garden / (m²/br)	11.5
Children's play space / (m²/br)	1.1
Sports facilities / (m²/br)	22.5

Workspace

Home office space / (m²/unit)	72
Area rentable workspace / (m²/br)	5
No. workspaces/ha (m²/br)	51

Transport

Private parking (sp/unit)	0.9
Car pool / (sp/unit)	0.02
Veg oil filling station / (sp/unit)	0.04
Charge points / (sp/unit)	0.27
Bike storage/ (bikes/unit)	1.2
Public transport	yes

Food

Communal growing space	yes
Private growing space	inc in garden
Farmers market / person	yes
Cafes	1.2
Shops	0.2

Biodiversity

Undisturbed wildlife habitat / ha	0.12
CO₂ saved per unit over lifetime	392 t

BedZED

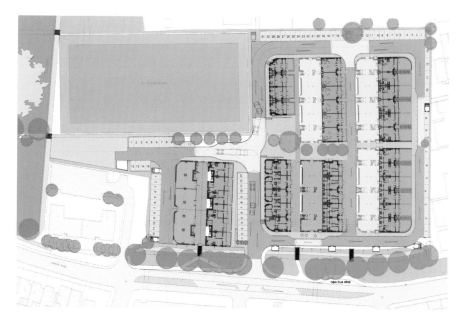

Energy – Heat and electricity is provided on site by a woodchip fired CHP unit with PV panels powering electric vehicle recharge points. In the CHP building is a water recycling facility and a public pavilion

Food – Roof gardens have 300 mm of topsoil and can be planted as gardens or vegetable patches

Energy

PV / (kwp/br)	0.8
Installed CHP / (kwe/br)	0.8
Ground source heat pump / person	no
Micro wind / (kwh/br/yr)	no
Onsite generation ex biomass	9%
Onsite generation inc biomass	100%

Amenity

Sunspace / (m²/br)	2
Public open space / (m²/br)	30
Private garden / (m²/br)	9.3
Children's play space / (m²/br)	3.3
Sports facilities / (m²/br)	26.2

Workspace

Home office space / (m²/unit)	79
Area rentable workspace / (m²/br)	9.6
No. workspaces/ha (m²/br)	76.4

Transport

Private parking (sp/unit)	0.5
Car pool / (sp/unit)	0.04
Veg oil filling station / (sp/unit)	0.02
Charge points / (sp/unit)	0.1
Bike storage/ (bikes/unit)	1.5
Public transport	yes

Food

Communal growing space	yes
Private growing space	20 m² minimum
Farmers market / person	no
Cafes	1.3
Shops	0.7

Biodiversity

Undisturbed wildlife habitat / ha	0.15
CO_2 saved per unit over lifetime	1236 t

Forest forever

Food – Imagine catching your own fish for supper. Half the development is centred around a catch and keep fishing lake

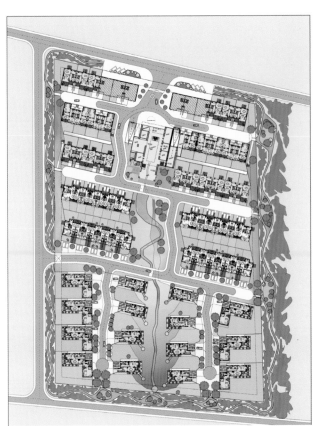

Energy

PV / (kwp/br)	1.1
Installed CHP / (kwe/br)	no
Ground source heat pump / person	1.4 cooling only
Micro wind / (kwh/br/yr)	2.25 commercial
Onsite generation ex biomass	100%
Onsite generation inc biomass	100%

Amenity

Sunspace / (m²/br)	5.3
Public open space / (m²/br)	11.8
Private garden / (m²/br)	2
Children's play space / (m²/br)	1.6
Sports facilities / (m²/br)	no

Workspace

Home office space / (m²/unit)	16
Area rentable workspace / (m²/br)	12.4
No. workspaces/ha (m²/br)	81.5

Transport

Private parking (sp/unit)	2
Car pool / (sp/unit)	0.04
Veg oil filling station / (sp/unit)	0.02
Charge points / (sp/unit)	0.06
Bike storage/ (bikes/unit)	4.5
Public transport	yes

Food

Communal growing space	no
Private growing space	inc in garden
Farmers market / person	yes
Cafes	1.5
Shops	0.25

Biodiversity

Undisturbed wildlife habitat / ha	none
CO_2 saved per unit over lifetime	1380 t

UrbanZED

Residential Density 120 to 150 Homes/ha

Typical applications

- creates high density low rise solar urban layouts
- suitable for urban estate regeneration
- suitable for inner city brownfield sites
- mainly residential, showing how larger family units with gardens can be achieved at higher densities
- opportunities for ground floor plinth to provide mixed-use active frontage, with retail or live/work
- requires car pooling and shared communal facilities

Prototype

BowZED tested this new residential typology on the site of a derelict workshop in Tomlins Grove, a stone's throw away from Bow underground station. ZEDfactory have tried to show how the ZEDstandards can be applied on small urban infill sites, maximising the opportunities of solar and wind energy harvesting at the same time as building respectfully in traditional durable materials (terracotta blocks and Stock bricks). Three floors of flats have been placed over a ground floor live/work unit, with functional rooms to the northern stairtower and living rooms opening out onto south-facing terraces and sunspaces – with interesting long distance views over adjacent low rise housing across the city to Canary Wharf. A wood pellet boiler and pellet store have been integrated into the ground floor, with passive heat recovery ventilation connecting all the kitchens and bathrooms to the rooftop wind cowls. Each home has both an external paved balcony terrace and a sunspace glazed with enough Glass / glass photovoltaic panels to meet about half of a typical flat's annual electricity demand. The remainder is planned to be supplied by two micro wind turbines, although the exposure and wind regime need more careful study. It is likely that BowZED will achieve zero carbon status over time when the current pellet boiler is replaced by a micro pellet CHP machine upgrade.

Production run

The wedge shaped block has now been designed to repeat on a linear site beside the canal at the old Leicester Bus Garage site, in Abbey Road, for the Metropolitan

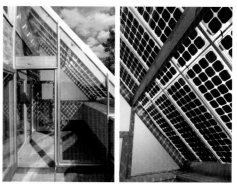

BowZED

Housing Trust. Here the same strategy employed at Bow has been scaled up so that every home has both a south-facing terrace (or outdoor living room) and a photovoltaic clad sunspace. The need to add larger three-, four- and five-bedroom family units to the scheme resulted in an interlocking cross-section, with north-facing maisonettes leaning over the south-facing homes to harvest south light, view and amenity. The northern half of the ground floor can then be devoted to parking and plant space for the biomass boilers and fuel store. The design has very little internal circulation corridor, and facilitates a wide mix of different size units within each linear terrace block. The housing terraces are spaced to minimise solar overshadowing, and all open space at ground level is allocated to each family home to avoid uncared for, left over public spaces. The aerodynamic roof shapes and thermally massive roof slab construction facilitate the future mounting of wind turbines.

Top – South view of typical UrbanZED block
Above – North view
Right – Cross-section showing family units with gardens on ground and upper-ground floors with flats above and almost no internal corridors
Below – View from the canal

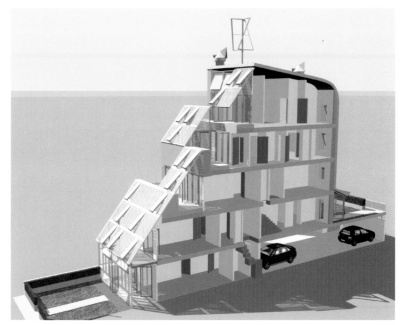

Leicester Bus

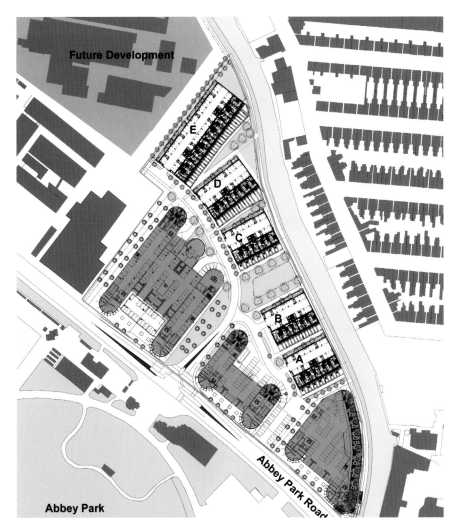

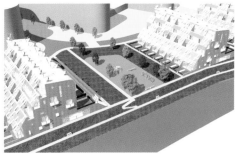

Amenity – in the centre of the site there is a central communal play area / outdoor space with views out to the canal

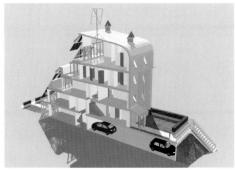

Transport – 1 undercroft parking space per dwelling. Loads of bike parking, secure in undercroft (see chart for figures). Good public transport links to city centre

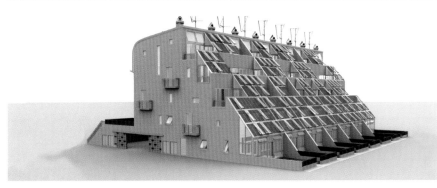

Energy

PV / (kwp/br)	0.2
Installed CHP / (kwe/br)	0.8
Ground source heat pump / person	no
Micro wind / (kwh/br/yr)	35
Onsite generation ex biomass	40%
Onsite generation inc biomass	100%

Amenity

Sunspace / (m²/br)	2.8
Public open space / (m²/br)	6.2
Private garden / (m²/br)	7.7
Children's play space / (m²/br)	0.9
Sports facilities / (m²/br)	4.2

Workspace

Home office space / (m²/unit)	0.5
Area rentable workspace / (m²/br)	no
No. workspaces/ha (m²/br)	no

Transport

Private parking (sp/unit)	1
Car pool / (sp/unit)	0.02
Veg oil filling station / (sp/unit)	0.03
Charge points / (sp/unit)	0.11
Bike storage/ (bikes/unit)	3.7
Public transport	yes

Food

Communal growing space	no
Private growing space	inc in garden
Farmers market / person	yes
Cafes	1.2
Shops	no

Biodiversity

Undisturbed wildlife habitat / ha	0.67
CO₂ saved per unit over lifetime	1067 t

CityZED

Residential Density 120 to 240 Homes/ha

SkyZED at Wandsworth roundabout

Typical applications

- creates high density high rise residential blocks
- suitable for densification around existing transport nodes
- creates new urban landmarks
- capable of being inserted into the existing streetscene
- with carefully designed mixed-use podium, can create complete urban blocks

Prototype

The first SkyZED project has been planned for Wandwsorth roundabout, an unloved traffic island beside an underused railway station one stop up from Clapham Junction. The idea is to replace a hostile and infrequently used pedestrian underpass crossing the roundabout with new retail outlets and offices – with toplit glazed atriums enhancing the pedestrian experience, as well as providing internal outlook for the new workspace away from the traffic noise. A beautiful new roof garden placed on the office roof, shielded by a storey-height glazed screen, will create a new amenity and public garden area for the 326 new one and two bed flats located in the residential tower placed at the centre of the site. The residential accommodation is split into two aerodynamic blades, connected every fourth floor with glazed bridges containing aerial herb gardens doubling up as high speed lift lobbies.The bridge links support cantilevered 15 kW wind turbines, placed between the two towers taking maximum advantage of the prevailing south-westerly and north-easterly winds. The focusing effect of the blade towers increases wind velocity in the centre by somewhere between one-and-a-half and twice ambient wind velocity, moving the average windspeed towards the level experienced on a Welsh hilltop. More or less enough electrical energy is harvested annually by each floor to more or less meet annual electrical demand, showing how high rise buildings can be achieved without excessive energy or carbon penalties. Solar thermal collectors mounted at each floor level, with photovoltaic rainscreen cladding and a biomass CHP placed in the plinth, ensure that the CityZED block is overall carbon neutral. The tower floorplates have been designed with lifts and circulation beside the central turbines, with habitable rooms and living rooms benefiting from the best panoramic views. The ZEDstandards construction with heat recovery ventilation, thermal mass and superinsulation with triple glazing ensures that residents are never troubled by turbine noise even at high windspeeds. Most of the time, the turbines make less noise than the surrounding traffic.

SkyZED

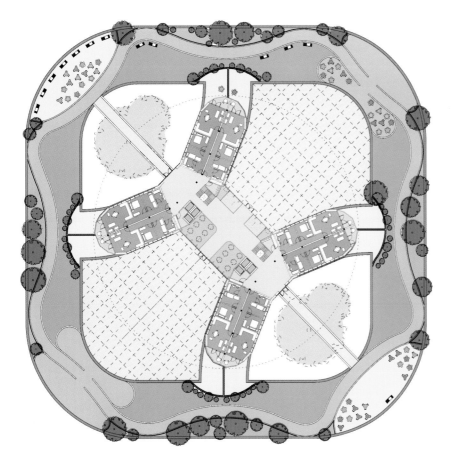

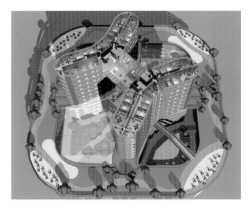

Energy

PV / (kwp/br)	0.1
Installed CHP / (kwe/br)	0.4
Ground source heat pump / person	no
Micro wind / (kwh/br/yr)	705
Onsite generation ex biomass	100% residential
Onsite generation inc biomass	100%

Amenity

Sunspace / (m²/br)	3.5
Public open space / (m²/br)	1.4
Private garden / (m²/br)	no
Children's play space / (m²/br)	0.6
Sports facilities / (m²/br)	1.1

Workspace

Home office space / (m²/unit)	bedroom sockets
Area rentable workspace / (m²/br)	37.4
No. workspaces/ha (m²/br)	2235

Transport

Private parking (sp/unit)	0.52
Car pool / (sp/unit)	0.02
Veg oil filling station / (sp/unit)	0.01
Charge points / (sp/unit)	0.04
Bike storage/ (bikes/unit)	0.8
Public transport	yes

Food

Communal growing space	yes
Private growing space	no
Farmers market / person	yes
Cafes	0.21
Shops	no

Biodiversity

Undisturbed wildlife habitat / ha	none
CO_2 saved per unit over lifetime	2366 t

ZEDquarter

Residential Density 100 to 250 Homes/ha

Typical applications

- creates medium density perimeter block layouts
- suitable for expanding new towns
- creates new suburban districts
- suitable for urban estate regeneration

Several ZEDquarters are currently being planned all over the world. The idea is to set up new viral urban districts that can begin as possibly just one building exhibiting the 'powerdown' principles of ceasing reliance on fossil or nuclear fuel, and then spread the concept radially outwards, until whole districts become exemplar low or zero carbon communities. All aspects of both the lifestyle, workstyle, food supply and infrastructure need to be designed around the limited quantities of renewable energy systems available within the natural landscape topography contained within a radius approximately 60 to 100 km from the settlement core

All the old European cities were divided into political / religious / ethnic identities, however most of the time a harmonious co-existence was achieved. The ZEDquarter provides a new concept for major regeneration sites based on environmental awareness, however without threatening the existing business as usual of its host city. If its demands are too extreme it will simply be rejected by its

Velocity – view from Brick Lane

Velocity – aerial view

surrounding host community as being too alien too quickly. Instead the ZEDquarter must expand because it genuinely offers a better quality of life, and – most importantly of all – a cultural framework for a civilised society that can continue indefinitely without accelerating climate change.

This is the 'ZEDquarter' – a new urban district of both new and existing buildings where people of all sects, creeds and backgrounds can unite under a common aspiration – to create a zero waste–zero carbon society – achieving a stepchange reduction in environmental impact at the same time as increasing most ordinary peoples' quality of life. The ZEDquarter is far more than a simplistic emphasis on carbon footprinting, it represents a fresh set of social priorities and cultural values – perhaps best represented in the United Kingdom by two magazines, *Resurgence* and the *Ecologist*. In time this thinking will develop a new aesthetic, new artistic movements, new critical and philosophical polemic, new social structures and new ways of inhabiting and modifying the infrastructure we have all inherited. This community has decided to live within their 'earthshare' – looking forward to a future without guilt or despair. These communities will generate new cultural values that will significantly enrich a larger cities' vitality, and will provide a living demonstration of a clean green future that the wider city outside will be able to choose without the need for coercive legislation.

This enables the ZEDquarter to spread by consensus – radiating outwards, repairing the damaged urban fabric all around, with a mixture of renovation, regeneration and wholesale recycling.

The examples included are a mixture of the practical and theoretical.

Prototypes

Velocity

The first ZEDquarter was proposed for a GLA competition – called Living in the City – held in 2000. Here a disused goods marshalling yard at Bishopsgate, on the edge of the City of London's financial district – was turned into three artificial hillsides. Offices and dealing floors were fitted into the northlit cavernous interiors under the slope while meandering pedestrian and cycle streets climbed the southern face – covered with prefabricated two storey family houses with sunspaces and roof

Velocity ZEDquarter concept

gardens. Two open air bicycle lifts take the strain out of hillclimbing, and downhill walkways enable cyclists to freewheel down to their front doors. A mountainbike training track runs around the perimeter, hung off the building, and passing through the centre of two office blocks straddling Brick Lane. The entire development could be powered by a mixture of biomass CHP with the car pool powered by waste vegetable oil from all the surrounding restaurants. All the homes have enough photovoltaics to meet half of their annual electric demand. Velocity has been designed to celebrate the efficiency, fun and convenience of cycling, and show how this simple device can transform the high density mixed use urban block into a place where the boundaries of living, working, leisure and sport are all blurred into one cohesive way of life. We think this development would have a similar cost to the high spec monofunctional office blocks proposed for this site – and it would be much more fun to visit, inhabit and work in.

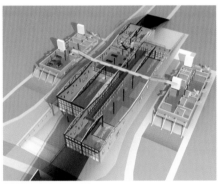

Residential block – built over work and retail space, combined to create a gently undulating landscape

Changsha

A 5 ha urban expansion to Changsha – the regional capital of Hunan province – was previously planned with twenty storey residential towers adjacent to a new drive in hypermarket. ZEDfactory proposed a new mixed use urban form with linear east / west axis residential blocks, overlooking lower rise commercial and leisure development. Undulating linear parks built on the workspace roof provide green amenity space and transpiration from vegetation, and allow the prevailing wind in summer months to blow away stagnant hot / polluted urban air – effectively reducing the urban heat island by around 3°C. This reduction in cooling load allows the homes to be powered by solar electricity from the south-facing terrace shade louvres, with ground water cooling, modest use of heat pumps and horizontal wind driven ventilation concepts effectively reducing demand to a third of a typical local home. A biomass powered CHP plant fuelled by rice husks will be installed as the number of completed homes provides sufficient critical mass.

The concept will be tested by a smaller demonstration building, containing a hotel, showflats and offices in the side blocks – with sports facilities including a swimming pool and café under the central garden.

A fresh urban landscape derived from combining passive building physics with a mixed-use programme

Gallions Reach, ZEDquarter

Gallions Reach

A proposal to transform a hostile island site surrounded by dual carriageways beside the City Airport into a zero carbon Zedquarter. The same turbine that had run for 4 months without objections on central Londons' Southbank cultural quarter in Christmas 2005, now forms the southernmost anchor to the site. A photovoltaic clad, wedge-shaped accommodation block rises to the east, while a new village square connects to the adjacent Docklands Light Railway. A south-facing residential tower rises from the square, with a café, car pool and community facilities embedded in its base. An undulating central communal garden joins the southern square to the existing northern woodland copse, with a terrace of family homes and back gardens contributing to the wide range of different sized homes. A small biomass powered CHP plant completes the zero carbon technologies, with the woodchip consumption kept well below the national personal biomass quota of 600 dry kg / person / year above 50 homes / ha. An on site renewable energy target of 25 per cent annual demand was achieved – despite the high density layout – allowing the CHP plant to meet the thermal demand of the year round domestic hot water load. The competition project team resisted the temptation to simply double the installed CHP capacity, effectively doubling the annual biomass consumption – so that theoretical carbon neutrality could be achieved with the lowest initial capital cost. However when the development is completed by the winning alternative team in 3 years time, public awareness of the limited stocks of the national biomass reserve would be likely to have exposed this short term strategy as being irresponsible, and not in the nation's best interests.

Milton Keynes

This scheme celebrates the rigorous Masterplan grid of Central Milton Keynes. The perimeter blocks facing the road are sheer sided with stone skins, eroded at pavement level to allow for the colonnade and retail activities, and indented at higher levels to provide the recessed balconies for the residential.

Towers pierce the smooth skin as glazed crevices, with the corner further eaten away to persuade visitors to enter the inner courtyard square.

These polite, permanent and somewhat inscrutable blocks rise towards the corner of the site, signalling the gateway to the new CMK 'Green Quarter'. A specially designed vertical axis with spherical blade configuration spins in the lightest wind

Milton Keynes ZEDquarter showing market square

– special LEDs on its vane creating an image of the earth generated from real time satellite images. The LEDs are dynamically tuned into the Green Quarter's electrical consumption, changing colour from green to red via orange as the community's power consumption exceeds its allocated allowance.

This is a community planning its own future. Rigorous weather and calendar compensated CO_2 targets are set, and the LED globe provides immediate feedback on whether they are being exceeded in real time with the beacon signalling this achievement to the wider city.

Passing under the glazed canopy, collecting window shoppers from both the arcades on Witan Gate and Avebury Bouvlevard, reveals an intimate relaxed urban square flanked by pavement cafés and lime trees. The pedestrian prioritised square provides a more intimate social focus to the Green Quarter, with parking giving way to cobbles, benches, market stalls and in one corner the new Community Hub. This houses the zero CO_2 transport hub, the carpool administrations and mechanics to repair bicycles and small electric scooters, as well as receiving food box deliveries from the local organic farm. As the new community grows, activities could include childcare, telecommuting shared facilities and possibly even a green tomato taxi service running off locally produced biofuel.

A timber staircase climbs from the market square over the double height biomass square CHP wood chip loading bay doors, leading into a new hidden courtyard – the informal heart of the Green Quarter.

Now the perimeter housing blocks step and stagger to catch the sun. Every roof surface becomes a terrace or garden. Each flat peers around or over its neighbour to catch a snatch of sunlight. Oiled FSC cedar cladding wooden patio doors and the colours of earthen lime render create a more relaxing urban landscape.

A lush cascading garden with edible plants and ponds covers the underground car park, with a skateboard ramp and a long distance vista out of Central Milton Keynes downhill towards the adjoining housing estates.

Each ground floor home opens out onto its own garden, framing the communal parkland, and each common stair connects to the central promenade route allowing upper-floor residents easy access to the outdoor space. The same glazed stairs feed small clusters of single aspect flats with each corridor leading onto communal roof gardens.

Oval towers roofed in solar electric panels break up the southern terrace. Following the landscape downhill, a visitor arrives in an open courtyard of terraced three storey town houses. South-facing bay windows and roof terraces give privacy and long distance views over Milton Keynes with a secure children's playground completing the sequence of increasingly relaxed and private communal gardens. From the roof terraces the cascading diamond shaped solar panels framing the penthouses along Witan Gate give the Green Quarter a reassuring city wall, further emphasised by the sentinel vertical axis turbines spinning between each oval tower.

The transition from low carbon specification to carbon neutral has been achieved by replacing the off site gas powered CHP plant with three on site biomass powered Talbot CHP units. The three Talbot units generate approximately 8 per cent more electrical energy than the community requires over a year, which over a 60 year period should offset the CO_2 embodied in the original construction, together with the carbon footprint of planned maintenance and replacement. The biomass furnaces, hot air turbines and

View of the central island block

chip store have been carefully planned into one corner of the inner courtyard square, with a double height woodchip loading bay and a small section of underground car park converted into a compact plant room. Special chimney flues integrated into the massing of the corner residential block deliver the non-toxic aromatic woodsmoke high enough to avoid the adjacent urban blocks. The CHP uses the latest hot air turbine technology, is certified for use within the Clean Air Act Zones and avoids the high decoking and maintenance regimes that make gasified wood power plants uneconomic with excessive downtime. Ten years after their experience with the first urban wood chip CHP at BedZED, the team are now confident that this technology represents the most cost effective way of producing a zero carbon high density urban quarter – with the efficiency of the building fabric and mixed uses ensuring efficient loadmatching with modest amounts of excess summer heat potentially used to provide trigeneration cooling using absorption chillers for the retail units. If the Central Milton Keynes power plant concept is still pursued at a later date, it is both sensible and economic to connect the biomass CHP units into the central CMK district heating main and private wire network – using the Woking precedent to encourage a complementary range of different microgeneration technologies working within a coordinated and future proofed framework. All the large scale microgeneration devices, including large-scale communal rooftop photovoltaics and micro wind generation, are linked into one Energy Services Company with remote billing facilities and overall responsibility for both the private wire electric supply and the district heat main supply, predominantly domestic hot water. Wood chip deliveries from three medium-sized 15 tonne tipper trucks could be required once a week, and these would take place on weekday mornings – freeing up the market square for the weekend stallholders.

Individual householders can then choose to incorporate and fund more solar electric panels on their home if they want to reduce or eliminate their electric bills. An energy mortgage service will be investigated with a major funding institution which can supply the capital required for the initial installation, with monthly loans paid off with the cash that would otherwise have spent purchasing power from the grid in a more conventional home. Any power produced will meet the residual demand in each home, and if surplus energy is produced this will be exported to the communal private wire, providing credits that can be offset against imported power, or in some cases, a valuable source of additional income. Using this simple system of encouraging individual microgeneration, the Green Quarter in Central Milton Keynes not only meets its own heat and power demands, but stays within each UK citizen's fair share of the national biomass reserve (approx 500 kg of dry biomass per capita per year without loss of agricultural land area), but becomes a net exporter of energy, subsidising some of the surrounding city still heavily reliant on fossil fuel.

View of the village square with community centre and biomass CHP

Changsha

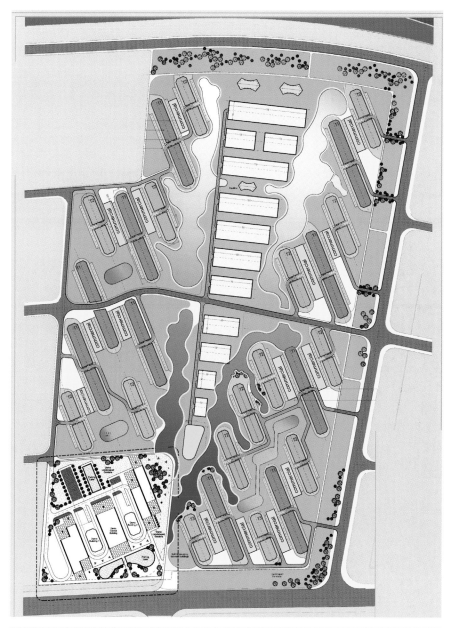

Energy

PV / (kwp/br)	1.2
Installed CHP / (kwe/br)	no
Ground source heat pump / person	1.5 for cooling
Micro wind / (kwh/br/yr)	no
Onsite generation ex biomass	100%
Onsite generation inc biomass	100%

Amenity

Sunspace / (m²/br)	no
Public open space / (m²/br)	2.3
Private garden / (m²/br)	no
Children's play space / (m²/br)	no
Sports facilities / (m²/br)	8

Workspace

Home office space / (m²/unit)	bedroom sockets
Area rentable workspace / (m²/br)	122
No. workspaces/ha (m²/br)	200

Transport

Private parking (sp/unit)	3.3
Car pool / (sp/unit)	0.05
Veg oil filling station / (sp/unit)	0.03
Charge points / (sp/unit)	0.04
Bike storage/ (bikes/unit)	2.3
Public transport	yes

Food

Communal growing space	yes
Private growing space	hotel n/a
Farmers market / person	yes
Cafes	13.6
Shops	1.5

Biodiversity

Undisturbed wildlife habitat / ha	none
CO_2 saved per unit over lifetime	5750 t

Gallions Reach

Energy – Gallions Reach has a feature x MWh Turbine along with a wood chip fired CHP and ancilliary PV panels. This will not only power the site but allow an ESCO to be set up to provide power to the local area

Energy

PV / (kwp/br)	2.2
Installed CHP / (kwe/br)	0.2
Ground source heat pump / person	no
Micro wind / (kwh/br/yr)	593
Onsite generation ex biomass	55%
Onsite generation inc biomass	100%

Amenity

Sunspace / (m²/br)	1.7
Public open space / (m²/br)	4.8
Private garden / (m²/br)	4.2
Children's play space / (m²/br)	0.2
Sports facilities / (m²/br)	no

Workspace

Home office space / (m²/unit)	bedroom sockets
Area rentable workspace / (m²/br)	no
No. workspaces/ha (m²/br)	no

Transport

Private parking (sp/unit)	disabled only
Car pool / (sp/unit)	0.01
Veg oil filling station / (sp/unit)	0.01
Charge points / (sp/unit)	0.01
Bike storage/ (bikes/unit)	1.5
Public transport	yes

Food

Communal growing space	yes
Private growing space	inc in garden
Farmers market / person	yes
Cafes	0.6
Shops	0.12

Biodiversity

Undisturbed wildlife habitat / ha	0.1
CO$_2$ saved per unit over lifetime	1691 t

Milton Keynes

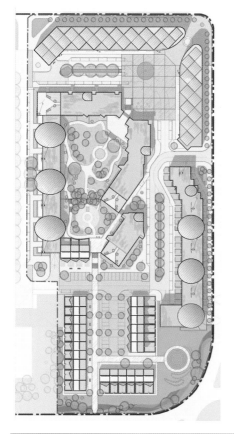

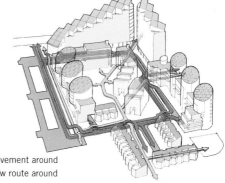

The diagram (right) shows the hierarchy of movement around the site. Pedestrians being the dominant yellow route around the site, cyclists green and vehicles red

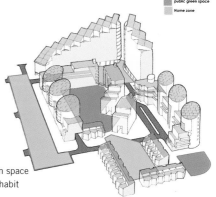

public green space
Home zone

Shows the areas of 'Home zone' and public green space which create areas in which the residents can inhabit comfortably

Energy

PV / (kwp/br)	0.3
Installed CHP / (kwe/br)	0.1
Ground source heat pump / person	no
Micro wind / (kwh/br/yr)	91
Onsite generation ex biomass	20%
Onsite generation inc biomass	100%

Amenity

Sunspace / (m²/br)	3.4
Public open space / (m²/br)	2.5
Private garden / (m²/br)	1.2
Children's play space / (m²/br)	0.8
Sports facilities / (m²/br)	no

Workspace

Home office space / (m²/unit)	bedroom sockets
Area rentable workspace / (m²/br)	0.6
No. workspaces/ha (m²/br)	24.4

Transport

Private parking (sp/unit)	1
Car pool / (sp/unit)	0.01
Veg oil filling station / (sp/unit)	0.02
Charge points / (sp/unit)	0.05
Bike storage/ (bikes/unit)	3.4
Public transport	yes

Food

Communal growing space	yes
Private growing space	inc in garden
Farmers market / person	yes
Cafes	0.6
Shops	0.4

Biodiversity

Undisturbed wildlife habitat / ha	adjacent
CO₂ saved per unit over lifetime	4718 t

Community/conference hall at Jubilee Wharf

Notes

Introduction

1   www.london.gov.uk

1.1 Make carbon history

1   www.environment-agency.gov.uk/yourenv/639312/#
2   US Department of State, US Climate Action Report 2002, Washington, D.C., May 2002.
3   The six greenhouse gases addressed by the Kyoto Protocol are: Carbon dioxide (CO_2), Methane (CH_4), Nitrous oxide (N_2O), Hydrofluorocarbons (HFCs), Perfluorocarbons (PFCs) and Sulphur hexafluoride (SF_6).
4   Carbon Dioxide Information Analysis Center (CDIAC): http://cdiac.esd.ornl.gov/pns/current_ghg.html (February 2005 update) and http://cdiac.esd.ornl.gov/pns/faq.html
5   www.unep-wcmc.org/climate/impacts.htm
6   Cox, P. M., Betts, R. A., Jones, C. D., Spall,. S. A. and Totterdell, I. J. (November 2000) 'Acceleration of global warming due to carbon-cycle feedbacks in a coupled climate model'. *Nature*, 408 (6809):184–7.
7   www.stabilisation2005.com/impacts/impacts_ecosystems.pdf
8   Intergovernmental Panel on Climate Change Working Group 1.
9   United Nations Framework Convention on Climate Change.
10   Marland, G., Boden, T. A. and Andres, R. J. (2006) 'Global, Regional, and National CO_2 Emissions'. In *Trends: A Compendium of Data on Global Change*. Carbon Dioxide Information Analysis Center, Oak Ridge National Laboratory, US Department of Energy. See http://swivel.com/data_sets/show/1002617
11   Hillman, M. and Fawcett, T. (2004) *How We Can Save the Planet*. London: Penguin.
12   The idea of DTQs even made it as far as a UK Parliamentary Bill – though it failed to get adopted. See www.teqs.net for more information.
13   OECD Report on Bangladesh and Climate Change, www.oecd.org/dataoecd/46/55/21055658.pdf
14   BBC News Report 20 September 2004, news.bbc.co.uk/1/hi/world/south_asia/3672050.stm
15   Swiss Re (2002) 'Opportunities and risks of Climate Change'. www.swissre.com
16   Brooks, Nick and Adger, W. Neil (in press) 'Country level risk indicators from outcome data on climate-related disasters: an exploration of the Emergency Events Database'. *Ambio – A Journal of the Human Environment*.

17   Marland *et al.* 'Global, Regional, and National CO_2 Emissions'.

18   www.globalpolicy.org/socecon/hunger/2003/1001globalwarming.htm; *Nature* November 2005, 438: 310–17.

1.2   Design out fossil fuels

1   We see little point in covering the issue of peak oil in detail when others have written so knowledgeably and eloquently on the subject. Readers are referred to: Paul Roberts' book *The End of Oil: On the edge of a perilous new world* (2004. New York: Houghton Mifflin); Kenneth Deffeyes' *Hubbert's Peak: The impending world oil shortage* (2001. Princeton, NJ: Princeton University Press); Heinberg, R. *The Party's Over: Oil, war, and the fate of industrial societies* (2002. Vancouver: New Society).

2   Elliott, Larry (27 June 2005) 'The black stuff has world order over a barrel: Everyone knows oil will run out one day, but some industry experts predict the decline will start as soon as 2008', *The Guardian*.

3   IEA (2005) *Resources to Reserves – Oil and Gas Technologies for the Energy Markets of the Future*. Available at www.iea.org/Textbase/publications/free_new_Desc.asp?PUBS_ID=1568

4   www.peakoil.net

5   See http://news.bbc.co.uk/1/hi/business/4077802.stm

6   www.osti.gov/EnergyFiles/; www.powerswitch.org.uk/Downloads/pos.pdf; and www.energyfiles.com

7   Changing IEA estimates are briefly explored in Mobbs, P. (2005) *Energy Beyond Oil*. Leicester: Matador.

8   Hallock, J. L., Tharakan, P. J., Hall, C. A. S., Jefferson, M. and Wu, W. (September 2004) 'Forecasting the limits to the availability and diversity of global conventional oil supply'. *Energy* 29(11): 1673–96.

9   Mobbs, *Energy Beyond Oil*, p.47.

10   www.kuwaittimes.net/localnews.asp?dismode=article&artid=37595069

11   Energy Green Paper *Towards a European Strategy for the Security of Energy Supply*. European Commission 2001, http://europa.eu.int/comm/energy_transport/doc-principal/pubfinal_en.pdf

12   It is telling to note that we had to revise this figure upwards several times during the drafting of this book.

13   www.businessweek.com/magazine/content/06_20/b3984001.htm

14   World Economic Outlook (2003): www.imf.org/external/pubs/ft/weo/2003/01/pdf/chapter1.pdf

15   www.earthisland.org/eijournal/new_articles.cfm?articleID=713&journalID=69

16   Diamond, Jared (2005) *Collapse: How Societies Choose to Fail or Succeed*, London: Penguin.

17   See www.museletter.com/Greer-on-Collapse.rtf

18   Michael Renner (October 2002) *The Anatomy of Resource Wars*. Worldwatch Institute Paper 162.

19   Richard Heinberg provides arguably the best summary and ample supportive evidence in his books *The Party's Over Oil, War and the Fate of Industrial Societies* (2003, updated edition 2005) and *Powerdown: Options and*

Actions for a Post-Carbon World (2004). Both are published by New Society Publishers, Gabriola Island, Canada, www.newsociety.com/

20   'Focus on World Energy: Iceland Pioneering the Hydrogen Economy', www.afsa.org/fsj/dec03/sigfusson.pdf; www.regeringen.se/sb/d/6791/a/63715 (speech by Swedish Minister for Sustainable Development, delivered May 2006).

21   Heinberg, *Powerdown*, p.149.

22   Heinberg, *Powerdown*,

23   Mobbs, *Energy Beyond Oil* – also see www.fraw.org.uk/ebo/intro.shtml

24   William Stanley Jevons wrote *The Coal Question* in 1865. See http://oll.libertyfund.org/Home3/Book.php?recordID=0546

25   See Elliot, D. (2003) *Energy, Society and Environment,* 2nd edition. London: Routledge.

26   'Oil Sands Fever: The environmental implications of Canada's oil sands rush', www.oilsandswatch.org/docs/osf-book.pdf

27   World Energy Council, 'What future for extra heavy oil and bitumen: the orinoco case'. http://www.worldenergy.org/wec-geis/publications/default/tech_papers/17th_congress/3_1_04.asp

28   Quinn, Thomas J. (July 2005) 'Turning tar sands into oil'. Available at www.energybulletin.net/7331.html

1.3   Reduce demand – run on native renewables

1   DTI (2002) *Managing the nuclear legacy: a strategy for action.* www.dti.gov.uk/nuclearcleanup/pdfs/whitepaper.pdf

2   For example, DTI (2003) 'Energy White Paper: Our Energy Future – Creating a Low Carbon Economy'. www.dti.gov.uk/energy/policy-strategy/energy-white-paper-2003/page21223.html

3   www.stormsmith.nl

4   www.stormsmith.nl

5   See DEFRA, www.defra.gov.uk/environment/statistics/radioact/kf/rakf11.htm

6   See 'Recommendations of the European Committee on Radiation Risk. The Health Effects of Ionising Radiation Exposure at Low Doses for Radiation Protection Purposes. Regulators' Edition', available from www.euradcom.org; and Busby (1995) *Wings of Death: Nuclear pollution and human health.* Aberystwyth: Green Audit.

7   This assumes that the heating and power loads can be balanced to meet demand, which can be a problem in summer when little heat is needed.

8   Assuming the efficiency with which fossil fuels are burned is improved (or if released carbon is reduced or captured in some other way) then this 80 per cent reduction in energy use will actually result in more than 80 per cent CO_2 reductions.

9   See The Royal Commission on Environmental Pollution's 22nd Report (June 2000) 'Energy – The Changing Climate'. www.rcep.org.uk/newenergy.htm

10   See, in particular, the work of Graham Sinden: www.eci.ox.ac.uk

11   DTI (2005) 'New and Renewable Energy: Prospects in the UK for the 21st Century: Supporting Analysis'. URN 05/1831.

12   1 tonne of oil equivalent (toe) = 107 kilocalories = 396.8 therms = 41.87 gigajoules = 11.63 megawatt hours. It is not a physical unit but a measure of energy.

13   All figures calculated from the Digest of UK Energy Statistics 2005. www.dti.gov.uk/energy/statistics/publications/dukes/2005/page19311.html

14   DTI (2002) *Future Offshore: A strategic framework for the offshore wind industry.* Available from www.dti.gov.uk

15   *Refocus* Magazine website article dated 3 May 2006: www.sparksdata.co.uk/refocus/showdoc.asp?docid=30172366&accnum=1&topics

16   www.scottishrenewables.com

17   www.defra.gov.uk/environment/statistics/land/

18   E4Tech (2003) 'Liquid biofuels and hydrogen from renewable resources in the UK to 2050: a technical analysis' – a study carried out for Department of Transport. Available forestry land (about 0.25 Mha of the 4 Mha total) is included.

19   Based on an average yield of 15 odt/ha/yr and an energy content of 18 GJ/odt.

20   Bugge, J. (2000) *Rape Seed Oil for Transport 1: Energy Balance and CO2 Emissions.* www.folkecenter.net/gb/rd/transport/plant_oil/9192/

21   Environmental Change Institute (2005) '40 percent house'. Oxford University Centre for the Environment, www.40percent.org.uk

22   This estimate uses a more realistic assumption about yields – assuming a usable supply of 10 odt/ha/yr (taking into account likely losses). This figure includes round 2.5 million odt of wood fuel (*Biomass as a renewable energy source* (2004) Royal Commission on Environmental Pollution. www.rcep.org.uk/biomass/chapter4.pdf). This is equivalent to about 14 TWh/yr (assuming no conversion losses) or about 40 odkg per person.

23   E4Tech (2003) 'Liquid biofuels and hydrogen from renewable resources in the UK to 2050: a technical analysis', a study carried out for the Department of Transport. See also *Biomass as a renewable energy source*, www.rcep.org.uk/biomass/chapter4.pdf

24   EST (2005) 'Potential for Microgeneration Study and Analysis: Final Report'. www.dti.gov.uk/files/file27558.pdf

25   Conventionally rated at 12 m/s (metres per second).

26   Based on 2.5 kWh/m2/day at 12 per cent efficiency. Note that panels are more likely to be inclined than flat.

27   C-Tech Biffaward Thermal Waste Treatment report. www.biffa.co.uk/files/pdfs/MassBalance_Thermowaste.pdf

28   For example, paper has a calorific value of 10.5 GJ/tonne. If burned at 25 per cent efficiency to produce electricity it generates 2.6 GJ/tonne of electrical energy. Yet it takes 22.7 GJ/tonne to produce virgin paper and 14.4 GJ/tonne to produce recycled paper. So for each tonne of paper burned – rather than recycled, 5.7 GJ of energy is being 'thrown away' needlessly. On average, about five times more energy is saved by reclaiming a material than is yielded by burning it.

29   Wood grown specifically for energy generation is dealt with elsewhere.

30   C-Tech Biffaward Thermal Waste Treatment report. www.biffa.co.uk/files/pdfs/MassBalance_Thermowaste.pdf

31   C-Tech (2002) *Agricultural Mass Balance: Opportunities for recycling and producing energy from waste technologies.*

32   www.restats.org

33   DTI (2002) 'Energy Consumption in the United Kingdom'. www.dti.gov.uk

1.4   Enable a high quality of life on a LOW footprint

1   WWF (2004) Living Planet Report 2004.
     www.panda.org/news_facts/publications/living_planet_report/lpr04/index.cfm

2   For a detailed explanation of the derivation of these figures, the reader is referred to Chambers, N., Simmons, C. and Wackernagel, M. (2000) *Sharing Nature's Interest: ecological footprints as an indicator of sustainability.* London: Earthscan.

3   Footprint data for more than 120 countries (data year 2002) has been published by the European Environment Agency, http://org.eea.eu.int/news/Ann1132753060/Global_footprint_data.xls. See also Global Footprint Network, www.footprintnetwork.org; and Best Foot Forward, www.bestfootforward.com

4   (1989) *Culture Shift in Advanced Industrial Society.* Princeton, NJ: Princeton University Press.

5   (2005) *Happiness: Lessons from a new science.* London: Penguin.

6   (2004) *A well-being manifesto for a flourishing society.* www.neweconomics.org/gen/news_wellbeingmanifesto.aspx

7   www.worldvaluessurvey.org/

8   Reported in 'Chasing the dream', the *Economist* 7 August 2003.

9   We have chosen 1974 as a start date for consistency with existing time series analyses. Satisfaction data from Veenhoven, R., *Trend Average Happiness in Nations 1946–2004: How much people like the life they live.* World Database of Happiness, www.worlddatabaseofhappiness.eur.nl/hap_nat/findingreports/TrendReport2005-1d.pdf
     Ecological Footprint data from National Footprint Accounts, Global Footprint Network www.footprintnetwork.org. All calculations by Best Foot Forward, www.bestfootforward.com

10   www.brandchannel.com/view_comments.asp?dc_id=17

11   Source: Merck Family Fund (1995) *Yearning for Balance*, Takoma Park, MD: Merck Family Fund (n = 4000).

12   'Redefining the American Dream: The Search for Sustainable Consumption' Conference Report 23–25 April 1995 Airlie House – Airlie, Virginia. www.iisd.ca/consume/mer_1.html

13   Diener, Ed, Horwitz, J. and Emmons, Robert A. (1985) 'Happiness of the very wealthy'. *Social Indicators* 16: 263–74.

14   Available online at: http://en.wikisource.org/wiki/Walden

1.5   The ZEDstandards: a checklist for ZEDliving

1   See www.ZEDstandards.com for more information.

2   See www.davidsuzuki.org/files/climate/Kyoto_Progress.pdf

3   'Energy – The Changing Climate', The Royal Commission on Environmental Pollution's 22nd Report, June 2000 (www.rcep.org.uk/newenergy.htm); 'Cleaner, Smarter Energy: Policies for a low carbon future' – a summary of the 2003 Energy White Paper.

4   See www.pointcarbon.com

5   Carbon Trust (July 2004) carbon trading predictions for the European Union. Trading started January 2005.

6   UN population statistics are at their website: http://esa.un.org/unpp/

7   http://themes.eea.europa.eu/Sectors_and_activities/households/indicators/consumption/index_html

8   Where small amounts of fossil fuel are used, in line with overall reduction targets, alternatives are provided.

9   Simmons, C., Gonzalez, G. and Lewis, K. (2006) WWF One Planet Business: Methodology for determining global sectoral material consumption, carbon dioxide emissions and Ecological Footprints. Available for download at www.bestfootforward.com/opb.html

10   Best Foot Forward (2002) 'City Limits: A resource flow and ecological footprint analysis of Greater London'. Available for download from www.citylimitslondon.com

11   Pimental, D. and Pimental, M. (1996) *Food, Energy and Society: Revised Edition*. Niwet, CO: University Press of Colorado.

12   Study by Best Foot Forward based on a shopping basket of 33 items. Due to poor information on the origin of the products, this study assumed all food travelled 640 km by road only. Though this is a reasonable estimate of travel within the United Kingdom, it is probably an underestimate as some foods will have additionally travelled by sea – and a few by air – over longer distances. Nonetheless this study illustrates well the relative impact of food miles.

13   Data from Mark Cottrell at Commonwork.

14   Source: Mike Cottrell at Commonwork.

15   Pimental and Pimental, *Food, Energy and Society*. This quotes two studies giving very similar figures of 19 and 20 kcal per kcal of protein.

16   Based on raw consumption data from Colin Tingle, Mike Cottrell and Jacqueline Leach at Commonwork.

17   An assumption of 90 per cent efficiency – see earlier chapter referring to the use of Pure Plants Oils as a transport fuel.

18   www.energetik-leipzig.de/Bioenergie/Bioenergie.htm

19   www.epa.gov/ttn/chief/conference/ei11/ammonia/mangino.pdf

20   www.dairynet.com/energy_resources/cowpower.pdf

21   (2002) 'An analysis of the energy available form agricultural byproducts'. www.easternct.edu/depts/sustainenergy/publication/reports/BIOMASS%20FINAL%20REPORT-Phase%201%20.pdf

22   Estimates produced by architects ZEDFactory, www.zedfactory.com

23   Heat demand was estimated to be 374,235 kWh/year based on the consumption of oil and LPG. Wood was excluded.

24   This figure would be much larger were it not for the fact that the electricity used by Commonwork is already purchased from renewable sources. It is

important that on-site sources are used where practicable to maximise the total supply of renewable energy.

25   At the time of writing, PV panels were available at £3,000 per kW installed. Assuming a 25-year life span and an output of 900 kWh per kW, this gives an average price per unit (kWh) of electricity as 13p. This is close to what is currently being charged to domestic consumers. If one considers that electricity prices will continue to rise, that the panels will continue to generate electricity beyond their guarantee and that the panels themselves have an asset value, then PVs are starting to look very attractive.

26   http://earthtrends.wri.org/pdf_library/data_tables/cli2_2003.pdf

27   Woodin, M. and Lucas, C. (2004) *Green Alternatives to Globalisation*. London: Pluto Press.

28   www.whokilledtheelectriccar.com

29   www.ev1.org

30   One litre of petrol contains about 10 kWh of energy. A very efficient car might consume 3 litres per 100 km. This equates to about 3.5 km per 1 kWh.

31   www.teslamotors.com

2.2   The ZEDphysics model

1   Total current dry wood fuel production divided by UK population = 130 kg per person or 650 kg per household. The RuralZED three-bed, five-person house pellet consumption with solar thermal = 670 kg.

2.3   Characterising a development for energy use and carbon emissions

1   www.iesve.com

2   www.retscreen.net

2.5   The effect of climate

1   Based on United Kingdom 2002 building regulations.

2.6   Building and upgrading houses to zero carbon standards

1   Assuming poly-silicate PV panels with nominal efficiency of 15 per cent. Output modelled with Retscreen software, www.retscreen.net

2   Using a monodraught 1,000 wind turbine. Output modelled with Retscreen software.

3   Based on the RuralZED layout with timber frame or BedZED style construction. Output modelled with IES software, www.iesve.com

4   Roaf, Sue (Summer 2005) 'Hot on the heels of coolth'. *Building For a Future* 15(1): 38–39.

2.9   ZEDfactory Wind Cowl passive heat recovery ventilation system

1   Images from report by Living Space Sciences, info@ls-sciences.com

2.10 Passive solar design

1   Assuming CO_2 emission rates of: gas 0.19 kg CO_2 / kWh, mains electricity 0.59 kg CO_2 / kWh.
2   BMT Fluid Mechanics Ltd with Arup, 30 March 2005 Project 43563/00.
3   For example these characteristics were calculated from tables in CIBSE Guide C Chapter 4.
4   Stack effect pressure difference calculated using CIBSE Guide A, equation 4.6.
5   Based on BRE Bredem 12 methodology.
6   Measurements carried out at BedZED by Ian Mawditt, Living Space Sciences in association with TracerTech GMBH on 11 October 2005.

2.12 Overheating risk assessment

1   Taken from: Gilbert, B (2005) *Thermal Mass and the Effects of Dynamic Heat Flow*. MSc Architecture thesis, University of East London.

2.14 Low energy air-conditioning, dehumidification and cooling

1   Taken from the Forest Research website, www.woodfuel.org.uk/WoodfuelsProject/pages/home.jsp

2.15 Providing a renewable electricity supply

1   www.retscreen.net

Index

Page numbers in italic denote illustrations and diagrams